D1559741

Utopia, NEW JERSEY

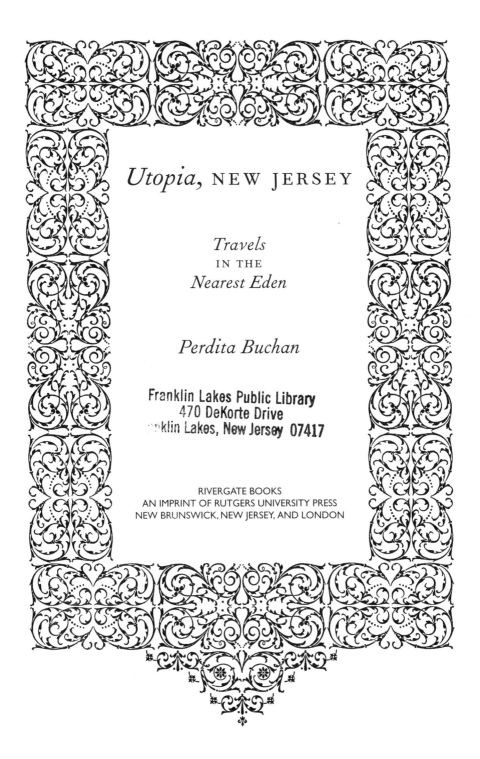

Utopia, NEW JERSEY

Travels
IN THE
Nearest Eden

Perdita Buchan

RIVERGATE BOOKS
AN IMPRINT OF RUTGERS UNIVERSITY PRESS
NEW BRUNSWICK, NEW JERSEY, AND LONDON

Library of Congress Cataloging-in-Publication Data

Buchan, Perdita, 1940–

Utopia, New Jersey : travels in the nearest Eden / Perdita Buchan.

p.   cm.

Includes bibliographical references and index.

ISBN 978–0-8135–4178–5 (hardcover : alk. paper)

1. Utopian socialism—New Jersey—History.   2. Immigrants—New Jersey—History.

3. Communities—New Jersey—History.   4. New Jersey—Description and travel.   I. Title.

HX655.N5B83 2007

307.7709749—dc22

2007000044

A British Cataloging-in-Publication record for this book is available from the British Library.

Visit our Web site: http://rutgerspress.rutgers.edu

Manufactured in the United States of America

for HEC

CONTENTS

Walking down a dirt road in Vermont some years ago, I came upon a field of wooden animals—a giraffe among them—paint weathered and faded, heads and tails broken off by storms or vandals. In the long grass were the remains of monkey bars and, in a grove of birches, boards that might have been a shed. It was late September, the crickets sang, grasshoppers whirred, and around me, woods and fields stretched to the edge of the mountains.

"That," an old timer told me, "that was the Communist camp."

Back in the 1930s there had been a camp for what we would now call inner city children. The organizers had been communists, or possibly socialists, and this had been their attempt to change the world by changing the world of those children.

The only legacy of Vermont's "Communist camp" seemed to be wry amusement among those who remembered it. But what difference might it have made in the life of a city child to climb monkey bars amid fields and mountains, to be shown another way to live? Utopian experiments, whatever their length and nature, inevitably leave something behind. Physically, it may be no more than a weather-beaten wooden giraffe, but socially something is altered.

My interest in alternative communities is probably inherited. My English great grandfather was a composer, a friend of the painter Edward Burne-Jones. Burne-Jones was a member of the Pre-Raphaelite brotherhood and a disciple of William Morris, socialist and guiding light of the Arts and Crafts movement. I grew up with stories of that world, with Morris-designed fabrics, Kelmscott Press editions of books, and Burne-Jones drawings. I didn't know much about Morris's utopian socialism, but a group of people living for art at romantic Kelmscott Manor beside a sleepy Thames seemed paradise enough.

Utopia, I have since learned, takes many forms. Vermont, when I lived there, was a major locus for hippie communes. I knew of a number, some of shorter and some of longer duration: Packer Corners lasted; Johnson's Pastures burned to the ground one disastrous April night in 1970. I remember dinner at the Fish Farm, a crumbling farmhouse that satisfied my interest in both community and dereliction. I cooked with Adelle Davis and studied *Living the Good Life*, Scott and Helen Nearing's tale of subsistence farming at the foot of nearby Stratton Mountain. When my daughter was born, I read A. S. Neill and determined that I would have to return to England to send her to Summerhill, his progressive school. For one heady moment, some could believe that the world was changing, and that children would have to be educated for something freer and better. We would be living on the land in concert with nature. I read Henry Beston's *The Outermost House* and *Northern Farm*. I read Louis Bromfield. I admired my Vermont neighbors, although they regarded us, the interlopers, with some suspicion.

The first time I left Vermont was for a "commune" in a big Victorian house on the New Jersey shore, established in the waning days of the Vietnam War by my then-husband's draft lawyer. As a convert to life in New England, I did not go willingly. I did not want to return to the Jersey shore of my childhood summers. This commune had much in common with Upton Sinclair's Helicon Hall, a group of professionals, lawyers, and professors trying to combine domestic life with their work. Like those at Helicon Hall, we too cooked and took care of children in rotation, meeting on Saturday nights to plan the week. When one person's patience with a three-year-old was exhausted, someone else took over. I loved it. This, I thought, was the way to live. But it didn't last.

For the next twenty or so years, I lived and worked in another kind of intentional community—a boarding school in Concord, Massachusetts, home of Emerson, Thoreau, and Bronson Alcott. I often drove up to Fruitlands, Alcott's failed utopian experiment, on its high hill. I swam in Walden Pond and explored the replica of Thoreau's hut. I read Hawthorne's *Blithedale Romance* and tried to understand the convoluted ideas of Charles Fourier, whose philosophy was the basis for Brook Farm and the North American Phalanx in Red Bank, New Jersey.

One sabbatical year I became a "colony bum." With a novel to finish I traveled from artists' colony to artists' colony, from New England to Virginia to Lake Forest, Illinois, and back to New England. Most artists' colonies came into being during the same time period as the utopias I write about here. Like these utopias, artists' colonies often embody someone's, usually a woman's, dream for temporary freedom from domestic responsibilities and distractions, a community where art is central.

Ragdale, in Lake Forest, was an Arts and Crafts mansion set on a stretch of virgin prairie where I skied through January snow. Here the multitalented Shaw family, writers and painters, had entertained Lake Forest at their open-air theater. Virginia Center for the Arts was a farm where cows would appear out of the autumn mist as I made my way to my studio in the converted barn. In one New England colony, I shared a crumbling, one-room stone cottage in the woods with an established colony of mice. Since the roof leaked, I kept a bucket in the middle of the floor. At night, the mice would run across the bed and fall in the bucket, and I would have to get up to rescue them. I also helped prepare meals and wash dishes in the kitchen where the Cummington Press had printed first editions of the likes of Marianne Moore, Allen Tate, William Carlos Williams, and Wallace Stevens. The children of resident artists lived in the Children's House, with a hired counselor and volunteer parental help. If I'd known about Stelton at that point, I'd have seen the parallels.

Moving among all those different people had its challenges. Looking back, I think of Upton Sinclair's remark that "there is no standard test for cranks." Happily, there weren't too many of those—application procedures are fairly rigorous. More memorable were the friendships formed and the feeling of being joined in a cause, albeit a somewhat solipsistic one.

Eventually, I left New England. Something pulled me back to the mid-Atlantic and New Jersey. It's a paradox that, living in a state that tears down and rebuilds at a frightening rate, I am constantly aware of the past. It is almost as though New Jersey has compressed centuries of archaeology into a short space of time. It's like living in Troy IX on the site of numerous previous cities. I am always digging. That's how I felt when I found my-self on Phalanx Road, all that remains of the North American Phalanx, al-though I'm told that the ruins of the Phalanstery were there into the 1960s.

Writing in *California's Utopian Colonies,* Robert Hine maintains that between 1850 and 1950, California saw the founding of seventeen utopian colonies—more than any other state—and that New York, Washington, and Wisconsin were runners up with three each. That's no surprise. Utopia in California is not hard to imagine. If there is a "golden medina," this is it: the ocean, the sunshine, citrus groves in valleys ringed by mountains. I have climbed the tower at Tor House in Carmel, built stone by stone by the poet Robinson Jeffers, and felt nostalgia for that tight little community of like-minded people under the Monterey pines. I have driven to the bottom of Tassajara Canyon to spend a day in the Zen community there.

Paradoxically, again, I found at least ten utopian communities in New Jersey that had existed during the same time period discussed by Hine. Re-membering Kelmscott and Cummington and the wooden giraffe in the Ver-mont field, I went looking for the physical and spiritual remains of some of them. Instead of driving down canyons, I drove down New Jersey high-ways and back roads. And from those explorations come the descriptions of what remains of each dream, followed by the histories of the communi-ties themselves.

I defined the term *utopian* broadly in choosing communities. My *Random House Dictionary* defines *utopia* in ever less qualified terms, from its origin as Sir Thomas More's fictional island, perfect in laws, politics, and so forth, through a "place or state of ideal perfection," to "any visionary sys-tem of political or social perfection." Although none of the communities I describe here achieved either political or social perfection, all were vision-ary. Nowadays, the words *intentional* and *utopian,* as applied to communal experiments, are seen as interchangeable. Intentional communities, how-ever, encompass any kind of grouping according to shared goals and ideals, and can include anything from student co-ops to shared houses. Utopian, in contrast, implies a broader focus, a shared dream or vision of how society, or some segment of it, should function.

Because I was more interested in communities whose populations were ideologically diverse, I did not choose any religious communities. Nor did I choose any "planned communities," like Radburn, New Jersey, which are mainly engaged with the planning of physical space, although such a concern obviously has philosophical implications. I chose the ones I did because they interested me and because each attempted to create, in some way, a better world.

ACKNOWLEDGMENTS

Many people helped in the writing of this book, but some I especially thank: Laurel Hessing, with her encyclopedic knowledge and generosity of spirit, who really started me on this road, and Dr. Fernanda Perrone, archivist, of Special Collections and University Archives of the Rutgers University Libraries, who was unfailingly helpful and efficient. I also thank Jillian Jakeman, of the Dyer Library in Saco, Maine, for prompt and intelligent help, as well as the staffs of the following libraries: Rutgers Special Collections, the New York Public Library, the Philadelphia Jewish Archives, the Asbury Park Library, the Neptune Library, and the libraries of Englewood, Union, Spotswood, Ocean County, Ocean County Historical Society, Cape May County, and Vineland. I also thank the many people who took the time to talk to me: Helen Barth, Tom Beisler, Terry Conner, David Freedman, Peter Goodman, Martin Hrynick, Allan Mallach, Sal and Tami Passalacqua, Clare Nadler Sacharoff, Leonard Sacharoff, Marjorie Rosenfeld, Rodham E. Tullos, and Lydia Wolniansky. I am also grateful to the Schlesinger Library at Radcliffe for a Carol K. Pforzheimer research grant that allowed me to look at unpublished papers in its collection and in the Ishill Collection at Harvard. Thanks also to Charlie Spiler and everyone at the UPS store for copying help. I owe a special debt of gratitude for all kinds of help and support to my daughter, Cressida, my son-in-law, Tom, and to HEC, who joined me on some fairly peculiar expeditions. It's been quite a journey.

Utopia, NEW JERSEY

Helicon Home Colony
A Cooperative Living Community

I take the turnpike north, which reminds me how close Englewood is to New York City. I hope I'll get the exit right and not end up on the George Washington Bridge. I do get it right and make my way through Englewood's comfortably dowdy downtown to the public library. I want to look at maps and get directions. I know that Helicon was on the Palisades above the town, but as directions go, that's a little vague. Helicon turns out to be quite far from the center of town, in the direction, of course, of the river. I get back in the car.

I turn onto Woodland Avenue, passing on my left the private Dwight Englewood School. On the right is a tangle of tall trees. Near the top of the hill, the houses begin. At the corner of Woodland and Walnut, where Helicon Hall once stood, is a large brick colonial. I get out of the car. The March wind blows hard on this hilltop. The view, however, is not toward the river some streets away but out to the west, over the Ramapo Valley, a broad view that would have been a lot emptier in 1906.

The houses along Woodland Avenue, at the top of the hill, are mainly Spanish-style, huge mansions with tiled walls and wrought-iron gates, set back along sweeping driveways. They were probably built in the 1920s when the style was so popular that it invaded incongruous East Coast landscapes. The houses are imposing, yes, but lost amid pines and oaks; missing are the palms, citrus trees, and agapanthus beds of the other coast. Houses like this don't belong under this gray-blue March sky of racing clouds. They need a still, clear sky and an azure sea.

I walk along Woodland at the top of the hill. The leaves of rhododendrons curl in the cold beside a heavy wooden gate in a brick wall. A number of houses seem to be for sale, as announced by the signs of high-end real estate companies. No traffic rumbles past save for delivery vans and the occasional sleek, black SUV. It's hard to imagine Helicon's collection of bohemians here.

Walnut Street runs downhill. On one side is the Dwight Englewood playing field, on the other side more big house of other styles—English Cotswold, mini Monticello. Which, I wonder, would have been here the night Helicon burned, when the rich took in their bohemian neighbors? A truck with a snowplow rattles past. There were snow squalls this morning.

Heading back along Woodland, I pass one house, scruffier than the rest, with several cars in the driveway. It looks as though people might be sharing it, school faculty perhaps? Certainly not the writers and artists of Helicon's day. It's hard to picture one of today's best-selling writers buying a big house in a fancy suburb to start a cooperative community. Or neighbors who wouldn't object.

We stood in the snow and watched our beautiful utopia flame and roar, until it crashed and died away to a dull glow.

━∙★ UPTON SINCLAIR ★∙━

The Autobiography of Upton Sinclair

Upton Sinclair's novel *The Jungle* has been a staple of high school reading lists for generations. Most people don't know much about its author, or even that he wrote the book not to reform the dangerous sanitary practices of the meatpacking industry but to expose the cruelties of capitalism. As he himself ruefully said, "I aimed at America's heart and hit it in the stomach." Still, it is *The Jungle* for which he is remembered, although he wrote more than eighty other books, ran for governor of California, and was a lifelong socialist and backer of radical causes.

Helicon Home Colony, or Helicon Hall, the utopian community he founded in 1906, was in many ways anomalous. Although Sinclair championed the working class, Helicon was an attempt to address "the servant problem," a topic popular in middle-class households of the day. Sinclair based his ideas on the works of Charlotte Perkins Gilman, the early feminist author of *Women and Economics*. Of course when Gilman herself envisioned a utopia in her 1915 novel *Herland*, it was an island world without men. And Sinclair was hardly a feminist. Had he, like the male characters in *Herland*, wandered accidentally into that perfect female world, he would have been dealt a lot of hard lessons.

Gilman, who was a supporter of most liberal causes, gave *The Jungle* a favorable review, but no reader of Sinclair's 1906 novel, which brought the young author fame and fortune, could consider it an endorsement of feminist principles. The novel belongs to its hero, Jurgis Rudkus, a Lithuanian peasant, superhuman in his strength and determination. In the opening chapter, which describes his wedding, he is Jurgis "with the mighty shoulders and giant hands," while his bride, fifteen-year-old Ona, is "small for her age" with a "wan little face." She stands there overwhelmed by the music and dancing as she will later be overwhelmed by the hardships of their life. She is often ill with "female troubles," bears the child that he must support, and is driven eventually to prostitution. As Jurgis describes their subsequent relationship: "There came one of those hysterical crises that had so often dismayed him. Ona sobbed and wept, her fear and anguish building themselves up into long climaxes . . . it was as if some dreadful thing rose up within her and took possession of her, torturing her, tearing her. This thing had been wont to set Jurgis quite beside himself." [1]

The women of the novel, and the offspring they produce, remain a constant burden for Jurgis and the other men. Prostitution seems about the only reliable way the women have of redeeming themselves or the family finances. As Sinclair himself admitted in the preface to *The Jungle:* "The physical and mental sufferings about which you read in the story were those not merely of the Stockyard workers, but of a youth who had supported himself through nine years of college and university study, and was determined to survive as a writer or not at all." [2] Implicit in this statement are Sinclair's own domestic arrangements for the years during which he worked on the novel. In May 1903 he moved his wife and baby to a cabin, sixteen by eighteen feet, a few miles north of Princeton, New Jersey. Eventually, these cramped quarters became impossible, and he was able to buy an old farm nearby, with a house and sixty acres on which to realize impractical rural dreams. [3] Sinclair spent his days working in a smaller cabin built partly by himself, with its interior painted black because that was the cheapest paint available. His wife, a city girl, was left to manage farm and child as best she could. There is not a great deal of sympathy in Sinclair's account for the loneliness of his young wife or for the baby he describes as a "trap." As the child becomes a toddler, his demands bewilder his young parents. The wife suffers from female troubles. In fact "Ona was Corydon speaking Lithuanian but otherwise unchanged." [4] In his autobiography, Sinclair coyly renames this first wife, Meta Fuller, Corydon and himself Thyrsis. It is not entirely clear why he chose the names of the two dueling shepherd poets of Virgil's Seventh Eclogue unless it was to emphasize competition over cooperation. It is clear that Corydon gets in the way of the literary heavy lifting, as Ona gets in the way of the ambitions of Jurgis. It seems that it was this situation, as much as any political principles, that spurred Sinclair to use most of the proceeds of *The Jungle* to create an experiment in cooperative living, the New York Home Colony, later called the Helicon Home Colony or Helicon Hall.

Upton Sinclair may have been a situational feminist, but the early part of the twentieth century was also a time of considerable political and social ferment. It was the era of the Progressives and their reaction to Victorian culture with its strict rules and pious propriety. New institutions and new ways were deemed necessary for the new century. The era was the culmination of the women's suffrage movement, and many voices were raised in support of changes in the roles of women. One such voice was that of Charlotte Perkins Gilman, who wrote extensively about the need for economic and psychological independence without which women would be unable to develop their full human potential. After Gilman's positive review of *The Jungle*,[5] Upton Sinclair became very taken with her major work, *Women and Economics*, although her novella, *The Yellow Wallpaper*, about a wife driven mad by her overbearing husband and circumscribed life, might have been more pertinent to his circumstances.

Gilman's main point in *Women and Economics* is that women will never be free as long as they are economically dependent on men. And to gain economic independence, they must escape the time-consuming drudgery of housework and childcare. "Work the object of which is to serve oneself is the lowest. Work the object of which is merely to serve one's family is the next lowest. Work the object of which is to serve more and more people, in widening range, till it approximates the divine spirit that cares for all the world, is social service in the fullest sense, and the highest form of service that we can reach."[6]

Gilman's plans for making this kind of work possible for women owe something to Edward Bellamy's 1888 utopian novel *Looking Backward*.

When its hero, Julian West, who had fallen into a hypnotic sleep in 1887, wakes in the year 2000, young Edith Leete explains modern housekeeping to him: "Not only is our cooking done at the public kitchen as I told you, but the service and quality of the meals are much more satisfactory if taken at the dining house."[7] Gilman feels much the same:

> If there should be built and opened in any of our large cities to-day a commodious and well served apartment house for professional women with families, it would be filled at once. The apartments would be without kitchens; but there would be a kitchen belonging to the house from which meals could be served to the families in their rooms or in a common dining room, as preferred. It would be a home where the cleaning was done by efficient workers, not hired separately by the families, but engaged by the manager of the establishment, and a roof garden, day nursery, and kindergarten, under well trained professional nurses and teachers, would insure proper care of the children.[8]

This is hardly a blueprint for a cooperative way of life, but Sinclair handed out copies of the book to prospective Helicon colonists nonetheless. Certainly he must have felt that a wife with fewer burdens would be happier and less demanding.

On July 16, 1906, Sinclair published a letter in the *New York Times* under the heading "For a Cooperative House." In it, he announced a meeting to be held the next night at the Berkeley Lyceum in New York City. This meeting was to involve some one hundred people interested in "a plan to establish a cooperative home in the vicinity of New York." Hoping for even more "congenial" recruits, he outlined the structure of the colony. Although Sinclair intended *The Jungle* as a criticism of capitalist society, he was careful to dissociate the planned colony from socialism, assuring the public that "very few" of the prospective colonists were socialists but rather that they were working people "who believe they can spend their incomes to better advantage in co-operation."[9] Everyone could build his or her own home in whatever way he or she wanted, but, in line with Gilman, these homes would not have kitchens or nurseries. Cooking and childcare were to be carried on cooperatively in a central kitchen and a building something like a central nursery school. Also planned were rooms and suites for those who might not want a separate house. The community would own sufficient property to raise some of its own food, fruits and vegetables presumably; whatever else was needed could be bought in bulk. Business affairs would be under the control of a democratically elected board of directors. "Members would thus be entirely relieved from the worry and waste incidental to the management of small scale household industries."[10] Nor would children ever come into contact with servants, one of Gilman's particular concerns in her later treatise *Concerning Children*. Most servants, she felt, could not provide the intellectual and moral guidance desirable, at least for a middle-class child.[11]

If the colony were of sufficient size, it would have a hall for lectures and concerts, reading rooms, a circulating library, gymnasium, recreation grounds, bathhouses, a boat and carriage livery, and a cooperative store. Socialist muckraker or no, Sinclair envisioned a utopia that was definitely a comfortable middle-class one. He did not escape his own bias toward individualism, maintaining that if the colony were large enough, people could avoid anyone they found uncongenial. He made it clear that he intended this protection for himself as well. It seemed that his colony would be a cooperative largely in name—a way for artists and intellectuals of the middle class unable to find reliable domestic help to avoid the much discussed "servant problem."

Nor was the colony intended for everyone. Each prospective colonist was required to fill out an extensive questionnaire, no doubt to establish congeniality. The most basic requirements for admission were clearly defined. "While in general accepting the formula that the colony should be open to any *white* person of good moral character who is free from communicable disease, it is necessary to recognize the fact that there are exceptional individuals whose habits and ideas would render them uncongenial. There should be a Committee on Membership which would meet personally all applicants, and which should be empowered to reject any person."[12]

The colony was pledged to equality, although obviously not along racial lines. No domestic service would be performed by anyone who could not be admitted to the full privileges of the colony. Part of the servant problem was, after all, the indifference and irresponsibility of hired workers. All members of the colony, who obviously had a vested interest, should be able to provide some domestic service for which they would be paid. Another unusual idea was that college students might be hired for menial work. With a fine confidence, Sinclair, said the *Times*, declared himself sure "that if the colony were put somewhere near Princeton quite a number of Tiger boys would be glad to serve the community." [13]

Throughout the summer of 1906, meetings continued to be held and duly reported on by the *New York Times*. While the *Times* tended to dwell on discussions about whether bare feet would be tolerated in the common dining hall, or whether pickles and candy are good for young children, or whether parents should be allowed to visit their children in the school or nursery at will, the actual structure of the colony was being hammered out in private meetings of various committees, including one held on a sailboat in Barnegat Bay. [14]

A corporation with stockholders would be set up. This corporation would raise the capital necessary to purchase a property. The property would then be leased to the Home Colony for three years. The colony would elect a five-person board of directors, which technically would govern the operation, although a salaried manager appointed by the board would run things on a day-to-day basis. [15] Sinclair himself put up a total of about $16,000 from his own resources, the proceeds of *The Jungle*. He had chosen as temporary chairman for the project the millionaire socialist H. Gaylord Wilshire. Wilshire, a Harvard dropout and wheeler-dealer who eventually gave his name to Wilshire Boulevard in Los Angeles, was likely to attract the kind of investors needed to make the colony a success.

In October 1906 a suitable property was found in Englewood, New Jersey. Englewood's founder, one J. A. Humphreys, had described the town's future as "a pleasant dream of gilded hopes," and by 1906 it was both pleasant and gilded. Built above a valley on the reverse slope of the Palisades, shaded by elms and with a view out across the Hudson to New York and back across the Ramapo Valley, about an hour from New York City, it was a peaceful spot with great appeal to affluent New York bankers and other businessmen. The East Hill section of Englewood is still today its most prized real estate, and it was there that the New York Home Colony found Helicon Hall.

In Greek mythology, Helicon is the mountain home of Apollo and the Muses. Helicon Hall had been a boys' school run by the Reverend John Woolsey Craig, an eccentric Episcopal clergyman, who bought the land at the corner of Woodland and Walnut streets at the top of East Hill, with its view back over the Ramapo Valley. Craig had strong aesthetic notions. He believed that boys exposed to grace and beauty, and who were required to wear dress suits to dinner, would become civilized and cultured citizens. To this end, it appears, no expense was spared. The large building, with its pillars and porticoes, was set on about nine acres of cultivated land, backed by a fifteen-mile forest stretching northward along the Palisades. But there was more to it than a graceful exterior and a bucolic setting. It was filled, according to the *New York Times* of October 7, "with everything that the traditional ascetic does not want," including a swimming pool, a bowling alley, and a theater. The interior was built around a glass-roofed courtyard with a brook flowing through it, crossed by Japanese-style bridges and bordered by tropical plants. Palms grew twenty feet high and goldfish swam in the brook. Niches held statues, among them a Venus de Milo. At one end was "a vast fireplace open on all four sides about which fifty or sixty people could sit or lounge." [16] Near it stood a large pipe organ on which the Reverend Craig had been wont to play "Now the Day Is Over" when the boys had been put to bed of an evening. About fifty rooms surrounded this interior courtyard, enough to house the eventual sixty or so colonists. As one young colonist, actress Undena Eberlein, later a colonist at Free Acres, described it: "The house has a big court in the middle full of giant rubber plants and ferns that reach to the glass roof and a brook flows through with rustic bridges etc., and mossy banks and statues, etc." [17]

Clearly the Hall was in "move in" condition, because by November 1, 1906, the first thirty colonists were in residence. Anna Noyes, wife of Professor William Noyes of Columbia Teachers College, agreed to take on the job of manager. Noyes was a disciple of Charlotte Perkins Gilman and proved, luckily, to be, with her husband's help, a competent administrator.

None, however, of the assorted artists and intellectuals who made up the group had any real training for running such a complex enterprise.

Among the original colonists were Edwin Bjorkman, literary critic, translator of Strindberg, and editor of the Modern Drama Series with his suffragist wife, Frances Maule; William Pepperell Montague, who taught philosophy at Barnard, his wife, and two sons; and Michael Williams, his wife, and two children. Williams, a young writer and something of a protégé of Sinclair's, would eventually become the editor of the Catholic weekly *Commonweal*. The novelists Alice MacGowan and her sister Grace MacGowen Cooke, with her two young daughters, moved in as well. Another member was Upton Sinclair's secretary, Edith Summers Kelly, who later became the author of *Weeds*, a successful novel of working-class southern women. Obviously this was a group of artists and intellectuals with wide-ranging views. All were committed to some degree, and for varied reasons, to the women's movement, and many had socialist leanings. Beyond this a great number of ideologies were represented. There were anarchists, single taxers, vegetarians, aesthetes, and spiritualists. Such diversity was a magnet for outsiders, both admirers and detractors, "like a gypsy van stopping in a Methodist camp-meeting and throbbing with a perpetual brainstorm of radicalitis!"[18]

From its inception, Helicon ran into criticism from the outside world. Few, in 1906, would have taken serious exception to the exclusion of blacks; in a long letter to the *New York Times*, however, one would-be resident complained of discrimination against Jews. Mr. D. C. Serber, who had paid his initial fee of ten dollars and been involved in all the July and August 1906 planning meetings, was told in October that there would be no room for him. On investigating this peculiar circumstance, he was informed by "a member of the colony now living at Helicon Hall . . . that Hebrews will not be admitted to the colony, and that this step had been practically decided upon at the Berkeley Lyceum meeting at a caucus held by the executive committee."[19] Upon his continued protest, he received a personal check for ten dollars from Upton Sinclair and a letter stating that this was a decision of the majority and not his fault.

Another letter to the *New York Times* of July 22, 1906, from well-known socialist reformer John Spargo and headlined "Facts for Mr. Sinclair," took on the colony's plans for the raising of children. As a reformer, Spargo was particularly involved in the movement to end child labor. He considered himself a friend of Sinclair's, but he disapproved of Sinclair's advertisement of his Home Colony. "If Mr. Sinclair and any number of his friends choose to co-operate in the purchase and management of their homes, that is no business of anybody except themselves. Mr. Sinclair, however, has made it everybody's business by the offensively noisy manner in which he has claimed public attention for the private business of himself and friends." Spargo went on to condemn the proposed childcare arrangements:

> Had Mr. Sinclair been half as familiar with the history of co-operative home colonies, co-operative nurseries and the like, as he is with conditions in the meat packing trade he would have know that long and sad experience has clearly shown that no amount of science and skill can adequately take the place of maternal care and affection. . . . I am not interested in the long list of amateurish questions which Mr. Sinclair has deemed necessary to submit to those who would join his "colony" but I am interested in the fate of the children. To propose communal child raising, in the light of the tragic experiences so universally encountered, is to propose child murder upon an extended scale.[20]

Interestingly, Sinclair seems to have been far less bothered by these substantive criticisms than the more frivolous but of course more constant and intrusive criticisms of the press. For the New York papers, particularly the *New York Sun,* Helicon was perfect fodder. Here was a group of bohemians living in palatial surroundings only an hour away from the city. Reporters could, and did, show up at any time. Despite Sinclair's early disclaimers and the middle-class ambience of the colony, the public persisted in seeing it as a hotbed of radical thought and its corollary, free love. Sinclair would describe this later in his exposé of the press, *The Brass Check:* "Here were the newspaper-editors of New York City who were supposed to report the experiment, and who behaved like a band of Brazilian Indians, hiding in the woods about Helicon Hall and shooting the inmates full of poisoned arrows." [21] Perhaps it was their failure to take the experiment seriously that upset him most. He was convinced that the colony was the way of the future, that "when our universal system of dog-eat-dog has been abolished and the souls of men and women have risen upon the wings of love and fellowship, they will look back on us in our twenty million separate kitchens as we look upon the Eskimos in their filthy snow-huts lighted with walrus blubber." [22] (It need hardly be pointed out that Sinclair had no feeling for native peoples.)

During the course of its brief six-month existence, the colony was visited by many of the notable intellectuals of the day, including educational reformer John Dewey and the young Will Durant. Dewey, who had in fact been active in the planning stages, had considered bringing his family to live at Helicon but ultimately changed his mind. William James, fresh from giving a famous series of lectures on pragmatism at Columbia University, spent an evening, according to Sinclair, quite fascinated by one colonist's use of the Ouija board. Another visitor was John Coryell, originator of the Nick Carter detective series, who also wrote romances under the name of Bertha M. Clay, making him a key figure in Bernarr Macfadden's publishing empire. In 1911, he and his wife Abby became two of the first teachers at the Ferrer School in New York City, which would shortly become the nucleus of the utopian community at Stelton, New Jersey. Durant would succeed them as a teacher there. Sinclair had even invited the poet Edwin Markham, author of the famous social protest poem "The Man with a Hoe," to join the colony, but he had declined.

Another eventually more famous writer and Nobel Prize winner spent a month tending Helicon's temperamental furnace. Sinclair Lewis and his friend, the poet Allan Updegraff, dropped out of Yale and arrived one day at Helicon, thus fulfilling one of Sinclair's early hopes for the colony— college boys as workers. Upton Sinclair should have remembered his literary history, however. An earlier writer, Nathaniel Hawthorne, had spent some time at the famous Massachusetts utopian community Brook Farm, which became the subject of his comic novel, *The Blithedale Romance*. Lewis spent about a month at the colony and sold his story, "Two Yale Men in Utopia," to Sinclair's nemesis, the *New York Sun*.

Lewis's description of his arrival at Helicon Hall is less than romantic. He remarks on "bedsprings in the main hall and the remains of packing boxes in the wooded court." Nor is he particularly happy to be offered the position of janitor, but still he decides to join, opining that the "author of *The Jungle* did it. For three solid hours I sat in his office while language flowed from him in a scintillating stream. It took him thus long to explain that my duty was to be firing a furnace. But after he had told how the cook was a Cornell M.A., the laundress a well-known assistant muckraker, the scullion a Tennessee lawyer and Poe critic, the other janitor a wealthy Providence wholesaler, it made my objections to janiting seem weak and unnatural." [23]

Lewis goes on to describe heated philosophical discussions in the kitchen as dinner burns and a mothers' meeting "discussing soulfully whether the institutionalized children should be allowed to drink six or seven times a day." [24] Through his eyes we see lawyers and literary critics beating rugs, valiantly trying to peel potatoes, and doing battle with a primitive forerunner of the washing machine, as well as Lewis's own scrambling to feed the monster furnace with kindling. He pokes mild fun at Sinclair's boyish enthusiasm about the "bully" swimming pool and the "jolly" bowling alley—and his conviction that servants are unnecessary, that all the colony work can be done by "socially 'possible' people who would earn enough to support themselves by a working day of six or seven hours," [25] allowing them to devote the rest of their time to "science, philosophy, art and literature." Although Lewis soon tired of "janiting" and the demands of the furnace monster, one feels his affection for the place: "This is a mighty pleasant place some ways. Take the evenings when I am not working. From the third-story gallery one looks down through the jungle of palm and rubber trees to the leaping flames of the great fireplace. It has an appealing, exotic charm. . . . A weird gray bat who inhabits the patio whirrs past and the moon gleams strangely through the big skylight over the court. A good place, say I, and redolent of dreams." [26]

Lewis was not the only visitor who went to the newspapers with an account of his experiences. There was also the incident of Sadakichi Hartmann. Hartmann, who cut quite a figure in the artistic/bohemian circles of his day, was an exotic from an exotic background: the product of a

German merchant father and a Japanese mother who died soon after his birth. Brought up by a wealthy uncle in Hamburg among books and art treasures, he was sent to the naval academy at Kiel, ran away to Paris, was disinherited by his father, and sent to relatives in Philadelphia in 1882. Discovering that Walt Whitman lived across the river in Camden, he made friends with the poet and recorded their conversations over fried eggs. He became a poet, a painter, and a respected art critic, who also wrote about the emerging art of photography. Hartmann wrote plays, including a cycle of symbolist dramas about religious figures—titled *Christ, Mohammed, Confucius, Buddha,* and *Moses*—and organized perfume concerts as well as sound and light shows. He spent time in Hollywood. He had theories about things like "soul atoms," which could travel across the centuries from one great artist to another. But he was also known as a sponger and a boozer. He arrived one evening at Helicon with the sculptor Jo Davidson and a young female companion. Hartmann was drunk, as Sinclair recalls it, and Sinclair, who had suffered an alcoholic father, had no time for drunks. When Hartmann's request to stay the night was refused, he left in high dudgeon, denouncing the whole operation. The next day he wrote letters to all the newspapers claiming that he and his companions had been thrown out at one o'clock in the morning and left to wander the Palisades in the dark. More fodder for the newsmen.

The press, however, was more interested in the possibility of a socialist love nest than the grievances of an art critic. Sinclair was at pains to correct this impression of the colony. As he maintains in his autobiography, "I do not know of any assemblage of forty adult persons where a higher standard of sexual morals prevailed than at Helicon Hall. Our colonists were for the most part young literary couples who had one or two children and did not know how to fit them into the literary life; in short they were people with the same problem as myself." [27]

On this topic, however, Sinclair may have been disingenuous. In *Upton Sinclair: American Rebel,* Leon Harris asserts that Sinclair called his wife Meta to a meeting with himself and Anna Noyes to tell Meta that he and Mrs. Noyes had fallen in love and were having an affair. Anna told Meta not to worry, that it wasn't practical for her and Upton to run off together, and that she was planning to tell her husband.[28] No doubt in the close and clearly romantic quarters of Helicon Hall, with its wooded courtyard, extensive grounds, and evening gatherings around the fireplace (with talk of dedicating its four sides to science, philosophy, politics, and the arts), some sexual experimentation went on in the name of liberating society and escaping bourgeois ethics. Certainly many were influenced by H. G. Wells's book *A Modern Utopia* and Edward Carpenter's *Love's Coming of Age*, both of which called for a more open kind of marriage and an end to monogamous sexual relationships.

Whatever the more sensational aspects of Helicon, it was in many ways a successful experiment. For the more ordinary colonists like Undena Eberlein, it was a godsend:

I have such news! Last week I took Bunch [her baby] out to Helicon Hall, Englewood New Jersey—that is the home of the Sinclair Colony—and we stayed all night and met the celebrity himself. Likewise his wife and little boy. It is a lovely place and I could hardly bear to come home. . . . Mr. Sinclair, when he learned that I would like to live out there with Bunch, became very enthusiastic. They have about a dozen children now but none under 2 years. They are anxious to start a department for babies younger. Several have applied already. We had a long talk about it, and the result was my putting in for membership, providing Lisbeth (we've really named her that) will be in it too. I will probably have charge of the nursery part of the time. . . . I am so worked up about the colony. I think of it all the time—especially on Lisbeth's account. She needs to be with other children.[29]

For others, like Michael Williams, it was a mixed blessing:

Never since the tower of Babel, I dare say, has there existed a place so saturated in language as Helicon Hall. Everybody there was more or less of the "advanced," or "radical" order of chemical make-up, or of soul development; and it is a scientific fact that this type is continually effervescing in monologue, sizzling in conversation, detonating in debate, fuming in argument, flashing in expressions of opinion and exploding in many theories. . . . That flimsy house fairly throbbed with criss-cross currents of diverse temperaments and purposes.[30]

Williams and his wife roomed next door to a lady spiritualist who saw visions and talked to them. Down the hall was Edwin Bjorkman philoso-phizing among his books and the MacGowan sisters dictating novels to an amanuensis. Helicon also provided the peace and the setting for Wil-liams's rumination on "the problem with which so much of my life has been concerned—the problem, namely, of whether we are immortal souls or merely ephemeral products of a casual chemico-mechanical process."[31] Certainly a dilemma to ponder as he walked along the wooded Palisades on winter afternoons. Like Sinclair Lewis, Williams found Helicon appealing in its better moments, as he conveys in a sentence worthy of Henry James.

Sometimes by night, when a glowing fire of crimson coals was sus-pended in the iron basket in the fireplace, and the lights were turned out, and the moon streamed dimly through the glass roof, splashing like noiseless silver water on the palm trees in the court, and someone played a violin or something on the organ, and the talk mellowed and modulated from sociological arguments to a more meditative mood, then it seemed as if some influence sweet and pensive, friendly and melting, flowed like incense over and through us all; and for a while we could dream that our dreams could and would be realized—and the Socialist lived for the moment in his co-operative commonwealth, and the anarchist in Egoland, and the spiritualists divined the pres-ence of their departed friends in the swaying shadows by the foun-tain, and all the ideals and dreams and fantasies, and all the impossible illusions of that assemblage of modern dreamers seemed to material-ize, seemed to be real things, and the world of fact evaporate quite out of existence.[32]

Sinclair himself always felt that the greatest success of the colony was with the children.[33] In many ways, Helicon anticipated the progressive education movement that would develop over the next twenty or so years. Approximately thirteen children took over the building's theater and were cared for there by one full-time employee and a roster of mothers. Cooperation among the mothers, except for a few incidents such as a mixing up of toothbrushes, was successful. The plan didn't quite fit that of Gilman—to remove children from their mothers completely—but it was a step on the way to what we know today as day care or perhaps cooperative nursery schools. The children even had their own parliament to discuss issues important to them. Mothers who participated in the care received reduced fees and had the advantage of company while carrying out their duties. They were also relieved at night, when social life and intellectual talk took place around the fireplace in the courtyard, known in Helicon parlance as the patio. Children became more self-reliant and delighted in having the run of the place, sometimes, as legend has it, in the nude.

Helicon did not entirely conquer "the servant problem." The original plan to use college students as a better class of workers did not materialize. Lewis and Updegraff, tired of feeding the furnace and carrying out the laundry, left after about a month, and no one turned up to replace them. The alternative—hiring servants for reasonable wages and making them part of the colony to increase their motivation—turned the "servant problem" into a "staff problem." [34] Most of the colonists, however, were relieved of the great part of their domestic duties and thus had more time for intellectual and other pursuits. Certainly the colony was perceived as an answer by enough people to have a waiting list by early spring 1907.

It is hard to know how long Helicon would have lasted, or how its difficulties would have been resolved, because on March 16, 1907, at three in the morning, Helicon Hall burned to the ground.

The headlines of the *New York Times* for March 17, 1907, shouted "Fire Wipes Out Helicon Hall" and "Upton Sinclair Hints That the Steel Trust's Hand May Be in It." As Sinclair explained in *The Brass Check*, he had in the building at the time the records of months of investigations into "the armor-plate frauds," which he claimed indicated that Carnegie Steel Company had robbed the U.S. government of millions of dollars. He asserted, for instance, that the plates for the conning towers on certain battleships were defective and would have "splintered like glass if struck by a shell." [35] It was also alleged that a stick of dynamite had been found on the premises some weeks before. Whether the cause was arson or whether it was, as found by the courts, defective gas pipes, the conflagration was a disaster for the colony and for its individual residents. For writers and artists, years of work went up in smoke. Or as Michael Williams told the *New York Times* reporter: "I went through the San Francisco earthquake and what I didn't lose there I lost in this fire. Two typewriters in such a short space of time is rather hard." [36]

The Helicon colonists may have been less than expert at housework or carpentry or cooking, they may have argued over whether or not eggs should be on the Sunday breakfast menu, but they proved themselves cool-headed in a crisis. When the flames broke out at three in the morning, it was, according to the *Times* report, Sinclair himself who gave the alarm, his wife having been woken by "a series of heavy crashes." He sent her to the ground floor to get their five-year-old son out of the children's dormitory while he ran along the balconies above the interior courtyard, shouting and banging on doors. Already the fire was well under way.

> If I live to be a hundred, I shall never forget that sensation; it was like a demon hand sweeping over me—it took all the hair from one side of my head and a part of my nightshirt. I escaped by crouching against the wall, stooping low and running fast. Fortunately the stairs were not yet in flames so I got down into the central court, which was full of broken glass and burning brands, not very kind to my bare feet. I ran to the children's quarters and made sure they were all out; then I ran outside, and tried to stop the fall of two ladies who had to jump from windows of the second story. [37]

The ladies in question were Alice MacGowan and her sister, Grace Mac-Gowan Cooke. The men were unable to keep the blanket from hitting the ground, the *New York Times* reported, because the two women were "not light." Mrs. Cooke's children had been safely caught when they jumped. Anna Noyes, meanwhile, after helping Emma Williams, who was in charge of the children's first-floor dormitory, pass them out of the window to those outside, ran down the icy road in her bare feet to a tower containing an alarm bell. Reaching the base of the tower, she discovered that the bell had no rope. Undaunted, she climbed up the side of the tower and swung the clapper. She did it, she said, not so much as a fire alarm as to summon medical help. In the melee, many people suffered injuries from burns or falls. The head cook, Helen Fichtenberg, jumped from the third-floor balcony to the floor of the interior court. Another woman took off her nightgown, tore it into strips, and made a ladder of it. Ironically, one colonist, Edwin C. Potter, had protested the absence of any kind of fire ropes. Though teased by other colonists, he had walked into Englewood and bought a ninety-cent rope. With this rope he saved himself, his wife and children, and several other colonists. Miraculously, only one person died. Lester Briggs, a hired carpenter, who had been drinking and was apparently a heavy sleeper, did not heed the alarm. Ernest Eberlein described his experience in a letter to his wife Undena, who was touring with a play in San Francisco:

About 4 o'clock Sinclair himself woke me saying "get up there's a fire in the building." I thought first that it had started somewhere and we were to be prepared, he acted so calmly and quiet. As he came back from the next room he saw me dressing. I had turned up the gas and got my trousers. "You had better hurry the place is burning fast. Help the children." The tone was enough this time and smoke poured in. Nothing but the baby on my mind then. Grabbing the balance of clothing in sight I groped through the dense smoke to Davida's room with sickening uncertainty of the baby and myself. Flashes of flame penetrated the darkness. The skylight was crashing into the court with a sinister noise. . . . Groping, fearful of losing my way, I came to what I thought or felt was Dovey's [Davida de Guibert, his sister-in-law, who was helping with the baby] door. I hurled myself against it. It gave way and I landed in the dormitory whose stairway was next to hers. She was not there. No one was interested except in their own children. I could not leave in that uncertainty. The terrifying racket in the court only made me wilder. I was up the stairs again like a monkey.

21

The interior was a seething furnace. I crawled into Dovey's room. The beds were empty. Crawling back, I held my breath and slid down into the dormitory [for the children]. It was empty and the side belching flames. I passed out through the back laundry. . . . I put on my coat but had no shoes. The rough ground was frozen and snow covered. Davida was standing with the brown shawl around a grimy wondering little pup. . . . Near her was Mrs. Potter ready to faint, nothing on but a thin nightgown and Lloyd [her baby] naked in her arms.[38]

To their credit, the millionaire neighbors of Helicon took in the stunned refugees and provided food and clothing. The building's location, at a distance from the center of town and at the top of a steep hill, prevented the Englewood Fire Department from saving anything. "In less than ½ hr.," wrote Ernest Eberlein, "the place was leveled, only the fireplace stood and the foundation." "We stood in the snow," Sinclair recalled, and "watched our beautiful utopia flame and roar, until it crashed in and died away to a dull glow. Then we went to the homes of our fashionable neighbors who hadn't known what to make of us in our success but were kind to us in our failure."[39]

Because one person had died, a coroner's inquest was necessary. Attending its sessions, Sinclair discovered exactly what the town had been thinking of the little world on East Hill. First of all, the jurors censured the colony "for not making adequate provisions for the saving of life from fires in a building containing 62 souls."[40] This reprimand was revealing, since no such provisions had been demanded of the Reverend Craig's establishment when it was a boys' boarding school. There were even suggestions that the fire had been set for insurance money and that ways had been devised to avoid paying debts to local tradesmen. Jurors also spent a good deal of time discussing the propriety of the sleeping arrangements in the large third-floor art studio, where curtains had been hung as temporary room dividers for the hired servants.

At the end of the day, the Helicon Home Colony had insurance and had not been carelessly run. Sinclair and his board were scrupulous. All its debts were paid and provision made for colonists left destitute. Had he had the money, Upton Sinclair declared, he would have started another colony. Instead, wanting to write another novel, he took his family to a rented cottage at Point Pleasant, New Jersey. Going back to the single-family way of life was, he maintained, "like leaving modern civilization and returning to the dark ages. I felt that way about it for a long time." In fact, it was a difficult summer. Meta suffered an attack of appendicitis and was taken by her family to the Battle Creek Sanitarium to recuperate while Sinclair himself had to "flee," as he put it, to the Adirondack wilderness, leaving child and nursemaid in Point Pleasant, "in order to get away from the worry and strain of it all."[41]

Some months later, however, he was plotting with Michael Williams to start up "a perambulating colony, a Helicon Hall on the hoof; a migratory home, warranted fireproof, and free from landlords and steam-heat and taxes. Our wives will escape flat-hunting; the servant problem will be solved, and dress will cease to worry us. We shall set out about the first of the year, with a couple of big surveying wagons and teams in South California." The party would consist of Sinclair, Williams, their wives, three children, a governess, a stenographer, and a cook—as well as "two young poets who will help with the men's work."[42] This true gypsy caravan would travel north with the season up the Pacific Coast. There were plans to follow up this itinerary with tours of England, France, and Italy.

"Helicon Hall on the hoof" never came to pass, and Upton Sinclair never founded another utopian colony himself, but other people's utopias continued to figure in his life. Two years later he made his first trip across the continent, with a fateful stop at the university in Lawrence, Kansas, to meet young Harry Kemp, the "hobo poet." He also visited his friend Gaylord Wilshire's gold mine and ended up in Carmel, California. Carmel had been a bohemian settlement since the first artists staked their claims after the San Francisco earthquake and Mary Austin wrote in her tree house. Sinclair arrived to stay with the poet George Sterling, whom he had met in New York, half hoping to be able to start a Helicon West. Carmel, with its silver beaches, twisted pines, and rugged mountains, was a far cry from sedate Englewood. Although he spent only a happy six months in that Pacific paradise, Helicon West, in a sense, got started without him. Alice MacGowan and Grace MacGowan Cooke with her two daughters followed the road to Carmel, where they bought a bayside house. Needing a secretary, they remembered the young man who had briefly stoked the furnace at Helicon and sent for Sinclair Lewis. Lewis was not much better suited to secretarial work than he had been to janitorial; he preferred to busy himself partaking of the town's bohemian festivities or working on his own stories.[43] Michael Williams also returned to the West, describing California as an earthly paradise and ending up in a hut in Carmel, a part of that enduring literary colony.

Sinclair returned east via Key West, Florida. His next visit was to Bernarr Macfadden's sanitarium. Sinclair had been reading Macfadden's *Physical Culture* magazine, for which he would eventually write, and became something of a disciple. He and Meta went there in 1909, fasted, and then went on a milk diet, which Sinclair claimed cured his persistent headaches and digestive trouble. They were also visited there by the peripatetic Harry Kemp on one of his tramping trips.

Restored to health by Macfadden's eccentric program, Sinclair decided that because he had no colony of his own, he "would try other people's."[44] He took his family first to Fairhope, a single-tax colony in Alabama, where they spent the winter in three tents. Fairhope, like Helicon, was a community of intellectuals, affording Sinclair the opportunity for debates with the likes of the young Scott Nearing, but without the responsibility of running the show. No one would come to him about missing lemons or eggs on Sunday. After Fairhope, he moved his family to another single-tax colony, Arden, in Delaware. It was in that place, named for Shakespeare's forest of tangled romance, that poet Harry Kemp reappeared and commenced the affair with Meta that would end the Sinclairs' shaky marriage. Arden, as Kemp describes it, "was a community as William Morris or some Guild Socialist of a medieval turn of mind might have conceived." Much of the last chapters of Kemp's autobiography are taken up with the affair and the ways the lovers found of deceiving the remarkably unsuspicious husband. One favorite and somewhat archaic pastime was to go into the woods, complete with a reference book, to collect mushrooms. "Down vistas of forest we often pursued each other . . . often got lost so that it took hours for reorientation . . . once, for awhile, to our great fright, we could not rediscover our clothes, that we had lightly tossed aside on the bank of a brook lost and remote—that had never before laved a human body in its singing recesses of forest foliage . . . for I had been playing satyr to her nymph, pursuing her." [45]

After Arden, Sinclair returned to ordinary single-family life, marrying twice more and living in California, where he ran for governor on a platform with utopian overtones.[46] However, as he maintained in *The Brass Check*, "I look back on Helicon Hall to-day, and this is the way I feel about it. I have lived in the future; I have known those wider freedoms and opportunities that the future will grant to all men and women. Now, by harsh fate I have been seized and dragged back into a lower order of existence and commanded to spend the balance of my days therein. . . . I have lived in the future and all things about me seem drab and sordid in comparison." [47]

If not for the fire of March 17, 1907, Helicon Hall might well have continued for some time. The waiting list for places in the colony was variously estimated at twenty-five to eight hundred names. Even though many disapproved, many were obviously attracted. Helicon Hall was the brainchild of one man, but that man did not insist on control. Sinclair was in fact happy to hand it over to others so that he would be free to do his work. For many women of narrow means, struggling with housework and children and unable to find, or afford, help, such a colony was a light in the darkness. It recognized women's need to have their own lives and children's need to have some sort of educational experience outside the home, which is common today in nursery school and prekindergarten programs. Living cooperatively is certainly a less wasteful alternative to single households. As resources dwindle and economies tighten, it is beginning to be revisited.

Interestingly, Charlotte Perkins Gilman herself was not impressed by Helicon: "Cooperative housekeeping is inherently doomed to failure. From early experience and later knowledge, I thoroughly learned this fact, and have always proclaimed it. Yet such is the perversity of the average mind that my advocacy of the professionalizing of housework—having it done by the hour by specially trained persons, with the service of cooked meals to the home—has always been objected to as 'cooperative housekeeping.' Upton Sinclair's ill-fated Helicon Hall experiment he attributed to my teachings, without the least justification." [48]

25

Free Acres
A Single-Tax Colony

I am in the middle of the central New Jersey commuter belt on my way to Free Acres. It's a relief to leave the speeding crowd on Route 78 and head toward Berkeley Heights. The traffic doesn't let up, but it moves more slowly.

"Turn at the Getty station," my directions read. I drive past the cul-de-sacs of identical houses off Emerson Lane, past the Tyvek-shrouded construction rising on a ridge of the Watchung Hills. At the old red farmhouse, I turn again, dropping down a road that is barely one SUV wide, into Free Acres, a utopian community approaching its hundredth birthday. There are no streetlights, and everywhere are trees, hanging over the road, abutting the houses, in all the places that worry the suburban driver and homeowner. These trees have presence, like the trees in a fairy-tale forest. Most of the late October leaves have fallen now, exposing an eccentric collection of camps and cottages, a few new houses stark among them. About eighty-five leasehold properties border the nine roads in the roughly seventy-five acres that make up the Free Acres Association.

Free Acres really began as a summer colony, but when people decided to live here year-round, little cabins and cottages grew like Topsy. Buildings had to skirt those magical trees—permission from the association was required to cut one down. And if that permission was given, a new tree had to be planted. Free Acreites loved their woodlands. The old houses are by now an organic part of the landscape, whereas the new ones, the kind that would be at home in any subdivision, look perched and a little uncomfortable.

All the roads in Free Acres are narrow, lanes really, with names like Appletree Row and Fern Way. There are no sidewalks, but any path you take will lead you onto another path or a road. Fences are not allowed. Paths meander through the communal woods, behind and between houses and across the stream.

The two centers of Free Acres community life are the red farmhouse, original to the property, and the swimming pool. The swimming pool began as a dammed-up swimming hole, on whose muddy banks colonists caper in old photographs. Now it is a regular modern pool, set in concrete and surrounded by a chain-link fence. The trees still shelter it. Like all swimming pools in autumn, it has a melancholy, abandoned look. But I find it peaceful sitting on a bench at the edge of the woods, facing the pool, as the leaves drift down. A few leftover flowers bloom in planters. Children ride by on bicycles. Despite the muffled rush of Route 78 on the southern boundary, there's a woodland stillness.

I walk back up Appletree Row toward the farmhouse. Near it, two small children are romping in the playground, a clearing with play equipment. I climb the rise to the farmhouse itself. This hill, in spring, will be covered with buttercups. I reach the deck where generations of Free Acreites have danced or listened to speakers or argued politics. Inside the old building, the monthly association meetings are held. It is the community's heart and a reproach to the anonymous development across the way.

* * *

I have been back to Free Acres many times since, in early spring when the woods are golden with celandine and in summer when gardens bloom. Always, when I leave Emerson Lane and drop down through the trees, I feel that I am leaving the world of impatience and anger. People who live here love it as a place apart. And even most newcomers are soon caught up in a sense that this place is different. Your neighbor is not just the guy always making a racket with the leaf blower; he is someone you have to take into account. You govern this little place together. There's the pool in summer and the annual Halloween parade. Here, too, the flora and fauna matter; they are not something to be ripped up or shut out. That is the legacy of those early colonists who loved the trees, studied the birds, catalogued the wildflowers, and staged plays together in the woods.

As a whole, the woods and the sky and the colonists were like one. The people living there enjoyed every minute of the day.
 DR. BENZION LIBER
A Doctor's Apprenticeship

My earliest memory," wrote Konrad Bercovici, "is of a winter afternoon when a caravan of Gypsies crossed the frozen Danube in front of the home of my parents."[1] Bercovici was a Romanian Jew, son in a prosperous and cultivated household, who spoke several languages including Rom, the language of the Gypsies, who were his lifelong friends. The world he describes in his autobiography is a world of Gypsies and peasants, of villages populated variously by Hungarians, Tartars, Greeks, and Germans fiercely defending their turf. Free Acres, where Bercovici lived for a time after pogroms drove his family out of Romania, was the antithesis of his childhood world. Its founder, Bolton Hall, saw land in an entirely different light. Born in Ireland in 1854, Hall was also an immigrant; he moved with his family to New York in 1867 when his father was made pastor of the Fifth Avenue Presbyterian church. Eventually Hall graduated from Princeton and became a lawyer and disciple of single-tax advocate Henry George.

As a young man, Henry George had been haunted by the gulf between rich and poor in a country as prosperous as America. He set out his answer to this gap in his famous *Progress and Poverty*, in which he argued that man has a right to labor and to natural resources, but that as the population increases, land values soar, creating wealth for landowners and distress for everyone else. George believed land should belong to the community, not to individuals. Instead, individuals would pay a "tax rent," which would be regulated by the cost of providing services and other improvements. He believed that in America, a new country, the land could set people free. In a country without a long history of contested land, it seemed possible to create a new way.

He was not alone. Between 1895 and 1927, ten single-tax colonies were formed in the United States. Fairhope, Alabama, was the first and Free Acres, New Jersey, the fourth. Henry George himself was skeptical of them, but they were a way of experimenting with the single-tax principle without the endless and probably futile task of trying to get national legislation changed. Obviously, such colonies had to abide by the tax laws of the state in which they were founded, and all were set up in essentially the same way. Each began as a nonprofit corporation that bought land, using the corporation as a holding company. Real estate taxes were billed to the corporation, which would pay the taxes in a lump sum after assessing the colony's residents on the value of their landholdings according to George's theories.

Bolton Hall was one of the early leaseholders (1894) of the single-tax colony at Fairhope, Alabama. A friend to radical causes, he also promoted the Garden City movement, important later to Roosevelt, New Jersey, and the Modern School movement, which eventually produced the anarchist community at Stelton, New Jersey. He was a frequent visitor to Upton Sinclair's Helicon Hall and a particular friend to his famous contemporary, the anarchist Emma Goldman. After the McKinley assassination, he gave her a farm in Westchester County as a place to retreat from police harassment. She described him as an "unconditional libertarian and single taxer . . . emancipated from his highly respectable background except for his conventional dress. His frock-coat, high silk hat, gloves, and cane make him a conspicuous figure in our ranks." [2]

Like his mentor Henry George, Hall believed that control of the land created wealth and power. The only fair tax was a land tax. As George explained it, "if we tax houses, there will be fewer and poorer houses; if we tax machinery, there will be less machinery; if we tax trade, there will be less trade; if we tax capital, there will be less capital; if we tax savings, there will be less savings. All the taxes, therefore, that we should abolish are those that repress industry and lessen wealth. But if we tax land values, there will be no less land."[3] If all were taxed equally for land, regardless of improvements, then wealthy landowners would not be able to profit by sitting on land until it became, by virtue of location or other resource, valuable, and then cash in.

Hall was interested in the ideas of many contemporary Europeans such as English artist/designer William Morris and the Russian "anarchist prince" Peter Kropotkin. He maintained a correspondence with writer and philosopher Leo Tolstoy, whose ideas on education much influenced the Modern School movement.

Hall was a shrewd businessman and not above some speculation in land. He did not lose money on the Free Acres Colony, eventually selling the section he had reserved for himself back to the Free Acres Association.[4] But he was a complex character with a mystical, Tolstoyan side. Hall was almost a practitioner of "Buddhist economics." His system, he believed, would prevent people from harming each other: "Happiness is to be found in the service of our fellow creatures, through which we come to be one with the mind of the Universe. It does not depend on what success we may see in this service. The effort to remove the causes of the sufferings of others and especially enable them to think rightly, so that they may themselves avoid evil is, in itself, a joy."[5]

Like William Morris, Hall nursed a nostalgia for the old ways of tiny village communities based on personal relationships. Morris, in his utopian novel *News from Nowhere,* posits a world in harmony with nature and the old crafts. Hall, in his opposition to what he saw as dehumanizing industrial progress, also admired Elbert Hubbard. Hubbard's Roycroft Colony in Aurora, New York, an enclave, like Morris's Kelmscott Manor in England, was dedicated to handcrafts and the printing of books and pamphlets. Hubbard invented for himself a mock medieval persona, a priest, Fra Elbertus, and named one of his periodicals *The Fra.*

Hall believed that freedom for the individual could come through community. To test his theories, on July 23, 1910, he conveyed the Murphy Farm, a property he owned in Berkeley Heights, New Jersey, to the Free

Acres Corporation in a deed of gift. He divided the land into leasehold properties of sizes varying from one-quarter to one acre, with sections set aside as communal property. Leaseholders would pay rent on the annually appraised value of their land excluding "improvements," that is, buildings. The rents collected were to be used for local taxes and for the public expenses of the association. Although the land would belong to the association, leaseholds could be transferred if the transfer was approved by a majority vote at two consecutive association meetings.

Over the years, some land was added to Hall's original grant but nothing could be subtracted. Hall was a lawyer and a practical man, and as such he set up the community of Free Acres so that it still exists in modified form today.[6] A penalty clause in the deed of gift ensured that if the association were ever to sell or mortgage, rather than rent, any portion of the land, the proceeds and the land itself would revert to Bolton Hall and his heirs. Thus Hall insured Free Acres against the fate of many utopian communities: the eventual sale of the land to provide cash in hard times.

Besides the deed of gift, Hall structured his community with a corporate charter and a constitution. The corporate charter established Free Acres as a nonprofit corporation under the laws of the state of New Jersey. The constitution, probably written by Hall himself,[7] set forth in its preamble the goals of the community: "We the leaseholders and residents of Free Acres, desiring to create a community for the study and demonstration of problems of self-government, social progress and taxation where all shall be mutually helpful and free from all forms of monopoly of natural resources, in order to secure to all equality of opportunity and to each a full reward of efforts, have this day organized ourselves under the name of the Free Acres Association."

The constitution included a prohibition against monopolies entering Free Acres property and gave women the right to vote almost ten years before the U.S. Constitution did. Each leasehold had one vote, which could be split between husband and wife. Under the constitution, Free Acres would have three trustees, a clerk, and a treasurer. A chairman would be chosen at the time of each monthly association meeting, open to all colonists.

Committees were formed to take on the mundane affairs of colony life, which over the years would evolve into the management of roads, water, health and safety, forestry, swimming pool, and farmhouse.

The Murphy Farm property, set about four hundred feet above sea level on the side of the second mountain in the Watchung chain in east central New Jersey, was about twenty-seven miles west of New York City, although, in the words of one early colonist, "in rural remoteness it might be one hundred miles away."[8] Hall reserved a corner of the property, about five acres of meadow with the farmhouse, for himself. He may in fact have intended to use the farmhouse as an inn or general store.[9] Otherwise, the land was open meadow and dense woodland.

Hall recruited renters to his community in the usual way: a series of meetings held in New York. These took place in Greenwich Village, at the studio of cofounder Ami Mali Hicks. Hicks was a well-known stage designer who had worked with Max Reinhardt and Norman Bel Geddes, and a craftsperson. She was much influenced by the Arts and Crafts movement and shared William Morris's ideas about the beauty of useful objects. During 1901 and 1902 she supervised the Cranberry Island Rug Project, a rug-making venture that employed the wives of Maine fishermen who had much time on their hands during the Maine winters and little ready money. Hicks designed the patterns and gave instruction in dyeing. Her philosophy is clear in this admonition from her book, *The Craft of Handmade Rugs,* published in 1914: "Handicraft is only beautiful when ornamentally restrained, and meaningless decoration impairs its usefulness." As the person in charge of distributing the leaseholds, Hicks was active in administering the colony.

That first summer, a group of intrepid souls moved out to the Murphy Farm to camp in makeshift accommodations, mainly tents, without electricity, plumbing, or a reliable water supply. Berkeley Heights was the nearest train station, and from there it was a walk of two miles uphill to the entrance of the colony on what is now Emerson Lane. Bolton Hall had a tent constructed on his property "big enough to contain a cot, a washstand, a table, a small stove, innumerable shelves racks and books [as well as] a Dutch door and two windows with wooden shutters that open[ed] up and out, affording protection from rain or sun." [10] Other summer settlers cobbled together what they could in the way of tents and shacks. One imaginative, if ill-fated, dwelling had three walls and the roof constructed of chicken wire, patched with mud in which beans grew. A rainstorm unfortunately caused the roof of this ingenious construction to fall in. [11]

The Murphy Farm, as those first Free Acreites describe it, was a place of great natural beauty. Meadows were filled with daisies, Queen Anne's Lace, honeysuckle, bayberry, and wild roses. Dense woodlands boasted oak, birch, chestnut, walnut, ash, tulip, and dogwood trees. "In the southern section of the colony flowing in an easterly direction through low, boggy ground was Green Brook. Behind it, on slightly higher ground, was a grove of cedar trees." [12] Into this wild and beautiful place came an odd assortment of characters. Varied as they were, all were glad to leave the city for so Edenic a spot and willing to rough it there. Surrounding farms provided vegetables, milk, and even freshly baked bread. There was a peach orchard where early Free Acres children would gather peaches and hide them in their bloomers. [13]

Most people lived in tents with wooden platform floors. Bolton Hall made some repairs to the dilapidated farmhouse, and his secretary, Ella Murray, lived there for a time, providing lodging of an undoubtedly basic nature to visitors. [14] Hall himself lived outside the colony, although he spent many weekends in his tent and puttering in the old chicken coop he had made into a workshop. Several colonists commuted to New York on the train from Berkeley Heights, which led to the forming of the Horse Association, a group that purchased a horse and a couple of carriages and was run originally by Mrs. Murray's nephew, Arthur Tiffin. Letters survive from Ella Murray to O. G. Fischer, Free Acres treasurer, concerning the misappropriation of the horse and "depot carriage." The complaint is against one Mr. Tucker:

> Although Mr. Tucker knew that Miss Goodwin, Arthur and I were going to town today on the 5:08 train, with luggage, he, entirely on his own responsibility without consulting Arthur who was still in charge or even to let him know what he was about to do, took the

covered carriage and left for Plainfield at noon, not to return until after 5 o'clock. The light wagon suitable for two was sufficient for his use but not for ours, and by his discourteous act, we, who had engaged the depot carriage for that train, were compelled to walk down. I wonder if this is an evidence of the "Broad Spirit of Co-operation"? [15]

This relatively minor problem betrays the difficulty of Hall's idea of freeing the individual through community. Those who responded to Hall's plan to create Eden in the wilds of New Jersey had to be strong individuals—with traits that might not easily accommodate cooperation. One assumes that the Mr. Tucker mentioned in the complaint is the same John Francis Tucker, socialist and free spirit, who built a house on Water Lane in 1911, including an outdoor sunken bathtub surrounded with marigolds. [16] In one way or another, most of those early residents were free spirits. Dr. Mary Hussey, who was also a member of Fairhope, was a suffragist and a gardener. O. G. and Emma Fischer were lovers of the outdoors rather than single taxers: O.G. was fabric director of Belding Brothers, a silk company, and Emma kept bees and began the Young People's Dramatic Club. Their daughter, Ethel, was ten when they first came to Free Acres. Interviewed at seventy-one, she described the "joy" of childhood in Free Acres when "the sky was so blue, the grass so green and the trees so beautiful." [17] Gertrude Moore, with her husband Arthur and sons Ulric and Donald, arrived in 1911 to introduce the colony to "mental motor rhythmics." [18] She directed classes for adults and children. She also helped found the Garden Guild, one of the first of Free Acres' many guilds. [19] Harry Kelly, a self-proclaimed anarchist who had traveled to England where he had met Peter Kropotkin, admired by Bolton Hall, came for a time. His companion at Free Acres was Mary Krimont, a suffragist whose sister was involved in the Whiteway Colony, a utopian/anarchist experiment in the English Cotswolds. [20] Later, Kelly and Krimont would be central to the establishment of the Modern School and Stelton Colony near Piscataway, New Jersey. Another pioneer was Dr. Benzion Liber, Romanian born and brother-in-law of Konrad Bercovici. Liber had studied medicine and psychiatry in Paris and Vienna but was also something of an artist, having studied in New York with Robert Henri. As he remembers the early days:

There was a warmth permeating the place . . . a feeling of fellow-ship, and a good humor that cemented the entire membership. . . . The majority were intellectuals or artists or people interested in books and art. They all loved nature and humanity and were radically inclined. With one or two exceptions, we were all poor and not interested in making money. We were all happy to leave the city behind and to come here to build and grow things, each in his own way, usually un-like how it was done in any other community. No one ever appeared ridiculous to his neighbors, although outsiders, whenever they visited the colony, found much at which to poke fun.[21]

Dr. Liber was a friend of John Francis Tucker's, and in fall and spring, when fewer people were around, the two would run naked through the woods to bathe in the brook. Tucker was also considered the socialite of the colony; a fine gardener, a gourmet, and the employer of a butler named Higgins. He is said to have entertained Upton Sinclair at his leasehold.

Hyperion Bercovici, Konrad's son and Benzion's nephew (known to his uncle as Rion, "let us laugh"; his own son was named Amour Liber, "Free Love"), described an early trip to Free Acres made while he and his parents were living in another radical/artistic colony in Croton-on-Hudson, New York:

While at Croton, I broke up the monotony by visiting the single tax colony of "Free Acres" at Scotch Plains, New Jersey, founded by Bolton Hall. I was the guest of an uncle of mine [Dr. Liber] who lived there. I was surprised, but not shocked, when the whole family—my uncle, aunt, cousin, and I—went bathing nude in a stream behind the house . . . a young lady artist of Free Acres asked me to pose for her in the nude. This proposal shocked me, though I myself had drawn and modeled from the nude in art schools in New York and Montreal.

I could imagine posing for a group. But to be alone in a room naked with a female stranger. . . . That was too much![22]

All was not bucolic, however, in those first summers. Water and sanitation were pressing problems. Water from a spring in the pasture of a neighboring farm was potable, and Bolton Hall paid to have a well dug near the old farmhouse. This solution was obviously not going to be sufficient for the long term, and in fact water remained a problem for twenty years, necessitating various bond issues to provide a pump house and other things, until eventually Free Acres was connected to township water. With the possibility of malaria ever present, colonists were warned of the need for proper drainage and for burning or burying refuse. One Mr. Monk, who seems to have been the general handyman, was paid two dollars a month year-round for looking after the outdoor toilets. Monk was an Englishman, a jeweler and watchmaker by trade, but clearly adept at general fixing.

During this time a swimming hole was dug largely by the useful Mr. Monk, with the enthusiastic if short-lived aid of the Free Acres children. This diversion would eventually metamorphose into the modern Free Acres swimming pool, still a center of community life today. In that first decade, Free Acres developed many of its characteristic occupations and interests. It was, in these years, essentially a summer colony. Pictures of the early dwellings show structures similar to the camps of the Adirondacks or of the New England lake resorts. The association's business meetings were held in New York during the winter months at various restaurants or at the Women's Trade Union League. Word spread in bohemian radical circles. The Bonis, friends of John Francis Tucker, came in 1913. Charles Boni and his wife, Bessie, were active socialists. Their sons, Charles Jr. and Albert, were college students who had spent their Harvard tuition money on a Greenwich Village bookshop. The New York Theater Guild was launched from the Bonis' bookshop and became the basis for other theater groups, including the Provincetown Players. Albert and Charles Boni became publishers. Albert joined Horace Liveright in the firm of Boni and Liveright, which published the Modern Library series in the 1920s. They published most of the great American writers of the time, including Eliot, Faulkner, Dreiser, and Sinclair Lewis.

This decade also saw the beginning of Free Acres' own Dramatic Guild. An open-air theater was created just south of Green Brook. The setting, among cedar trees and lit by moonlight and Japanese lanterns, was fitting for the ambitious 1916 production of *A Midsummer Night's Dream,* chosen to celebrate the three hundredth anniversary of Shakespeare's death, with sets and costumes designed by Ami Mali Hicks. Further plays were directed by Grace Colbron, a New York drama critic and single taxer who had been involved in theatricals at Arden in Delaware. Colbron was also a translator, and the author, with Augusta Groner, of a number of mysteries, such as *The Case of the Pool of Blood in the Pastor's Study,* featuring an Austrian detective called Joseph Muller.

As more people came, and more dwellings were built, the architecture became increasingly varied. As Grace Colbron described it in the April 1920 issue of *Touchstone* magazine, the houses were "architectural experiments which express a spirit of adventure in homemaking." This was understandable, she continued, because "Free Acres is an experiment and adventure in itself. If you want to build a home in Free Acres you can put all your money in the house, you need none for the land." [23] If individual camps were left to individual taste and means, however, the layout of the community was not. Open community land was maintained; properties were not to be fenced off. Paths wound through the woods from road to road connecting all sections of the colony. All the roads, with the exception of Water Lane, also led into each other so there was always a sense of the whole. Meeting in the woods, two people could take different paths and meet again by the brook or in the meadow. Nature mattered to the denizens of Free Acres, and next to nature, art.

In 1919, the Eberlein family came to Free Acres. Ernest Eberlein, an artist and lithographer, and Undena Eberlein, an actress, had been part of Upton Sinclair's brief Helicon Home Colony, although Undena had been on tour in San Francisco at the time of the Helicon fire. Undena brought the drama of the stage into everyday life at Free Acres, wandering the fields in flowing white dresses and dancing barefoot, Isadora Duncan style, in the woods.

One of the freedoms that Free Acres provided for women was freedom from conventional roles. There were those like Mrs. Ollie Newcomb, who in 1915 built her own house. Newcomb also helped others, as Undena Eberlein notes in a letter to her mother in 1920: "tonight Mr. Lutz and Mrs. Newcomb made a little porch with six [two by fours, which Undena had bought] . . . and tomorrow she is going to make me a table out of the other two (rustic legs from the woods, close by)." [24] As Undena also notes in a letter to her friend Cora Potter, a refugee from Helicon now at Arden, "We have so much freedom in the matter of dress and then, everybody lets everybody else alone . . . all do as they please. Of course there aren't many people and there isn't as much co-operation as one would like sometimes, but things go along very smoothly." [25] The strength of Free Acres in those early days may have been its residents' tolerance for various kinds of eccentricity. At one point, Bolton Hall even suggested that white flags be flown by colonists who did not wish to be disturbed at whatever they were doing. Free Acres was inclusive; Bolton Hall had never insisted that colonists be single taxers or anything else. As he wrote on a postcard sent to interest people in the colony: "It is not restricted to single taxers and includes wage earners, business and college people, artists, actors and writers." [26]

Early life at Free Acres was primitive even for a summer colony. The Eberleins, to save rent money, became year-round residents, and the cottage Undena describes was only 14 by 20 feet, a mere 280 square feet for a family that by then included several children. Cottages had no indoor plumbing, and they were heated by coal or kerosene stoves. These stoves proved dangerous in the often haphazardly built wooden "shacks," and there were several fires. The Fischer house burned down during a blizzard, forcing them to move into the farmhouse. Ten days later, the Eberlein cottage also burned. Roxanne Eberlein, one of the children, described it in 1986: "The night our house burned was clear and cold with snow still on the ground. We children ran bare-footed over icy patches up to the Inn [farmhouse], where the Fischers took in our family for the night, having found refuge there themselves after their fire." [27]

Unlike the fire at Helicon, which Ernest Eberlein and the oldest child, Lisbeth, had survived, a fire at Free Acres did not mean the end of the community. In fact it showed the essential nature of the place: everyone helped out. Free Acres embodied the anarchist ideals of individual freedom and mutual help. And this made it attractive to people like Harry Kelly, Joseph Ishill, and Alexis and Elizabeth Ferm, who were connected with Stelton and the Modern School. Amour Liber, the seven-year-old son of Dr. Benzion Liber and his wife Rosafine, had been one of the first pupils at the Ferrer Modern School when it began in New York. After moving with his parents to Free Acres, he continued to commute to the city for a brief period. According to his father, he sometimes made the trip entirely by himself. From the city, he would have to catch a streetcar to Christopher Street, then buy a ticket and take the ferry across the Hudson to get the Lackawanna train at Hoboken; the train stopped in Berkeley Heights, leaving him with a two-mile walk to the colony. Eventually he tired of the Modern School, complaining to his father of the other children: "They only fight there. . . . Nothing else happens." He was much missed by his teacher, the young Will Durant ("Tell Amour that I miss him very much.").[28]

In 1923, by the end of the colony's first decade, Bolton Hall seemed pleased with his experiment: "There is a little new colony in little old New Jersey which is on the road to showing that a landlord is a needless and expensive luxury, and whose plan may eventually help to open rich domains of earth to people without means, and even aid them in putting up a country home, shack, or bungalow—or whatever the preferred brand of country dwelling may be."[29]

By this time, the population had grown to more than fifty. "The community had a rudimentary water system, a swimming pool, a renovated farmhouse with an impressive platform. The Open Air Theater had already witnessed a number of stirring performances."[30] And word was beginning to spread. Advertisements still appeared in newspapers. David Neuman was a high school student in Jersey City who learned about Free Acres while browsing in the Jersey City Library, and he arrived on foot, with his brother Leon, in Berkeley Heights to check it out. Subsequently, his parents and a number of their cousins and friends found their way to the colony.

One Edmond Brown purportedly made the trip from Brooklyn by foot, obtained a leasehold, and built a shack out of soap boxes.

Some of Free Acres best-remembered characters came during the colony's first decade. Will Crawford was in his late forties when he came to Free Acres in 1917. He was a well-known artist, having begun his career as a newspaper illustrator for the *Newark Advertiser,* the *Newark Sunday Call,* the *New York World,* and the *New York Journal.* He then became a magazine illustrator, contributing to *Life, Colliers,* the *Saturday Evening Post, McCall's,* and the children's magazine *St. Nicholas.* In his youth he had traveled all over the American West, becoming friends with western painters Charles Russell and Frederick Remington and being influenced by their painting styles. He was also much interested in Native Americans, their stories, and their way of life. Legend has it that he first arrived with a Native American friend, who helped him build a teepee. Over time, the teepee metamorphosed into a tiny cabin with a huge fieldstone fireplace, where Crawford happily entertained visitors.

Crawford was in fact a New Jersey native, having grown up in Irvington, and the little wooded colony of Free Acres was a long way from the mesas and canyons of his beloved Wild West. Yet the place seems to have been as central to Will Crawford, or Uncle Bill, as he was known to generations of Free Acres children, as he was to it. Will Crawford was a storyteller and a nature lover. As town forester, he persuaded other residents who wanted to enlarge their houses to spare any trees. Sometimes that could mean actually building around a tree. He told stories to the children and led stargazing hikes on summer nights. He was a humanist and a socialist, a vegetarian and an atheist—embodying many of the colony's strains of thought. He also founded the archery club, the Locksley archers, and trained his archers well enough to win outside contests.

MacKinlay Kantor, author of Civil War novels including the Pulitzer Prize–winning *Andersonville,* who spent some time in the colony, described Will Crawford as "an elderly dwarfish Robin Hood. He wore a green felt hat, cocked and pointed in medieval style and adorned with pheasant feathers. A bow hung over one shoulder and a quiver of arrows over the other. He sported also a fringed hunting shirt."[31] Despite his western background,

Crawford was also under the medieval spell. In 1926, he tried to get acorns from Robin Hood's Sherwood Forest to plant at Free Acres. A letter from one Harry A. Dix apologized for his inability to find any acorns: "the trouble is that almost every autumn the farmers hereabouts all turn their pigs into the woods, and together with the squirrels etc, [they] soon make short work of the seeds. . . . I suppose it is only what one might expect 'Pigs *is* Pigs.'"[32] The writer promised to try again, but there is no record of success. Kantor described Free Acres as "a bizarre little single tax colony" and Crawford's cabin as containing "a windrow of Things, which started high against one wall and sloped down across the room. Anything and everything was in that pile: Dakota war bonnets, breakfast-food cartons, helmets, lumps of quartz, pressed flowers, overshoes."[33] Crawford illustrated several of Kantor's books, although in time he became careless of deadlines, preferring to work on carvings of signs for friends or presents for children. Konrad Bercovici remembered this gypsy of another kind as a wonderful teller of stories "like genealogical trees. They started with a root and then spread out branches and twigs and more branches and more twigs that twined and intertwined themselves. . . . Will Crawford spoke of Emerson, Walt Whitman, and Thoreau, of the Civil War, of Lincoln, and of the North and the South. He was America." Bercovici would read his own work to Crawford in the evenings, to test it on that most American ear. "When we touched him," Bercovici wrote, "we touched some of the best in this country."[34]

Crawford told the story of his first meeting with James Cagney, then an aspiring hoofer and Broadway actor, who, with his wife Billy, had rented a shack in Free Acres for five summers as a cheap holiday alternative. Crawford was building his cabin at the time and offered to pay the young actor for his help. Cagney began chopping so enthusiastically that he nearly brought the whole place down, but a friendship began that lasted until the end of Crawford's life, even after Cagney's big break took him to Hollywood. In his autobiography Cagney remembers: "Free Acres at the time was a single tax colony. Every kind of political philosophy was represented there. . . . When I got there at twenty-one years of age, I had no fixed political philosophy. . . . My big concern of the moment was where the next meal was coming from."[35] As Kantor recounts, Cagney helped take care of

Uncle Bill in his old age, paying for him to spend two winters in California. Uncle Bill insisted on visiting Cagney on the set of one of his movies, a western that took place in Oklahoma. The outing was ruined for Uncle Bill, however, because the deer's head in the bar scene was the head of an English fallow deer.[36]

Crawford is remembered today in Free Acres by the plaques he carved. The Free Acres sign he made out of twigs and branches that was once part of an arch at the entrance to Appletree Row deteriorated and had to be taken down. Laurel Hessing remembers him from when she was a child in the 1940s and he a very old man, living with the Boehne family, who looked after him. Too old to tell his stories, he still impressed her as "the magical old man in Mrs. Boehne's garden."[37]

Another resident, friend of both Cagney and Crawford, was the Broadway and Hollywood actor Victor Kilian. Kilian had begun acting as a teenager in 1909 and appeared in a vaudeville act with James Cagney. He became a successful character actor on Broadway and in Hollywood but was blacklisted during the McCarthy era and made no films for six years. At the end of this life, he had a successful run in the television soap opera spoof *Mary Hartman, Mary Hartman*, in which he played Hartman's father, the Fernwood Flasher. Kilian and his wife Daisy had a house in Free Acres from 1917 to 1953. For a time, Daisy turned the farmhouse on weekends into the Bide a Wee Tearoom, a place for conversation as well as tea and cookies.

For Konrad Bercovici, Stony Hill, as he calls Free Acres in his autobiography, was an escape from the darkness he found as an immigrant in New York City. Dramatic and romantic, a bit of a swashbuckler, and prone to fights, Bercovici was a musician, writer, and painter who, on coming to America, was forced to take jobs with a wrecking company and then as a claims investigator for a charitable institution. The Lower East Side sweatshops he investigated were dirty and airless; many workers were consumptive, but all had to drink water out of one tin cup. "I was sick with rage, impotence, pity and revolt. Charity wasn't even a palliative; it was one of the toys of the rich." Bercovici resigned and returned to Free Acres "to breathe fresh air again. The trees were only half clad that early spring, and the shack was cold, but it was clean, spacious and didn't smell sour and sweaty." He continued to write and compose, eventually having great success with his tales of Gypsy life, a number of which were published by Bernarr Macfadden's *Liberty* magazine. Bercovici maintained contact with the Gypsy underground in New York City, many of whose members had known his father in the old country. Bercovici's career eventually took him to Hollywood, where he became a friend of Charlie Chaplin's. Sent to Europe on assignments for various magazines in the years before World War II, he found himself in Vienna during the Nazi riots hanging out "behind the shuttered windows of the bar" with Sinclair Lewis and George Seldes. At this point, he clearly foresaw the rise of Hitler and its consequences.[38]

A writer and resident until his early death, very different from the flamboyant Bercovici and the rustic Crawford, but more famous than either, was Thorne Smith, author of *Topper,* a book that became a movie and a television series and that is still in print. He wrote other books, including *The Passionate Witch*, made into the 1942 movie *I Married a Witch*, with Frederic March and Veronica Lake, and later the inspiration for the television series *Bewitched*.

Thorne Smith began his career in advertising. For years before the success of *Topper*, he longed to leave the business. He lived in Greenwich Village and began bringing his wife and daughters to Free Acres in the summer to share a cottage with his wife's sister, her husband, and their two children. Blond and slight, he was described by Konrad Bercovici as "a frail and delicate fellow . . . witty, fantastic, with no consciousness of what was real or what was otherworldly. He cared little for single tax, socialism, or anarchism. It was no novelty to see Thorne Smith on a Saturday afternoon in the nude with a whiskey bottle in one hand and a wad of paper in the other running to the woods to climb his scrub oak."[39] He was also the owner of a gin-drinking duck named Havelock Ellis. Smith's whimsical and asocial take on life may have set him apart from the radical, political thinkers of Free Acres, but in some ways his spirit was close to the essence of the place. He gave his cottage the ironic name of The Flop—although it was here, seated at a table on the sunny lawn in tennis whites, that he wrote the tremendously successful *Topper*.[40]

James Thurber, writing in *The Years with Ross*, described Smith's brief stint on the *New Yorker* staff:

Thorne Smith doesn't properly belong in any *New Yorker* or, for that matter, any other category, but he underwent a stretch of torture, both give and take, as a member of the staff during the winter of 1929–1930. I had brought him in and introduced him to Ross, saying that he had given up an advertising job to write a book . . . and found himself unable to get to work. . . . Everything went wrong between Ross and Thorne, who once didn't show up for a week. "You ought to know where he is," Ross told me. "He's your responsibility." I said that Smith was God's responsibility, not mine or any man's. When he did finally appear, Ross said, "Why didn't you telephone and *say* you were sick?" Thorne had a lovely answer to that: "The telephone was in the hall and there was a draft." [41]

Many visitors came to breathe the rarified air of Free Acres, including the ubiquitous Harry Kemp, who arrived on the heels of his stay at Arden and his affair with Upton Sinclair's wife. Recalls Bercovici, "When Harry came to pay our 'colony' a visit, I saw a tall broad shouldered, lanky giant, with the eyes of a Savonarola and the high cheekbones of a Slav, who looked and spoke like a village priest. The Arden episode gave Kemp a great lift with a young Russian woman, married to an American, who howled like a madwoman after Harry left to let us know how much she suffered." [42]

As early as 1915, the colonists were referring to themselves as Free Acre Folk. Like one of their inspirations, William Morris and the Pre-Raphaelite brotherhood, they looked back to the Middle Ages for models of cooperative life. In Free Acres, the various clubs were known as guilds. By the 1920s there was the Dramatic Guild and the Children's Dramatic Guild, the Garden Guild, and the Library Guild—so many that a Folks Guild had to be set up to organize them. On Sunday afternoons, events called gemotes were held, weather permitting. *Gemote*, an Old English word, means "town meeting," but in Free Acres gemotes were usually lectures followed by discussion. When the Dramatic Guild was formed in 1915, its officers were a guildmaster, a bursar, and a scribe. Its choice of productions began with Shakespeare, at the suggestion of Ami Mali Hicks. By the 1922 season, however, it was suggested that "a popular show be given, such as a minstrel show or a circus." [43] A circus, remembered as the Great Circus, had Mr. Fischer as the hurdy-gurdy man, a ringmaster, a snake charmer with a stuffed snake, and at least one small boy in a monkey suit. It was apparently a big success.

Free Acres continued to function as a community both in its structure and, on a more informal level, through the cooperation and interaction of its members. The Free Acres Association met monthly at the farmhouse, variously called the Community House and Frank Stephens Hall, after one of the two founders of the single-tax colony of Arden, Delaware. By 1930, a library had been installed on the second floor; there social activities and the monthly association meetings could take place. A wooden platform had been built in front of the farmhouse, where dances were held on Saturday nights, the association could meet on warm, sunny days, and discussions be held. The grass field, or "common," around the building was the archery range. Nearby were swings for the children and the tennis court. Down Appletree Row were, of course, the swimming pool and the open-air theater. The colonists of those days had to make their own amusements, which included pageants, flower shows, spelling bees, and folk singing. These were all, of course, cooperative ventures. Where money was tight, services might be exchanged, such as piano lessons for dance lessons and the like. In her *Free Acres Chronicle*, Lillian Leon remembers shish kebab evenings on the common, when "under the supervision of some older person, the teen agers and small fry would gather wood all afternoon. . . . At dusk the procession began. Adults, laden with baskets, cushions and blankets, flanked by happy, boisterous children found a convenient spot around the fire which had been lighted earlier to provide 'coals' so necessary for the roast. . . . After the messy meal, the fire was replenished and singing began, lasting until way past midnight." [44]

In 1930, the twentieth anniversary of the founding of the colony was marked by a celebration over the weekend of the Fourth of July. The twenty-two-page program included an introduction by Bolton Hall and reminiscences of the early days by Ella Murray and Emma Fisher. Will Crawford did the illustrations. The celebration began with a pageant arranged by Will Crawford and continued with a line up of various speakers, including Grace Colbron and Bolton Hall. The festivities, which lasted over the next two days, were composed of such merriment as children's games, singing, dancing, baseball, archery, tennis, and folk dancing. The final event was a spelling bee: men against women.

Free Acres seems to have had little trouble with its neighbors. Unlike Helicon Hall's neighbors—the conservative, well-off denizens of Englewood—the Berkeley Heights and Watchung neighbors tended to be somewhat eccentric themselves. Up on Emerson Lane, a dirt road so named by Bolton Hall in honor of one of his heroes, was something called the Vegetarry Inn. There was also a group of naturists and various other sympathetic souls in a section called Freedom Hill. Konrad Bercovici made friends with the leader of the Italian colony, who had settled on neglected farmland and reclaimed it. She considered the Free Acreites fools for buying vegetables when they had land to grow them. The Burgmullers, owners of a nearby farm, had been helpful from the earliest days, and colonists maintained good relations with the owners of the small store at the corner of Plainfield Avenue.

Free Acres itself was always a hotbed of opinions. The association meetings were often fiery, and fights among colonists and their dogs were common, but people worked things out and friendships appeared to survive. Feelings and opinions spilled over into the pages of the colony newsletters, which often read like a cross between a high school newspaper and a slam book. Here are some typical excerpts.

Things We Hope For

That Thomson will not do the "Virginia Judge" for the entire summer

That Newman will learn a new song besides "Little John, Bottle John"

That Mrs. Eberlein will go a whole summer without doing
Shakespeare

That Friptu and Newman will have no fights at meetings and also that
the dogs will follow suit

That Mr. Prinz will not read more than one poem at shishkebab [45]

In the meantime, much as I dislike doing it, I am reading your de-
tested sheet to get the low down on my neighbors. But if you ever put
in a crack about me, no bullet-proof vest will save you. [46]

As is now known to a good many of us the system of taxation [un-
der] which we are bound to manage our affairs is wrong in principle,
hurtful to a majority of us, and unworkable within a society which is
functioning within capitalistic laws and regulations. [47]

The newsletters also contained reports from the various guilds, with Ida
O. Howell writing on the ferns of Free Acres and Uncle Bill Crawford on
the presence of copperheads. There were poems and jokes and, in the mid-
1930s, a letter from a Free Acreite, en route to Germany on a German ship,
that discusses the plight of the Jews. [48]

❋ ❋ ❋

Change, of course, was bound to come to Free Acres, and it came with
the Depression. Hard up, many of the "summer people" decided to win-
terize their "shacks" and save money by living in the country year-round.
Greater change came as a result of the property abutting Free Acres to the
south. Camp Elsinore began as a summer camp run by the philanthropic
Dr. Muldenka for children orphaned in the disastrous sinking of the *General
Slocum*, a paddle-wheel excursion boat, in the Hudson River on June 15,
1904. Eventually the children grew up, and Muldenka sold the property.
He claimed that he tried to sell the land to Free Acres but that they didn't
want to buy it. It was bought instead by a German hiking club, the Workers

and Sports Association of Greater New York. The German hikers found Free Acres with its rental land appealing, and in the early 1930s many of them bought leaseholds. Some were socialists, but they were also skilled craftsmen—carpenters, masons, plumbers. They helped each other build substantial houses, quite unlike the "architectural experiments" Isabel Grace Colbron had described. The German colonists were more practical householders than artistic free spirits. They also built roads and improved the precarious water supply. These improvements did not go unnoticed by the municipality, and taxes on the improved property began to rise. Municipal tax assessors did not subscribe to Bolton Hall's single-tax theory. Since each leaseholder was taxed only on his land, without improvements, this created considerable tension. Clearly, someone with a large piece of land would end up paying more in tax to the association than someone with a substantially improved smaller plot.

Appeals to Bolton Hall to modify the tax structure went unheeded. From 1934 to 1936, Hall was attacked regularly at association meetings, even denounced as a land speculator. Finally one of the colonists, Peter Berlinrut, came up with a "communal tax advantage" proposal. Assessments by the local authorities would be passed on to the individual leaseholders, who would then have to pay an additional assessment to be put toward internal Free Acres expenses. The community accepted this approach to the disgust of Bolton Hall. Hall left the community in 1936 and died two years later in Georgia. Although Hall had played God in the 1912 Dramatic Guild production of *Hiawatha*, for the colony he had played the God of the deist. After he had created Free Acres, he stepped back and did not really become involved in the daily workings of his creation. Thus neither his departure nor his demise seriously affected it.

Free Acres life went on with its dramatic productions, its lectures, meetings, pageants, and water carnivals. Camp Wanoga, a summer camp for children, was started and was indirectly responsible for bringing another well-known radical to the colony. Michael Gold, activist and social critic, writer for the *New Masses*, and linked with the Communist Party and Dorothy Day, came to Free Acres because his brother was director of Camp Wanoga. Friend and admirer of Upton Sinclair, Gold was nonetheless critical of Sinclair for making his fictional workers too much like "Walter Crane's Merrie England peasants." [49] He stayed, however, among the Folk of Free Acres and their guilds for a decade. He would later spend time at the Stelton colony.

More things changed at Free Acres. Emerson Lane was paved, and the electric and phone companies, monopolies both, were invited in. It may be true that Free Acres contained, as Konrad Bercovici described it, "bahaists, Buddhists, anarchists, spiritualists, all with a different creed and all agreeing to disagree," [50] and that it was never simply an enclave for single taxers, but all those devotees of various political and artistic philosophies were much the same at heart. They wanted to escape a world they saw as sadly flawed, whether that escape was temporary or permanent. They wanted a place apart from it, a place of natural beauty with none of the rules and prejudices of the outside world. Native born or immigrant, they would be new people in a new place. They were the dreamers and Free Acres was the dream. And the dream continued in the plays and pageants, the water carnivals, the baseball team, and the children's summer camp. Some tended their gardens; one resident raised champion cocker spaniels.

As the thirties merged into the forties, it became clear that Free Acres could not escape the greater world. One hears, in the words of Lillian Leon writing in the late 1940s, a refrain that sounds again and again right up to the present day—the split between the old people and the new people. Ironically, the new people of the early days had become the old people, conservative in their desire to preserve their woodland home:

They [newcomers] knew little of the old customs and traditions and were indifferent to the sacred cows. Finding Free Acres delightful, its charm was taken for granted. Ignorant of what made it so, they proceeded to fashion the place into their own mold, overriding the pleas of the old timers. THEY wanted comfort, lights, heat, water and covered pipes, drainage, sewers, a swimming pool and real roads, not ruts. In short they wanted Suburbia, while the older residents fought for real rusticity. [51]

The coming of World War II in Europe brought heated debates about the Second Front. It was hard for the German residents to believe that Hitler was really trying to exterminate the Jews. However, the only person probably ever voted down for membership in the community was someone who came to Free Acres in a car flying a swastika flag.

When America went to war, the outdoor theater was blacked out for fear of enemy bombers. The real threat to Free Acres, however, came at war's end. Suddenly, this little enclave with its wild bog garden, its protected, communal woods and fields, its quirky houses and bohemian customs, was directly in the path of the postwar real estate boom. The train commute of an hour or so from New York to Westchester or Connecticut or anywhere else became the staple of 1950s fiction—a liminal journey from the world of work to the world of family. Anything less like the suburbia of 1950s sitcoms, with its manicured yards and shockable neighbors, than Free Acres would be hard to imagine. John Cheever's swimmer could not have existed in Free Acres—swimming through an endless series of similar pools in an endless series of similar yards at the end of a summer just like any other. John Cheever, in many ways a fanciful writer like Thorne Smith, could not imagine a sunny world where things got better by magic. The magic in Cheever's stories is 1950s magic, claustrophobic and threatening.

But there Free Acres sat as the towns around it became bedroom communities, the farms were sold for development, and a number of corporate campuses, most notably Bell Laboratories, were established. Planning also began for Route 78, the superhighway that would eventually become the southern border of the colony, cutting it off physically and symbolically from what had been familiar woodland.

Although Bolton Hall's careful design had kept Free Acres together for some forty years, that was not the whole story. It seemed that Free Acres, in tune with its make-do beginnings, had an adaptable quality that allowed it to change just enough to stay the same. As values for surrounding properties rose, Free Acres leasehold transfers either took place within families or had to be financed by the sellers. Banks would not deal with the unique setup of Free Acres, which they considered high risk. Finally, the community decided to change the terms of the lease from one year to ninety-nine years with an option to renew. This made the banks less nervous and more willing to grant mortgages to Free Acres buyers and in effect opened up Free Acres to the outside world. By the 1960s the state had taken one lease-hold for the construction of Route 78. Emerson Lane boasted cul-de-sacs of suburban houses between Plainfield Avenue and Appletree Row. Free Acres was under siege from the modern world.

Yet it was still Free Acres. Children who grew up there in the 1950s and 1960s describe it in the same idyllic terms as did the children of those early summers. Terry Conner, a grandson of Thorne Smith who still lives in the Smith cottage, remembers it as "absolutely wonderful." There were still games on the ball field, winter sledding on the farmhouse hill, summers at the pool. The adults around him, he admits, were different from the adults that most of his friends knew. One had masses of birdhouses and talked to the birds all day long. Another liked to wash his car in the nude. Along with Edward Brown, who walked all the way to Gillette to get his mail and groceries because he had had a disagreement with the township of Berkeley Heights, they seemed ordinary to Terry until friends from outside called them weird. Free Acres children were welcome at association meetings and learned a lot about democracy along the way. Maybe there weren't as many artists and writers as there had been, but the scientists from Bell Labs were "just as crazy." "Not a lot of difference between artists and scientists."[52]

Reading a memorial essay for Billy Kluver in the *Free Acres Newsletter*, one would have to agree. Kluver, an electrical engineer and a member of the Physical Optics and Electronics Research Department at Murray Hill Bell Laboratories, who lived in Free Acres for almost forty years, seemed distinctly cast in the mold of the original Folk. Married to an artist, he helped many other artists, among them Andy Warhol, who wanted to make floating sculptures; John Cage, who wanted to generate sound through the motion of dancers; and Jasper Johns, who needed a portable neon sign that would hook into a painting. These notions evoke Sadakichi Hartman and his sound and light concerts. Another artist and friend, George Segal, used Kluver and his wife as models for *Appalachian Farm Couple*, now at the Franklin Delano Roosevelt Memorial in Washington, D.C. Kluver died in Free Acres in 2004.[53]

Europeans, posted to American corporate jobs in the area, found Free Acres appealing. It retained some of the old cosmopolitan atmosphere that made it more sophisticated and Old World than the surrounding suburbs. Nor did artists desert Free Acres in that period. Gershon Benjamin, perhaps the last of the "old" artists, remained until his death in 1985; his wife, Zelda, stayed for the rest of her life. Ceramicist Marjorie Abramson lived in Free Acres in the early 1970s. Artists and teachers Harriet and David de Long lived in Free Acres from 1964 to 1979.

Although it may seem that Free Acres was a playground for free spirits, one must remember that there were many people who had come to America after being persecuted in their own countries: Jews like Bercovici and Liber had left eastern Europe, and even the Germans who came later had been trade unionists and were fleeing Hitler. Certain people had always been drawn to Free Acres for its history and its Jeffersonian democracy, but as the 1970s and 1980s arrived there were other reasons to choose Free Acres. Most importantly, it was cheaper than the surrounding towns and a safe place for children. In many ways, society had caught up with Free Acres, and its quirks were talking points for real estate agents. Although Bolton Hall probably intended the name, Free Acres, to apply to the land, Free Acres pioneered many social freedoms that were, by the 1970s, being demanded in mainstream culture. Feminism, sexual and intellectual freedom, freedom from discrimination by race and gender, the questioning of the military industrial complex—all these strains in the larger society echoed the concerns of those artists and radicals arguing in their meetings and on the porches of the summer "shacks." Preservation had always been a watchword in the colony: the trees, the ferns, the wildflowers, the flora and fauna of the communal woods. In the outside world, concern for ecology and the land had culminated in rituals like Earth Day and beach cleanups. By the 1980s and 1990s, many of the individual freedoms the Free Acreites had enjoyed in their little world were taken for granted in the larger society. Free Acres could now be seen as forward looking rather than quaint or odd. Its structure even prefigured the condo movement.

In the 1980s, the Free Acres constitution was again rewritten to allow second stories to be built on houses. Before, if a leaseholder wanted to add onto his cottage, it had to sprawl, and only as far as the protected trees would allow. Also, a leasehold could now belong to partners other than husband and wife. These changes, combined with house prices that were lower than those in surrounding towns, brought many of the new suburbanites down Appletree Row and into the heart of Will Crawford's beloved forest.

One relative newcomer, Sal Passalacqua, owns Dimaio, a popular restaurant in Berkeley Heights. For years before he bought into the community he remembers hearing that people in Free Acres were weird, nudists maybe. Yet when a leasehold, complete with abandoned cottage, came up, he and his wife, Tami, bought it. The cottage couldn't be saved, so they tore it down and built a house. It's definitely a house, not a cottage, but the Passalacquas built with stucco and natural stone to make it compatible with the landscape they love. Sal shows me the woods outside the picture window, where he often sees deer. Tami has been chairman of the Pool Committee, and Sal would like to restore the open-air theater. What neither of them wants is to see Free Acres become an ordinary suburb. "If," Sal says, "I start to require that Free Acres put in curbs and sidewalks, then I'm costing the guy across the street." [54]

Certainly some leaseholders would like Free Acres to be tidier, less eccentric, more like the surrounding towns. After all, it's about property values now; Free Acres is no longer, they feel, a summer colony of "shacks" and cabins. Others, newcomers among them, want Free Acres to remain a place of opportunity for the greatest number of people; they believe that "suburbanizing" it would make it less diverse. Terry Conner remains philosophical. Between the old and new people, there "have always been battles fought." [55]

Indeed, the association meeting I attended presented an issue analogous to the Bevans case of the early 1930s. Then, one Mrs. Bevans was denied permission to build a studio on her property. Now, one leaseholder wanted to buy a second leasehold, tear down the existing cottage, and build a house to sell. Nothing written in the constitution forbade this, but in line with single-tax thinking, owning more than one leasehold had always been discouraged as a kind of speculation. On a vote the proposal was carried, but it had to be passed at a second meeting. In the meantime, feelings ran high. People anguished over the issue of individual freedom versus community interest—the first principle of utopia. At the second meeting, the proposal was defeated. Back in 1933, Mrs. Bevans left the community in disgust. Since this was 2005, the conflict eventually went to arbitration and the Free Acres Association lost. It seems, however, that the spirit of Free Acres lives: the second holding was sold to someone else while the legal tussle was going on.

Laurel Hessing, playwright and Free Acres' unofficial but most diligent historian, worries about its future. We sit on the deck behind her house with its sign carved by Uncle Bill Crawford. The birds are singing their heads off, and the early spring woods are full of celandine. It seems very peaceful, but Laurel sees the difficulty of keeping the community going in what she refers to as these "anxious times." Two-income commuting families simply don't have the time families once had. And some people don't care about the colony's history, although, she muses, that usually changes "if they stay." [56] Bolton Hall seems to have been right about the effect of the land, or at least this little piece of it, on people and community. The past still reaches out to the present. Some spirit still dwells in these groves. One can imagine a Thorne Smith scenario in which a materialistic and uninvolved suburbanite tears down an old Free Acres shack to build his suburban dream house only to be haunted by the old radicals who once lived there. As Smith would understand, the old Folk are not gone from Free Acres. There is something that remains, just as the trees, the woods, and the meadow remain, something that sets Free Acres entirely apart from the modern suburbia that surrounds it. According to Benzion Liber, "the woods were like one huge interesting body, filled with its own life, which one could never tire of listening to and admiring." [57] Most people who stay in Free Acres pick up the vibrations and find themselves involved in the debate over whether to spray for gypsy moth or the outcry when the farmhouse meadow was accidentally mown before the buttercups had bloomed.

Stelton
An Experiment in Education

I know my way to New Brunswick very well. For a while, it was my twice weekly commuting route. Route 18, like the Garden State Parkway, is an old road, built when driving was meant to be a somewhat aesthetic experience. I began driving Route 18 in the fall of the year after my move from New England. This is beautiful, I thought, as the trees flamed into color—who says you have to go north for the leaves? Then November came, the leaves fell, and I saw the housing developments—acres of them, only yards from the road. Driving north this time, the month is April, and the green haze on the trees, the clumps of blooming serviceberry, are not enough to hide those houses.

I cross the river at New Brunswick and drive through Highland Park, past bakeries and coffee shops, an arts center. As Route 27 bends north, the scenery changes, as though another set of leaves had fallen, disclosing auto shops, furniture stores, and strip malls featuring liquidations of one commodity or another. At the corner of Plainfield Avenue is a defunct Shell station, a lighting and fan business, and a liquor store.

I turn here into a dilapidated commercial area and follow the road past the gothic brick Stelton Community Center, a church, a cemetery, streets of small houses, and under the railroad bridge at the Edison train station. I note the Stelton Diner and eventually turn right on Ethel Road, at a large and very fancy blue and gold sign for the Timothy Christian School. Is Timothy Christian a person, I wonder vaguely, or is it a Christian school named for Saint Timothy?

I accidentally turn into a development full of blooming magnolias and kwanzan cherries before I finally find Brotherhood Avenue. That's what I'm looking for, along with Friendship Lane and Justice Avenue.

I am not surprised to find myself in a subdivision of modest capes and ranches that look as though they were built in the fifties and sixties. A few, those with uneven siding and rundown outbuildings, might have been part of the original colony. I stop to eat my lunch next to a weedy piece of open land with a PRIVATE PROPERTY/NO TRESPASSING sign. I imagine it could have been a communal garden, set diagonally across from a ragged patch of woods. The land is flat but, with modern paved roads, not the sea of mud described by the early colonists. As I drive on, I pass a house with a large plastic deer on the lawn. Off International Avenue, I find Jennifer Court, a cul-de-sac of garrison colonials in pastel colors. The contrast with the names of the original roads is obvious; we live now in a world of individuals, not of ideas.

I find one house, half hidden in a grove of trees, with a faded pastel banner flying over a cluttered yard. I know this house has been here a long time. Driving back to Ethel Road, I see American flags flying. At the corner of Freedom Avenue and Ethel Road is the parking lot of the Stelton A.M.E. church. Flags and churches. Hardly the legacy of anarchism.

I cross Plainfield Avenue, and the road, smoothly new, curves through an industrial park, with the familiar big box buildings and their conscripts of flowering trees. I turn right on Suttons Lane, then right again on School Street, so named because this was where the Modern School was built. On the corner is a red building that proclaims itself "The First Class" and seems to be a daycare center. I pass a house in the Bauhaus style of Roosevelt, another utopian community I've visited. Then, on a curve, I spy a strange building, cement, with bas reliefs of swans and cranes and fairy-tale cottage windows, as though a dacha had been lifted from the forests of Russia and dropped on the flat plain of central New Jersey. I'll return to look at that; no suburban contractor came up with that one. Now I follow the road through a landscape a bit shaggier and more rural until I reach the Kropotkin Library. On the first pass, I miss it. The name makes you expect something grander, something befitting "the anarchist prince." In fact, it is a small frame building, now painted gray, about the size of the one-room schoolhouse in which I once lived in Vermont. In front of the library is a boulder with a plaque that reads:

Site of the Ferrer Modern School 1915–1953

The modern school of Stelton was established in New York City in 1911, one of more than twenty such schools founded in memory of Spanish anarchist educator, Francisco Ferrer. It moved to Piscataway in 1915 to provide a rural environment for the children. The Modern School, the "Living House" for boarding children, and surrounding Ferrer Colony became a center of libertarian ideas, art, and politics. Based on the principle of "freedom in education," the children took part in running the school and were allowed to make their own educational choices, free of established curricula, conventional classes, examinations, and grades. It was the hope of the leaders of the colony that this educational process would foster citizens with a responsibility toward others and a profound belief that government is best when derived from the people. The house on this site was the Kropotkin Library that was adjacent to the school.

The school building is gone—it burned down—but I can walk from the Kropotkin Library to the stream where the children played, all day if they wanted. It is narrow, almost hidden by trees and underbrush, loomed over by electric pylons. The banks are littered with trash, but little fish still dart in the tea-colored water, and you can imagine them being chased by happy children. I stay for a while, imagining.

Then I drive from School Street onto Brookside Road. On one side, there are still woods. In front of a small house in a clearing, a black man sits in a chair reading. The colonists must have carved houses like this one out of the woods. On one side of the road is Clara Drive, on the other, a conglomeration of mini-McMansions crouched on small lots. The road ends at Metlar's Lane, facing a farm, a real honest-to-goodness farm. It looks as though it has always been there. The old Stelton was surrounded by farms. I decide to return to the dacha, passing a Baptist church on the way.

It seems that no one lives in the dacha; it is crumbling at the edges. Brown paint peels from the window frames, and on one of the panes someone has stuck a sun catcher. It's the sort of house you can imagine being commandeered by hippies in the sixties—if there was anything for hippies out here in Piscataway. In bas relief, the crane spreads its wings, the swan bends it neck.

There's a cherub of sorts and, by the door, an image of a man who looks like a refugee from Soviet art of the 1930s—the stalwart worker. Behind the house are some apple trees, remnants of an orchard. I am told later that this house belonged to Sam Goldman, a master of many things but not of making money. His wife kept cows. Out under the apple trees, I suppose.

Driving back through the industrial park, I notice another sign: "Bright Beginnings—Early Learning." Whatever it is, school or daycare, it is housed in a bleak, square building with few windows.

We know that our experiments will not convince many. We know that our fundamental convictions that the only method of education is experiment, and its only criterion freedom, will sound to some like a trite commonplace, to some like an indistinct abstraction, to others again like a visionary dream.

⤙ LEO TOLSTOY ⤚
"On Popular Education"

Her verbal instructions seemed to vanish in the spirit of her real activity, in which it always had its source. The result of her system was that each child was skilful, intelligent, and active to the full extent that its age allowed.

⤙ JOHANN HEINRICH PESTALOZZI ⤚
Leonard and Gertrude

he Ferrer Modern School was responsible for the founding of the anarchist colony at Stelton, New Jersey. Like Pestalozzi's fictional school and Tolstoy's actual school for peasant children on his estate at Yasnaya Polyana, the Ferrer Modern School was an educational experiment.

Francisco Ferrer y Guardia was born near Barcelona in 1859. He grew up with strong anticlerical views, became a radical Republican, and was forced into exile in Paris in 1885. There he lived for sixteen years, involving himself in various radical causes including the Dreyfus affair. Ferrer became particularly interested in education. He was influenced by the writings of Jean-Jacques Rousseau, Pestalozzi, Friedrich Wilhelm Froebel, Tolstoy, and Peter Kropotkin. This educational tradition, "rooted in eighteenth-century rationalism and nineteenth-century romanticism, involved a shift from emphasis on instruction to emphasis on the process of learning, from teaching by rote and memorization to teaching by example and experience." Ferrer saw most education of his day as a process of brainwashing by the state and the church—a system designed to keep both institutions in power. "Rulers," he said, "have always taken care to control the education of the people."[1] He founded the Escuela Moderna of Barcelona, an institution dedicated to his principles, where tuition was charged on a sliding scale so that both working-class and middle-class children could attend. Because Ferrer believed in lifelong education, he also sponsored lectures and classes for parents on evenings and weekends. Convinced of the power of libertarian education, he renounced his earlier ties to anarchism and violence.

In 1906, a young anarchist, Mateo Morral, attempted to assassinate King Alfonso XIII and his wife. Before he could be arrested Morral killed himself, but the authorities used the pretext of Ferrer's friendship with Morral to arrest Ferrer, whom they considered an enemy of the state. In 1909, Ferrer was found guilty of complicity in the anarchist plot and executed. Overnight, Ferrer's death became an intellectual cause célèbre. The execution was condemned by Maurice Maeterlinck, Anatole France, Peter Kropotkin, George Bernard Shaw, H. G. Wells, and Arthur Conan Doyle, to name a few. Ferrer's martyrdom created immediate interest in his ideas about education.

On June 3, 1910, the Francisco Ferrer Association was founded in New York. The association had no specific mandate other than "to perpetuate the work and memory of Francisco Ferrer." Ferrer's name was linked with earlier martyrs, among them the great teachers Socrates and Jesus. Of the association's anarchist founders, the best known was the charismatic Emma Goldman. Addressing an international anarchist congress in Amsterdam in 1907, Goldman had described the typical school of the time as a "veritable barrack, where the human mind is drilled and manipulated into submission to various social and moral spooks, and thus fitted to continue our system of exploitation and oppression."[2] Other anarchists involved in the association were Harry Kelly, Leonard Abbot, Joseph Cohen, and Alexander Berkman. Berkman had served fourteen years in prison for shooting industrialist Henry Clay Frick.

The trio of Abbot, Kelly, and Cohen were central to the Modern School movement. They were contemporaries, born in the same decade; all three died in 1953, the year the Stelton Modern School ended. Leonard Abbot was a New Englander who, "had he been born a generation or two earlier[,] . . . would have been a New England Transcendentalist and Non-Resistant of the Emerson or Garrison type."[3] Abbot saw himself as a socialist and an anarchist. Having spent much of his youth in England, he had been influenced by Peter Kropotkin and William Morris.

Harry Kelly, more outgoing than Abbot, came from English, not Irish, stock and grew up in Missouri. Kelly's family had been financially ruined in the Panic of 1873, so Kelly had to take up a trade, choosing printing. After loosing his job, he rode the rails as a hobo, ending up in Boston and espousing anarchism. All his life he was restless and a traveler, but he was also more practical than many of his fellow anarchists. Joseph Cohen, a Jewish immigrant from Russia, had served in the czarist army before arriving in Philadelphia in 1905. He was a more abrasive character than Abbot or Kelly and, although a good organizer, much less loved.[4]

Anarchists were not the only founders of the Ferrer Association. There was the usual smorgasbord of socialists, single taxers, and other progressive thinkers. Upton Sinclair was a representative socialist on the advisory board.

For the next five years, the association grew. Modern Schools were started in other cities. By the end of 1910, Modern Schools had been opened in Philadelphia, Chicago, Salt Lake City, and Seattle, and later in San Francisco and Los Angeles. Although there were plans for Modern School high schools and colleges, schools beyond the elementary level were never founded. Many were ephemeral ventures lasting a few years at best, and some were only Sunday schools. In contrast, the Modern School at Stelton lasted almost four decades.

Stelton was, however, four years in the future when the Ferrer Modern School began in New York City on New Year's Day, 1911. It was, at first, a center for adults. Bayard Boyesen, aristocratic son of America's foremost Ibsen scholar and himself an instructor in English at Columbia University, became secretary/director of the school and secretary of the association, while Bolton Hall, founder of Free Acres, was treasurer. Lectures on social questions were held on Sundays for an audience largely made up of working-class immigrants. A prospectus was drawn up for the children's school, which was to be run on libertarian principles, that is, without coercion. "Each pupil," Boyesen stated, "will be free to be his true self." [5]

A fundraising appeal for the Day School, as it was called, was successful, and adequate quarters were found at 104 East Twelfth Street, between Third and Fourth avenues. The school opened on the anniversary of Ferrer's death, October 13, 1911. The first child to arrive was Amour Liber with his father, Dr. Benzion Liber, who later lived for a time at Free Acres. Dr. Liber would become an important adjunct of the school, lecturing on physiology, sex, and dental hygiene. On October 4, 1912, the school moved to roomier quarters at 63 107th Street. Here the school was close to the upper reaches of Central Park, and Harlem had a large immigrant population.

The first teachers in the new school were John and Abby Coryell. John Coryell, friend of Upton Sinclair and frequent visitor to Helicon Hall, wrote the Nick Carter detective stories and was an important figure in Bernarr Macfadden's publishing empire. He combined his commercial success with his left-wing principles in a way that could have made him a successful double agent.

Most of their pupils were the children of anarchist parents. Three were Amour Liber's cousins, the children of Benzion Liber's sister Naomi and Konrad Bercovici, also Free Acres residents for a time. Another pupil was Stuart Sanger, son of birth control advocate Margaret Sanger. The children were fond of their teachers, but the older couple found them hard to handle. As one of their students, Rion Bercovici, remembers, "They were too serious. Mr. Coryell refused to tell us Nick Carter stories. He was ashamed of the one phase of his life that interested us." [6]

Emma Goldman herself went looking for the Coryells' replacement. Her first choices were the Ferms, Alexis and Elizabeth, who had been operating a libertarian school on the Lower East Side. It was this school, the Free School, that Konrad Bercovici described in his autobiography. Arriving penniless in the "filth" of the city, he found that the only ray of light in this bleakness was the "Free School" on Madison Street near the East River, established by Alexis Ferm and his wife. An empty store with a few chairs and a piano, the Free School was open to the children of the neighborhood from eight in the morning to seven in the evening. . . . By themselves and with no fanfare or outside help, these two people, themselves immigrants, did more for the morale of the neighborhood than the settlement institutions put together.[7]

Elizabeth Ferm, however, having been raised a Catholic, did not like the anticlerical posters on the Day School walls and refused the job. Goldman's next choice was a young man who had actually trained for the Catholic priesthood, Will Durant, recently graduated from St. Peter's College in Jersey City, New Jersey.

In June 1909, Durant had attended a lecture by Emma Goldman that, coupled with his reading of Spinoza and other philosophers, decided him against a theological career. He read Edward Bellamy's *Looking Backward* and Upton Sinclair's *The Jungle* and became converted to vegetarianism by Bernarr Macfadden's *Physical Culture* magazine. He started on a precarious career as a substitute teacher in Newark, surviving by eating "chiefly in Macfadden's Physical Culture Cafeteria."[8] In the summer of 1911, he spent a week at Macfadden's Physical Culture City, this time living on bananas. Durant and a Newark bookseller friend founded a group called the Social Science Book Club to discuss economics, sociology, literature, and history. This resulted in an invitation for Durant to give a Sunday lecture, which he titled "The Origins of Religion," to the Ferrer Association. The young and unsophisticated Durant was surprised by the anarchists he met, who did not seem to fit the stereotype of the anarchist as a bomb-wielding madman.

At the time, anarchism was a frightening concept for most people. In *The Man Who Was Thursday*, G. K. Chesterton's 1907 allegorical satire about anarchism, the anarchists keep rooms full of guns and bombs under a London pub. The anarchist creed, however, is not one of random violence and is perhaps best expressed by one of the heroes of the Modern School movement, Peter Kropotkin, who lived much of his life in exile in England.

> We want freedom, which is to say, we claim for every human being the right and wherewithal to do whatsoever he may please, and not to do what does not please them: to have all of their needs met in full, with no limit other than natural impracticability and the equally valid needs of his neighbors.
>
> We want freedom and we hold its existence to be incompatible with the existence of any power, whatever may be its origins and format, whether it be elected or imposed, monarchist or republican, whether it draws its inspiration from divine right or popular right, from the Blessed Blister or universal suffrage.
>
> Because history is there to teach us that all governments resemble one another and are much of a muchness. The best ones are the worst. The greater the hypocrisy in some, the greater the cynicism in others! At bottom, always the same procedures, always the same intolerance. . . . In other words, in the eyes of anarchists, the evil resides, not in this form of government, as against some other. But in the very idea of government as such, in the authority principle.[9]

If Kropotkin was one of the gods of the Modern School movement, others were Bakunin, Tolstoy, Rousseau, Pestalozzi, Froebel, and the Americans Ralph Waldo Emerson, Bronson Alcott, and Walt Whitman. Those in the movement looked more to William Morris's art-driven utopia described in *The News from Nowhere* than to the more mechanical world of Edward Bellamy's *Looking Backward.* As a center of radical thought, the Ferrer Association also attracted the intellectual rebels of the day. The years preceding World War I in New York were "a period of extraordinary intellectual brilliance, in which many of the seminal ideas of twentieth century politics and art were being developed. Anarchism, socialism, syndicalism, revolution, birth control, free love, Cubism, Futurism, Freudianism, feminism, the New Woman, the New Theater, direct action, the general strike—all were intensely discussed at the Modern [Adult] School."[10]

At the Ferrer Center, Moritz Jagendorf, a well-known folklorist, ran his Free Theater, which produced works by Sean O'Casey, J. M. Synge, and the mystical favorites Maurice Maeterlinck and Lord Dunsany; art was taught by Robert Henri and George Bellows. The association attracted lecturers such as writers Edwin Markham and Jack London, muckrakers Lincoln Steffens and Upton Sinclair, as well as birth control advocate Margaret Sanger and lawyer Clarence Darrow.[11] Then there were those center regulars who were known mainly as flamboyant characters, like Hippolyte Havel and Sadakichi Hartmann. Hartmann's coup was his trips to Camden to interview Walt Whitman. Despite his drinking, sponging, and womanizing, Hartmann was prized as a talented reader of Whitman's work. He also performed hand dances and gave his famous perfume concerts. Where Hartmann was tall and thin, Havel was short, round, and bearded. Half Czech and, he claimed, half Gypsy, he knew a number of languages, wrote and spoke with fluid brilliance, and became Emma Goldman's lover and eventually her friend. Havel found it hard to stick to anything except drinking, which led to outbursts directed at whatever "bourgeois pigs" he detected in his vicinity.[12] Another recurring character was hobo poet Harry Kemp, who contributed both to Emma Goldman's magazine, *Mother Earth*, and to the *Modern School* magazine.[13]

Meanwhile, in the midst of this volatile, bohemian adult world, the dozen or so pupils of the children's Day School prospered. Durant was popular with his charges. "When we learned that Durant had abjured his monastical vows . . . to enter the radical movement he acquired a mysterious aura. An ex-monk was a person of glamour."[14] For his part, Durant recalls all of his twelve pupils as "delightful even when troublesome." In 1912, in an essay in a Ferrer Association publication, he described a day in the life of the school:

> They come to school before me, most of them; and when I arrive they recognize my step, and come tumbling out of the classroom to meet me on the stairs; hardly a morning but I must mount those stairs with ten or twelve incorrigible angels hanging on my neck, my arms, my coat, and even on my legs. . . . What do I teach them? Everything

under the sun. . . . One of my children is beginning algebra . . . another is flirting with improper fractions. . . . In our reading lessons we kill two birds with one stone by reading, except in the case of the youngest children, from history. We have lessons in correct English every few minutes, when mistakes are made by the children or by myself. . . . And then we have lessons in French, for the few who have asked for them; we have writing lessons, music lessons, exercises in skill, and what I call industry lessons—as when we exhausted the article on the match-making industry in the encyclopedia which Mrs. Sanger has given the class. And of course we have our "art class"; Mr. Wolff comes every Thursday afternoon and develops the frail, easily crushed artistic, creative spirit of the children.[15]

Durant and the children made frequent trips to Central Park, and Rion Bercovici recalls a game called Cannibalism in which the teacher was chased around a fire in the school's backyard. If a pupil caught the teacher, he could burn his clothes. Durant, however, bought them off with bananas.[16] There were also frequent forays to the offices of *Mother Earth*, where they were entertained by Alexander Berkman and somewhat intimidated by Emma Goldman herself. School may have been free, but it was not apolitical.[17]

During Durant's second year of teaching, a new teenaged student appeared in his class. She was Ida Kaufman, the child of Ukrainian Jewish immigrants who had been helped to escape the pogroms by the Baron de Hirsch Fund. Durant renamed her Ariel and they fell in love, beginning a lifelong intellectual and romantic collaboration—but the Modern School had to find a new teacher. In May 1913, Cora Bennet Stephenson took over and ran the school successfully for one year. During that time she began a summer school, which included two weeks at an open-air camp in Maplewood, New Jersey, on land donated by Bolton Hall.[18] By 1914, the school population had grown to thirty. In the summer of 1914, however, everything changed.

On July 14, 1914, a bomb exploded in a tenement building on Lexington Avenue, killing four people. Arthur Caron, Charles Berg, and Carl Hanson, young men in their twenties, had visited the Ferrer Center regularly.

The fourth person, Marie Chavez, had attended occasional lectures. Supposedly, the bomb was intended for John D. Rockefeller. Feelings against the industrialist were running high in the wake of the crushing of the miners' strike in Ludlow, Colorado. No less a figure than Upton Sinclair had accused Rockefeller of murder. Caron, Hanson, and Berg had already tried and failed to plant a bomb at Rockefeller's Pocantico Hills estate; what their intentions were on July 14 is unknown.

The explosion had major repercussions for the Ferrer Association. Plainclothes police infiltrated lectures and meetings. Reporters were everywhere, and more moderate socialists such as Upton Sinclair resigned from the advisory board. Perhaps the most serious defection was that of Cora Bennet Stephenson, who resigned her position. School, however, opened as planned on September 15, 1914, under the capable direction of a young Harvard-educated couple, Bobby and Deedee Dana Hutchinson. Deedee's maternal grandfather was Henry Wadsworth Longfellow, while her paternal grandfather was Richard Henry Dana, who had taught at the Temple School, Bronson Alcott's Boston experiment.[19] They were a bright and energetic pair who took their charges to movies and the theater, to museums and factories, and to see Isadora Duncan dance. It was a busy year.

Meanwhile, during the infamous summer of 1914, Harry Kelly had gone to spend a few weeks with a friend, Mary Krimont, at a socialist cooperative called Fellowship Farm in Piscataway, New Jersey. The largely German, and German-speaking, socialist Fellowship Farm Cooperative Association had first met formally on Thanksgiving Day, 1912, in the manor house of the original farm they had bought, a "stately, wide-verandahed house of 22 rooms, with high ceilings, marble mantels and great shining mirrors, [which] was to be the center of the group's activities for many years to come." Although the property had been acquired collectively, it would be farmed individually. "Each member had bought shares in the corporation, and the land was leased in proportion to the number of shares he owned. Some leased one acre, others two or three, and some as many as four. Lots were drawn for the location of the plots. A plot of approximately ten acres was reserved as common land, for future use as a park."[20] Because the closest town was New Brunswick, four miles away, a cooperative store was opened in 1913. During his stay in 1914, Harry Kelly was impressed. The secretary of the cooperative suggested that the Ferrer Association buy an adjoining farm, divide it into plots, sell some to cover the purchase price, and leave the old buildings and a few acres for the school. It seemed important to Kelly to get the children and the school away from the atmosphere of anxiety and suspicion that had followed the July explosion.

Kelly presented the idea to the association on his return to the city. Leonard Abbot and Joseph Cohen were enthusiastic, especially Cohen, who remembered "the boundless fields and meadows" of his Russian childhood.[21] As they saw it, the school and the colony would be separate entities but mutually supportive. The school would provide the intellectual life often lacking in rural communities, and "the colony would help to shelter the school. The children would not be confronted by a hostile, alien world as soon as they stepped outside the classroom. Instead, all their experiences would take place within a single enveloping milieu. Meanwhile, the school would be enabled to survive for a time, in economic terms, by the 'profit' made on the resale of the land to the individual colonists."[22]

A meeting was called at the Ferrer Center on September 24 to discuss relocating the school and establishing a colony within commuting distance of New York. The Hutchinsons took pedagogical advantage of the situation by having the children use chalk to divide the auditorium into plots, on which they built orange-crate houses.[23] Eventually, in the real world, a farm adjacent to the Fellowship Farm cooperative was chosen, and sixty-eight acres known as the First Tract were purchased. Fifty acres were sold to Ferrer members at $150 an acre, while nine acres were reserved for the school. The remaining acreage was set aside for roads or left undeveloped.

On May 16, 1915, the Modern School moved to Stelton, New Jersey. The day was cold and rainy, a gloomy backdrop for the opening ceremonies held in the unfinished children's dormitory. Most of the major figures of the Ferrer Association were there, with the exception of Emma Goldman and Alexander Berkman, who were away on lecture tours. Speeches were made, and two lilac bushes were planted. The rain continued for most of the month, making the old farmhouse with its ramshackle outbuildings and the half-built dormitory even bleaker. Nor was the terrain beautiful: flat, overgrown with scrub trees, no rolling hills or lush meadows. The pioneers, six adults and thirty-two children, started off living in tents and temporary tar-paper shacks. They had no electricity, no heat, and no running water. The woods were infested with mosquitoes. Rain made the dirt roads a slough of mud. On July 4, 1915, a Second Tract of 40 acres was purchased, and a Third Tract of 32 acres was added later in the year, for a total of 140 acres. Gradually, trees and gardens were planted, the old farmhouse was refurbished, and the barn converted to include a library and a stage.

The first days of the colony were hard. The colonists, after all, were urban people with no real land-holding experience. They had to clear ground, lay out streets, build houses, and plant trees and gardens. On top of this, the soil was poor, lacking the necessary layer of humus for successful cultivation. An agriculturalist from Rutgers visited the colony that spring and asked Cohen how he expected to grow anything. The two struck a bargain: Cohen would explain how the colony could work without a government, if the agriculturalist would explain the composition of humus.[24]

As the writer Michael Gold described the colony, Stelton was "a strange exotic jewel of radicalism placed in this dull setting, a scarlet rose of revolution blooming in this cabbage patch, a Thought, an Idea of Hope, balancing its existence in the great Jersey void."[25] Few would have seen Stelton as a jewel or a rose. Houses "required no numbers to distinguish one from another. They were not even in rows. These imaginative idealists had not only widely differing ideas on the sizes, shapes and interior layouts of their homes, but apparently no two of them agreed on landscaping. One home might be set on the back of its acre, completely hidden in the natural woods or thickly set shrubs and evergreens, right next door to another built closer to the road with a neat lawn and hedges. Many had been built in the middle of weed patches across which the neighbors had trodden short-cut paths. Gardens were placed in front of the homes as well as alongside or back of them."[26]

Neighbors on the surrounding farms were wary. They suspected the Stelton colonists of being nudists (which they were not, although the rumor might have been caused by the fact that few could afford bathing suits) and advocates of free love (which they were). The school had a large bell, which would be rung on special occasions, such as an evening play or a lecture. The locals insisted that the bell was rung every midnight as a signal for husbands to change beds. At Stelton, however, free love did not mean promiscuity. For colonists, rejecting the authority of church and state meant rejecting the coercion that both institutions imposed through their promulgation of marriage but not necessarily rejecting the concept of fidelity.

Nor was Stelton a cooperative in the strictest sense. Colonists may have grown vegetables and kept a few animals to supplement their income (later, some raised poultry or boarded students from the school), but the majority supported themselves with jobs in New York or, in a few cases, New Brunswick or Philadelphia. Some stayed in the city, joining their families only on weekends. Most took the 5:45 A.M. train to New York on weekday mornings, convening in a group, well known to the conductors, that hotly discussed politics in a mixture of English and Yiddish.[27] Not every Stelton colonist was an anarchist: there were communists and socialists, Lovestonites, Shackmanites, social democrats, single taxers, and vegetarians. Stelton, like Free Acres, did not demand allegiance to any one political or social theory. Eventually, the colony bought a cooperative van for the two-mile trip to the station, and every month or so someone would be appointed to drive it whether or not he had a driver's license.

Stelton had to build itself from scratch. The Ferrer Association in New York had been a very different entity—a place for lectures and discussions and adult classes. The only element that came directly from New York was the school. And the school was at the heart of the colony. Children are indubitably any society's hope for the future. The colonists of Stelton saw this in a broad sense—that children brought up and educated outside the system would be able to change it. As Harry Kelly wrote, "the hope of the future lies in the ability of the rising generation to think and act independently without regard to the prejudices of the past."[28]

Bobby and Deedee Hutchinson moved with the school and built themselves a small cottage. Two months later, however, in July, they left to found their own school at Stony Ford, New York. Apparently, they wanted complete control of the children's world without interference from parents, which was not really possible at Stelton, where the parents lived close to the school and wanted a voice in its running.[29]

The Stelton Modern School once again needed a principal/teacher. Henry T. Schnittkind, a young Harvard Ph.D., was hired. He arrived, as he put it, seeing "in this school a real hope for a better, saner, more civilized system of education."[30] Although he turned out to be a brilliant teacher, he lasted only until Thanksgiving. His young city-bred wife could not cope with the hardships of the first Stelton winter. Most of the hastily thrown-together shacks lacked heating, as did the school's dormitory, a partially enclosed wing of the farmhouse.

That winter, only five families and the school's boardinghouse staff, plus the resident children, stayed at the colony. The isolation and misery were so great that Mary Krimont inaugurated communal dinners in the school's boardinghouse every Saturday night, which were enlivened by a Victrola and a few records.[31] For several months, the school had an interim principal in the form of Abe Gosner, from the Philadelphia Modern School. Rudimentary heating was installed in the kitchen and dormitory, improving comfort slightly. When the harsh winter ended and summer came, the colony burgeoned with summer residents, and so a pattern of crowded, busy summers and lonely country winters was established. To keep Stelton somewhat in the public eye, and in the minds of city radicals, Kelly and Cohen arranged two festive weekends each year—one in May or June to celebrate the establishment of the colony and one, the annual convention of the Modern School Association of North America, on Labor Day.

In the spring of 1916, William Thurston Brown arrived from Chicago to run the school. He and his companion, Elsie Pratt, who assisted him with teaching, moved into the Hutchinsons' house. Brown was at Stelton for three and a half years. Other than a somewhat greater emphasis on academics, he made few changes to the running of the school.

There was no segregation of the sexes in the boardinghouse or in the school. Attendance was voluntary. The children came and went as they pleased, pursuing what interested them and ignoring the rest. There was no discipline, no punishment, no formal curriculum. Above all, the methods of public and parochial schools were avoided.[32]

As the school was now in the country, the natural world became important. Many hours were spent hiking, swimming (naked and not segregated by gender), growing vegetables in a special garden, playing various games and sports, or just messing about in the stream that ran by the school. In *Daybreak*, Joan Baez, whose mother, Joan Bridge, attended the school at Stelton, describes the freedom: "There was one school she was sent to which she loved. They left her alone there, and she could sit by a brook and not go to class."[33] In 1918, the colonists dammed the brook to make a swimming hole, known as John's Pond. As Michael Gold wrote, "the whole green tract is their school, and they absorb the universal education that comes to man only through all his five senses, and that he misses if he reads only books and knows only abstractions."[34] Or as Peter Goodman remembers it: "we grew like weeds," going barefoot summer to fall so that when it came time to put shoes back on, they didn't fit.[35] School was not confined to regular hours: it began when the children got up and ended when they went to bed, an exhausting schedule for their teachers. Nor were there any holidays or vacations. In fact, the school was joined in summer by the children of the summer residents. Children cooked; they gardened; they put on plays, such as *A Midsummer Night's Dream*, outdoors. School was life, and life was school. Stelton was a friendly place where everyone was kind to the children and everyone knew each other. It was a safe background for the progressive freedom of the school.

From early days, the children had their own magazine, *The Path of Joy*, thanks to the work of printer Joseph Ishill. Ishill was a Romanian Jew who could nonetheless have wandered out of William Morris's establishment at Kelmscott. He had come to America, already an anarchist, in 1909. Few Jews in Romania were allowed to own property, but Ishill's father, as a war veteran, was allowed to choose where he wanted to live. Acquiring a plot of land in a small village, he made a life of subsistence farming. Ishill grew up with a deep love of the countryside. Although Stelton must have been the antithesis of the hills and meadows of his childhood, he described it as "pleasantly colorful."[36] There he built himself a one-room cottage and settled in to print the private editions that would make his name. He continued, like most of the colonists, to earn his living in New York, but he was also responsible for the design and printing of the Ferrer Association's publication, the *Modern School Magazine,* with its Rockwell Kent illustrations. In 1918 he moved to Berkeley Heights to be closer to his work and the Watchung Mountains, which reminded him of Romania. He bought a three-room bungalow near Free Acres from Bolton Hall, but he did not live in the community. He set up his Oriole Press in the bungalow's basement and continued to produce beautiful books until his death in 1966.[37]

There was always a connection between Free Acres and Stelton—Bolton Hall was an officer of the Ferrer Association and friend to Emma Goldman. It was he who had provided the site for the school's one-time summer camp. The Libers and the Bercovicis sent children to the Modern School and lived at Free Acres. The wandering Harry Kelly lived for a time at Free Acres. And even Sadakichi Hartmann got as close as Leonard Abbot's house in Westfield, protesting to Joseph Ishill about his problems with paying the rent, saying, "I surely do not want to owe anything to anybody in Berkeley Heights."[38]

Although Ishill spent only three years at the school, printing and the print shop remained a strong part of the curriculum. One student remembers setting type for the children's magazine before he could read and running the press, first with a foot pedal and then a motor.[39] Setting type was probably an excellent way to learn how to read, and the approach was typical of the Modern School. A child learned the basics while pursuing something of interest rather than being forced to sit at a desk and drill with dull readers.

In those early years the Stelton colonists were poor, and as a result the school also suffered financially. As Harry Kelly put it, "the five and a half years at Stelton have been one long and continuous struggle against poverty."[40] Tuition was kept low for egalitarian reasons, so money had to be found in other ways. Individuals, and in one case a trade union, made donations. The children put on skits and plays in New York, and once, Ray Miller recalls, "when funds were low, we trooped round the neighboring towns while Uncle Will [William Thurston Brown] harangued the public and we children tried to charm them with our singing and dancing, into parting with a few coins to keep our school alive."[41]

Although the Stelton colonists were poor, at least their rural location protected them from harassment during the Red Scare at the end of the First World War. In 1918, the Ferrer Center in New York was forced to close. During 1919–20, a number of anarchists were deported, most notably Emma Goldman and Alexander Berkman. The U.S. attorney general's office sent agents out to New Jersey, who suggested the entire colony be deported. The fact that these were property owners with children in school probably saved them.[42] At one point, a group of local vigilantes rode out to Stelton to haul down a red flag flying from the water tower. Stelton itself was split over whether the Russian Revolution could really be called a revolution since it was not an anarchist revolution. The discussion, Peter Goodman remembers, went on for years, as did the discussion he had with his father about why they were living in the country and not on the social barricades of the city.[43]

In the early years of the school, life in the boardinghouse was supervised by a constantly changing cast of adult volunteers, almost all of whom had quirky ideas about diet. The diet was mostly vegetarian, but under one regime the children ate only nuts and raisins; under another, all vegetables were eaten without peeling and with dirt still on for nutrition. Still another regime insisted that all fruit be soft, so that oranges, bananas, and the like had to be thrown against the wall. Children were exhorted to chew their food thoroughly. They were even served mud to purify the body. Until heat was installed, pupils and their caretakers ate these meals huddled in overcoats and blankets. One child, Margaret Sanger's daughter, Peggy, came down with pneumonia and died in November 1915. Finally, in the spring of 1917, the arrival of Jim and Nellie Dick provided stability at the boardinghouse. Both had been involved in other libertarian educational experiments and were remembered by the children as warm and kind.[44]

Stelton, by all accounts, was still a ramshackle place. No building codes were in force; the roads were unpaved. George Spayth, a journalist, who lived there with his family from 1930 to 1932 because it was cheap, described the house he rented as a structure "that would have been grotesque any place else, except possibly in the pages of an illustrated copy of Mother Goose. It appeared much taller than its greatest width. . . . The exterior of this strange structure had been covered with tar paper which the wind had removed in conspicuous spots, revealing the mongrel collection of second-hand boards, which would have been concealed had the owner ever gotten around to buying and applying the siding."[45] Some even described the colony as a rural slum.

Of the school's eighty pupils, about half lived in the colony with their parents, while half lived in the boardinghouse. Although Jim and Nellie Dick had brought some order to the boardinghouse, by the end of 1919, after the departure of Thurston Brown to run another school in the West, the school at Stelton was again in trouble. The turnover of teachers and the intervals between teachers had created a state of confusion. In 1920, Harry Kelly persuaded Elizabeth and Alexis Ferm to take the reins—which they did literally, selling their farm in Connecticut and traveling to New Jersey by horse and buggy.[46]

In the interim, a schoolhouse had been built through the cooperative efforts of an exotic weekend tribe of colonists and volunteers from New York and Philadelphia, who worked all day and sang songs in Russian, Italian, and Yiddish around a bonfire at night. Immediately, the Ferms changed the planned use of the classrooms by dedicating each one to a craft or some other sort of manual training. Only the library would remain an academic area. Jim Dick would run it, in case any child requested instruction. They renamed the boardinghouse the Living House and settled in to run the school according to their theories.

Elizabeth and Alexis Ferm, Uncle and Aunty Ferm to the children, shaped the Stelton School for the next five years. Elizabeth Ferm, twelve years older than her husband, was the dominant member of the pair. The daughter of Irish Catholic farmers, Elizabeth was raised Catholic, including a convent education in Montreal. Alexis was the son of a Swedish shoemaker who immigrated to the United States when the boy was two. Alexis had had to leave school at fourteen to make his way in the world. The two eventually met at the Brooklyn Theosophical Society, where they recognized a mutual interest in single-tax theory and reform. At the time, Elizabeth was teaching at the Brooklyn Guild Kindergarten. Later, she opened a number of schools of her own, including the one that caught the attention of Konrad Bercovici.

Elizabeth Ferm was dedicated to the principles of Friedrich Froebel, the originator of the kindergarten, and to the importance of play, which she did not consider as only the province of very young children. Under the Ferms, academics at the school took a back seat.

> Scot's English class is going on with large attendance but he says he has to remind them when it is time because they are so busy playing ball. I feel they are getting a great deal out of their ball playing for they are getting physical development and the play spirit. . . . When they are playing on the outside, they are really doing something themselves, while when they are merely memorizing something out of a book, they are really not doing anything.[47]

The arts and crafts curriculum was immensely varied for so small a school. It included, as it always had, printing, but also weaving (on real looms), pottery, leather and metal work, basket making, and carpentry. Sports were important, and music became central. Elizabeth Ferm had trained as a pianist, and every school day began with an assembly in which she played classical favorites on the piano and the children sang and danced.[48] It was, David Freedman remembers, "classical [interpretive] dancing that wasn't done anywhere else."[49] To this day, he says, he remembers "every piece of music they played at assemblies." Aunty Ferm would make songs out of pieces of classical music; years later Peter Goodman would recognize the melodies when he heard them played in concert,. One teacher, who also taught gardening and sewing, went down to Arden, Delaware, to learn weaving so that she could teach the Stelton children. During various breaks in the day, everyone would sit on the floor and read Shakespeare. Typical of the school's attitude is this excerpt from one of Alexis Ferm's reports:

> About six thirty I went over to get the little ones ready [for bed] when I found all of the older ones, boys and girls, having some kind of play in the middle dormitory amongst themselves. One boy had a crown all made of paper, another had a cap with a large feather on the side and all had capes or cloaks or something. They were Kings, Queens,

Lords, Princes and what not. All had swords. The little ones were in bed and Billie [a child] was dramatically reading them a story and would explain all the personalities as she went along. So there was nothing for me but to go back and not disturb the play.[50]

The children produced outstanding art work and continued to print their own magazine, which at this point was titled *The Voice of the Children* and was illustrated with wood and linoleum cuts. No attempt was made to correct grammar or spelling—pieces are dotted with eccentricities such as "valcanow" and "stormey." The art work is exceptional, the writing uneven. It was true, however, that many of the children came from families whose members spoke little English. A succession of well-educated, left-leaning intellectuals, with degrees from Harvard and other such places, spent time at Stelton; they were talented teachers who, without any kind of rules, got a lot out of their charges. Probably there was nothing quite like it until the 1960s, when young college graduates "dropped out" to teach in ghetto schools or in other ways to pledge solidarity with the working class.

Also reminiscent of the 1960s was the strong streak of anti-intellectualism shown by the Ferms. They were not great proponents of teaching children to read because they believed that stuffing a child's head with conventional facts would stifle creativity. The library, built next to the school building and named for Peter Kropotkin, seemed to function mainly as the home of anarchist Hippolyte Havel. From 1924 until almost the end of his life, Havel lived in the library, where he had a little kitchen, colonists recall, and spent his time drinking and reading. He was remembered by Stelton children who knew him as a nice man who was usually drunk and sometimes talked to them of anarchism.[51] Finally, ill and bitter and forgotten by his friends, he ended up in the Marlboro, New Jersey, Psychiatric Hospital, where he died in 1950.[52]

The Ferms were also against any kind of political propaganda in the school. Uncle had an ongoing debate with Havel on the subject, and in January 1925 he also engaged in a formal debate with Scott Nearing,[53] the socialist economist, at the Rand School on the subject "Has Propaganda Any Value in Education?" The Ferms represented a kind of cultural and artistic radicalism that clashed with the political radicalism of the Stelton community. The anticlerical Ferrer was not a sympathetic figure to Aunty, with her strong Catholic background. After all, those anticlerical posters at the Ferrer Association in New York had caused her to decline a position teaching at the school during its urban incarnation.

If the school represented the "inner" or self-directed route toward liberation, and the colony represented the external or political and social route, the two did not successfully merge.[54] The Ferms were believers in the William Morris hero: the artisan craftsman. Many of the immigrants at Stelton, however, knew this role too well and wanted their children to have white-collar professions.

Despite being a talented teacher, Elizabeth Ferm was in some ways unsuited to the educational movement she espoused. As one of her students told me, "I don't know how the anarchists ever glommed onto Elizabeth Ferm."[55] Others among her pupils described her as rigid and opinionated. During her regime, the sexes slept in different rooms and did not bathe together, except at the swimming hole in the summer. She held firm opinions about what was vulgar and could be prudish. On one occasion she called a girl who had worn a bandana to school "a whore"—none of the other children knew what she meant.[56] Such behavior seems in sharp contrast to the views she expounded in a pamphlet written for the Modern School Association in which she criticized "the trio—home, school and society—[which] have undertaken to develop us so that we may reflect their perfect plan or system. . . . It is intended to reproduce images of life, to perpetuate all forms of life, and to guard against the creation of new forms."[57]

Yet there is no question but that she was a charismatic person. Interviewing her for the *Modern School Magazine,* Jacob Robins described her in this way:

Elizabeth Ferm calmly knitted and rocked herself in her chair. The sunlight streaming in through the window behind her threw her face into bold dark relief. Had she been young in years Titian would have loved to paint her. She must have been very beautiful when she was young. Even now, the eyes—the truest barometers of the soul—

remain suggestive of beauty. . . . Most people become older through association with children. Their personalities fade, like strong colors in the sun. But here I felt a personality rich in contacts and yet not overwhelmed by them. There was a self assertive calmness about each of her movements, from the play of her knitting needles to the swaying of her chair. But underneath that calmness there was a white hot fire.[58]

Alexis Ferm, on the other hand, is remembered as warm and kindly. Yet he too betrayed a middle-class attitude toward what he saw as Stelton's squalor and lack of civic-mindedness. He complained in several of his principal's reports about litter: "It seems unfortunate to hear the children complain that they did not throw some of the things on the ground and that they were thrown by the adults." And again, "We still have some clearing up to do if we can only get the adults to refrain from throwing things outside."[59]

There was also a perception that the Ferms favored the Living House boarders, whom they saw as more thoroughly their own children than the children of the colonists. Mainly, the Ferms wanted total control of the school, while the colonists who had created it wanted a voice.

In 1925, the Ferms decided to leave Stelton. Aunty was so exhausted that she had to spend several months in Arden, Delaware, to regain her strength. Once again the school was leaderless. That fall, Abe Goldman, a Polish-born anarchist, Esperantist, and vegetarian, took over, but he left at the end of the year. The school closed down during 1927–28, although a Work and Play Center was set up in one of the colonist's homes, supervised by some Modern School teachers.

The Dicks, meanwhile, had been working at Mohegan, a colony in upstate New York built on land purchased from the Baron de Hirsch Fund by a committee headed by Harry Kelly. One important resident, George Seldes, had been one of the founders of the Alliance colony in South Jersey. In 1928, the Dicks returned to Stelton, where Jim Dick described the school as "demoralized to the extreme."[60] The Living House had to be renovated, the *Voice of the Children* revived, and the schoolhouse fixed up and painted.

The Ferms, who lived for a time at Free Acres, maintained contact with the school by attending the yearly fall and spring conferences. When, in 1933, the Dicks left to open their own school in Lakewood, New Jersey,[61] the Ferms agreed to return to Stelton. At this point, Elizabeth Ferm was seventy-three and Alexis sixty-five, but they plunged back into the work of the school. Nor had they changed their educational philosophy. If anything, over the years their views had become more entrenched.

Steltonites managed well enough through the 1920s, but the Depression made the 1930s very hard. The members attempted to start a cooperative garment factory. In 1936, the school received an inquiry from the state Board of Children's Guardians asking if they would take children referred by the agency. They would and they did. The city kids who arrived were used to a scrapping, disrupted life at school. A Stelton boy remembers that "they were sent so they could reform but they taught Stelton kids some tricks." One city boy proceeded to beat everyone up until he was told that kids at Stelton didn't do that, at which point he stopped. Many of the tough street kids came to love the place.[62] Jimmy Diamond, son of the gangster Legs Diamond, reportedly boarded at Stelton—what place could be safer than a shantytown of known eccentrics in the wilds of New Jersey? Apparently there were other sons of gangsters, and sometimes black cars with New York plates would appear on Stelton's dusty roads.[63]

Even the Ferms, however, could not bring the school back from decline. The Depression meant that many parents could not afford the school's fees and had to withdraw their children. In the mid-1930s, the Living House had to be sold as a private residence to keep the school afloat. By 1938, enrollment was down to thirty.

As the children grew older, parents began to worry about their lack of traditional academic skills. So, indeed, did some of the children themselves. Leonard Sacharoff took himself to the local public school when he realized that a boy at the colony, whom he considered not particularly smart, knew fractions.[64] Other children were sent by their parents. In most cases, they advanced rapidly and did well. The school that had given them a grounding proved to be sowing the seeds of its own destruction. As David Freedman put it, anyone who stayed in the school too long would be "educationally deprived." As he explains it, "there was no one and no place to bring things together educationally."[65] The Modern School, however, seems to have provided a grounding that allowed children to do well in the public system. Alexis Ferm quoted a visiting principal from the Plainfield primary schools, which were the public schools in the Stelton area: "They say that even if the children that come from this school may be lacking in a subject or two, they soon catch up and are easily ahead of the others in their school work."[66]

During the 1930s, the colonists and the Ferms were once again at loggerheads. The Russian Revolution and the First World War had created a different political climate. There were anarchists and there were communists, and, as described by journalist George Spayth, they were "natural enemies."[67] Anarchists believed in the sanctity of the individual, whereas to communists the individual was simply a cog in the social machine. Discussion and conflict were nothing new in the Stelton colony, but in these years the division became deeper and more bitter. As Laurence Veysey explains it, "the Communists constantly preached solidarity but practiced the fomenting of divisive conflict; the anarchists preached individual initiative and self reliance, but practiced something much closer to brotherly love and community feeling."[68] Even though communists often took their children out of the school and sent them to public school, and Stelton had a branch of the Young Pioneers, the community managed to survive.[69] One theory, advanced by Veysey, is that the political schism occurred mainly among the men, and that while they were away at work in the city, the women and children socialized as they always had.[70]

As Alexis Ferm put it in 1933, "we were simple enough to believe that different political opinions could be kept in the background so far as the children were concerned in the common desire for the best for the children."[71] In fact, many colonists, both anarchists and communists, believed that the school should foster a political agenda. This the Ferms refused to do. So the Ferms opposed the parents on two major issues: academics and politics.

On May 17, 1940, three days after the death, in Canada, of Emma Goldman, the Modern School celebrated its twenty-fifth anniversary with a dinner at the Hotel Diplomat in New York, presided over by Leonard

Abbot. The celebration gathered together most of the Ferrer Association war horses. The program printed for the occasion contains brief essays and letters from Henry Shchnittkind, Harry Kelly, Joseph Ishill, Dr. Benzion Liber, and others. Former students also contributed reminiscences, remembering happy times and gifted teachers. The golden glow would not last, however; both colony and school were declining.

After suffering a series of strokes, Elizabeth Ferm had had to give up her work at the school in 1937. She died in 1944. Alexis Ferm carried on as principal until 1948, when he moved to the milder climate of the single-tax colony of Fairhope, Alabama, dying there in 1971 at 101. Although he became more pessimistic as he aged, he noted that many of the ideas and methods of his teaching career had made their way into the nation's public schools. He also read and admired A. S. Neill's *Summerhill*, a book about Neill's progressive school in England. Neill's methods were reminiscent of Stelton. The parallel is clear in Neill's statement that "there is a great amount of good fellowship and love in humanity, and it is my firm belief that new generations that have not been warped in babyhood will live at peace with each other—that is if the haters of today do not destroy the world before these new generations have time to take control." [72]

World War II brought the demise of the Stelton colony. The threat did not come from within—if anything, the war in Europe united anarchists, communists, and others—and although there were National Socialists among the socialists of neighboring Fellowship Farm, there seemed to be little conflict between the two colonies. The Ideal Farm at the southern edge of the colony, however, was appropriated by the army for the building of Camp Kilmer. Ironically, the colony at Stelton was destroyed by another intentional community, an army base.

Camp Kilmer was activated in June 1942 as a staging area for the port of New York. During World War II, more than 2.5 million soldiers would pass through the camp. Troops were billeted there in preparation for transport to the European Theater, and it became the largest processing center for troops both going overseas and returning home. An army barracks is a community of rules, the antithesis of an anarchist community, and yet it was the lawlessness of the soldiers that helped to destroy Stelton. The soldiers heard about the "free love" community and came looking for action. There were stories of vandalism, robbery, and even rape. For the first time, colonists had to lock their doors, a problem because most doors wouldn't lock. The soldiers frequented a bar called the Nine O'Clock, and to reach it they had to walk through Stelton, often returning drunk.[73] Suddenly, the dearly bought rural peace was shattered, and the colony was under siege. People began to move away. Children were taken out of the school. By the end of the war, the colony was much diminished. Many houses had been bought by black soldiers, since Steltonites were the only people near Camp Kilmer willing to rent or sell to blacks. Probably Camp Kilmer accelerated what would have happened anyway as the radicals aged and their educated children scattered across the country.

By 1948, the school enrollment was down to about fifteen children, most of whom were of kindergarten age, although the school continued as a kindergarten and primary school through 1953. By the late 1970s, the colony "had dwindled to a single original resident, a former garment worker named Sally Axelrod."[74]

The school and community had lasted about forty years, a long time, and in the process had produced some interesting patterns. The community had been one of immigrants, most of whom were Russian Jews, but with a sprinkling of other nationalities (Spanish, Italian, English). It was a community centered on a school and an educational philosophy engineered by educated Americans, many of upper-middle-class backgrounds. This unusual synthesis was made possible because the community wanted what was best for its children. The good of the next generation is a powerful glue for holding together a disparate group of people. And it was an appealing idea—to change the world by changing the character not of institutions but of people.

Today, many of the Modern School's innovations are standard educational practice: learning by doing, and the incorporation of art, music, and drama into the curriculum. Relationships with teachers are less formal. And lip service, at least, is given to realizing the potential of every child.

The Modern School inspires a deep loyalty. Those Modern Schoolers still living gather for a reunion at Rutgers University every September, traveling from as far away as California. They are a lively group with a positive perspective that the years do not seem to have dimmed. Perhaps their feelings are best described by an old student writing in the Twenty-fifth Anniversary book:

> I like to remember Stelton: The walk to school in the morning and the feeling of being intensely alive with the trees, the brook, and the yellow cow lilies that floated on it in the spring. There was something inevitable about working and learning in Stelton, as when the location and environment of a tree are ideal it is inevitable that it should grow. . . . Living and learning in Stelton included not only the school and the hours we spent there but the colony and the people in it.[75]

Physical Culture City
The Kingdom of Health

Back on Route 18 again, this time I'm heading for Spotswood, a name on a sign that I have passed many times en route to work. I know this is where Bernarr Macfadden built his utopia, but I have never explored it. Now I swoop down the exit ramp, around to the right, and onto Main Street. The center of Spotswood is small: the library, post office, a strip mall, and an old tavern building. Physical Culture City existed a little beyond Spotswood, mostly in the section called Outcalt, partly in Helmetta. I drive on as Main Street becomes Route 615.

Physical Culture City is the most grandiose of utopian names, but of Macfadden's city little remains save the layout of the streets. Turning left on Daniel Road, I cross Manalapan Brook by the VFW building, probably the site of the old mill that became Macfadden's publishing operation. I take a turn onto one of the lettered avenues. Physical Culture City was laid out as a grid of numbered streets and lettered avenues with spaces of woodland between them. This Lower East Side alphabet soup seems incongruous in such suburban territory, where roads are usually named for trees or for the developer's female relatives. The wooded buffer zones have long since been sacrificed to housing.

At the end of this road I find myself on South Shore Drive, which winds around, with the ends of the avenues on one side and overgrown deciduous woods on the other. Where the woods are would once have been the shore of Lake Marguerite, Macfadden's artificial lake named for his first wife and long since dried up.

Trash litters the edge of the woods. A rusted trailer with a FOR SALE sign stands next to a mailbox. At first I wonder if some eccentric holdout could be living down among the trees in the old lakebed. Then I realize that there are a number of mailboxes and that, for some reason, they belong to the houses across the street. A white cat peers at me from a REWARD FOR LOST CAT poster duct-taped to a telegraph pole. The cat went missing somewhere on Avenue I.

I drive on. At the end of Avenue K, where a meadow is becoming a new subdivision, I can see the pines massed against a sunny blue sky. These are the remains of Macfadden's healthful pine woods. The houses on these streets are small capes and ranches, with backyards cluttered by children's bright plastic play equipment. In some driveways, RVs wait under blue plastic tarps. Here and there appear a few scaled-down McMansions, as though the contractor hit the shrink button while copying plans. Off Avenue K, Dynasty Estates offers only a few houses and a lot of empty ground.

On North Shore Boulevard, some refurbished cottages, including a little red log cabin, might date back to Macfadden's settlers, although most of the bungalows and ranches look newer. Avenue E even boasts a house with a pair of stone lions, beloved of New Jerseyans, flanking the path.

On one of the numbered cross streets, I find a white cottage, built on blocks and with a glassed-in porch that was once probably screened. It is definitely a summer cottage, although it may date from a period after the demise of Physical Culture City, when the area remained a working-class summer resort. I wind back by the defunct lake, noticing that the trees are mostly oaks and that there are paths leading to a sort of wild common area. I get out of the car to walk. It is very quiet, with just the wind in the trees on this February day. On Avenue C, I pass a bungalow of the right period, screened by huge pines. Otherwise, the architecture is pretty much bastard suburban: southern pillars, fifties bay windows, stone mixed with gingerbread frame.

I wind back to the bridge over Manalapan Brook by the VFW building. The brook is wide and muddy brown, the water eddying around the fallen branches of the trees that lean over it, some grown with ivy. It would be a cool tunnel in summer. After the demise of his colony, Macfadden is said to have returned to this bridge from time to time, to muse and say that his heart was here in his abandoned City. Today, the February wind blows in the branches, and sun glints on the current-ruffled surface of the water. Even with passing traffic, it feels peaceful. The air is soft, and once there would have been the breath of the pines.

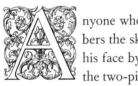

≺≺≺≺≻≻≻

If you are ailing, move to our City and get well. If you would remain well, live
with us. If you would bring up your children to be strong and healthy men and
women, locate to our City.

ADVERTISEMENT FOR PHYSICAL CULTURE CITY

nyone who read comic books in the 1950s probably remembers the skinny kid on the back cover getting sand kicked in
his face by a bully—apparently to impress the curvy girl in
the two-piece bathing suit. That was until the skinny kid discovered Charles Atlas and his bodybuilding program. Behind the famous
bodybuilder was another just as famous in his own time. Charles Atlas
was a protégé of Bernarr Macfadden, bodybuilder and health guru. Macfadden himself was once that ninety-eight-pound weakling, but he survived
a Dickensian childhood and adolescence to build an empire of health and
fitness and found his own utopian city in the New Jersey pines.

Bernard Adolphus McFadden was born on August 16, 1868, on a rundown farm in the Ozarks. His father was a hard-drinking Union army veteran. His parents divorced when Bernard was about five, and his mother
sent him, despite his frantic pleadings, to a school for orphans in Missis-
sippi. Thus began McFadden's hard-knock childhood. When he was nine,
his mother retrieved him only to send him to live with relatives who ran
a hotel in Mount Sterling, Illinois. There he scrubbed floors, carried lug-
gage, and did all the odd jobs no one else wanted to do. Finally his mother
died of tuberculosis, and he was sent as a "bound boy" to a nearby farm.
Bernard had been a weak and sickly child, and it was clear to him that his
relatives thought he would not long outlast his mother. He determined that

he would survive. Work on the farm was hard, but as he plowed, split logs, and fed and milked the cows, Bernard began to grow strong. At twelve, he ran away from the farm to St. Louis, Missouri, where his sister, Mary, was living with their maternal uncle and grandmother. McFadden found a job as a clerk, but the sedentary life made him ill again. His consultations with various doctors proved fruitless. "They simply promised cures they rarely if ever accomplished."[1] This was the beginning of McFadden's distrust of the medical establishment, which lasted throughout his life. His pursuit of health would take an entirely different track.

The end of the nineteenth century saw the growth of a physical fitness movement, so it is not surprising that a dispirited McFadden should wander one day into a gymnasium. Impressed by what he observed, he bought a set of dumbbells and began to exercise daily, including in his regimen a three- to six-mile walk. As he grew stronger, he became convinced that the body could heal and strengthen itself under the right conditions. From then on that would be his life's crusade under the rallying cry, "Weakness is a crime; don't be a criminal."

Determined to maintain his regained health, McFadden took a job on a Kansas farm. But the restless spirit that had allowed a boy of twelve to make his own way from Ohio to Missouri returned. McFadden became a hobo, keeping his dumbbells with him and exercising regularly in the box cars. When he took jobs, they were physically demanding ones: chopping wood, working in a coal mine, even holding patients down in the dental chair.[2]

Eventually, in 1886, he returned to St. Louis, where he took a variety of jobs and joined a gymnasium, prophetically located in a converted church. He started wrestling, at which he was almost immediately successful. Wrestling is a sport that involves the mind as well as the body, and McFadden was gifted with intense determination and focus. Although he was not a big man, standing only 5 feet 6 inches tall and weighing 142 pounds (a weight that never varied significantly throughout his life), he defeated Frank Whitmore, the heavyweight champion of Chicago. After this exploit, he opened his first studio, hanging a sign from his apartment window:

BERNARD MCFADDEN

KINISTHERAPIST

TEACHER OF HIGHER PHYSICAL CULTURE

McFadden, who carried a dictionary around with him, liked the Greek origin and meaning of the word *kinistherapist;* it sounded important. It's doubtful that anyone else knew what kinistherapy was, but the late nineteenth century was the heyday of strange enthusiasms. Phrenology attempted to assess character by charting the topography of a person's skull, spiritualists communed with the dead by means of table rapping and spirit guides, while mesmerists hypnotized their subjects. It seemed that religion alone was no longer enough for people; they needed other beliefs to sustain them.

Although his studio drew patrons, McFadden was still restless. He had begun to realize that he was hampered by lack of a formal education. To remedy this deficiency, he took a job as an athletic trainer at Bunker Hill Military Academy in Illinois, where his employment allowed him to take classes in English, history, and other subjects. He returned to St. Louis and continued to wrestle, but he now called himself Professor B. A. McFadden. He tried writing a novel that combined romance with physical culture but was unable to get it published. He also taught and coached at a military academy in Sweet Springs, Missouri. He continued to be successful as a wrestler and to pursue other athletic promotions. He also began to develop the ideas about health that he would preach under the name of physical culture for the rest of his life.

McFadden's crusade was really nothing new. Health reform was as American as the cornflakes and shredded wheat that it produced. From the 1830s on, dissatisfaction with the doctors and drugs of the day had created an interest in natural healing. Among these early reformers, Sylvester Graham, originator of the graham cracker, was perhaps the most famous. Reform of this kind often had its origin in religion. Graham was a Presbyterian minister who believed that white flour and white bread were poisoning the nation. His rationale was that man had "put asunder" the natural ingredients of wheat by refining out the bran—a sin with terrible conse-quences—and so he promoted the whole wheat "graham flour" that bears his name. He also stressed exercise and was known to take morning ice baths. He preached the value of a vegetarian diet and the avoidance of al-cohol and tobacco. Graham's theories appealed to many utopians of the pe-riod: they surfaced at Brook Farm, Oneida, and Bronson Alcott's ill-fated Fruitlands, where vegetarianism extended to not taking wool from sheep or wearing leather shoes.

Anyone who ever sent in a collection of cereal box tops to gain some of-fered prize knows the name of Battle Creek, Michigan, the cereal capital of the United States. Here the health rulers, John Harvey Kellogg and C. W. Post, set up their rival empires and made their fortunes.

Kellogg was the son of John P. Kellogg, a Seventh-Day Adventist and follower of the renowned Sister Ellen White. Sister White, who had opened a Western Reform Health Institute in Battle Creek in September 1866, tapped young John Harvey for medical school to fill the institute's need for a resident doctor who could legitimize the its regimen. When John Harvey Kellogg took over the institute, he made peace with the various medical as-sociations, installed electricity, and added massage, and gymnastic classes to the course of therapy. He also changed the institute's name to the Medical and Surgical Sanitarium, soon abbreviated by its patients to the "San." He was quick to gather testimonials from the likes of Bronson and Louisa May Alcott. As more health seekers flocked to Battle Creek, Kellogg bought real estate, leased cottages, put up new buildings, and even added a truck farm. The Simple Life at the San emphasized sleep, exercise, and plain and whole-some food. The Sabbath was taken up with religious services and lectures.

Cereals, like oatmeal and granola, were staples, but it was not until one Henry D. Perky invented Shredded Wheat that Kellogg set out to create a popular breakfast cereal. Perky had offered Kellogg a share in Shredded Wheat, which he had declined. When Shredded Wheat became a sensation, however, Kellogg got busy perfecting the flake method that would culmi-nate in the famous corn flake, which first appeared in 1898 under the name of Sanitas Corn Flakes. In 1903, the Adventists moved their headquarters to Takoma Park, Maryland, because the atmosphere at the San had become too worldly. Kellogg's scientific orientation was probably responsible for the gradual downplaying of the Adventist religion at the institute. The "Battle Creek Dynamo," as Elbert Hubbard called Dr. Kellogg, had made the San a resort where people went to recover their equilibrium.

McFadden eventually bought the Phelps Sanatorium from Kellogg's competitor, C. W. Post. Renamed the Macfadden Health Home,[3] the sanatorium became a retreat for many famous people. Soon after the fire at Helicon, Upton Sinclair's wife had gone to Kellogg's sanitarium to recuperate. In 1909, Sinclair himself, who had long suffered from stomach troubles and had become a convert to Macfadden's principles of diet and fasting, had stayed there. According to Sinclair, Macfadden was an

> athlete, showman, lecturer, editor, publisher, and health experimenter . . . to the highbrows he was a symbol of the vulgarity and cheapness of America. And it won't help for me to defend him, because I may also be on that list. I merely state what Macfadden did for me—which was to teach me free, gratis, and for nothing, more about the true principles of keeping well and fit for my work than all the orthodox and ordained physicians who charged me many thousands of dollars for not doing it.[4]

In the 1890s, however, this fame, or notoriety, was all in the future, and Macfadden was still struggling to bring his message to the people. At the end of 1893, or early 1894, he ended up in New York City, rented two rooms, and "placed in his doorway framed photographs of himself posing as Hercules, David, and Samson, among others, [and] advertised a free 'Physical Culture Matinee,' invited the press, and ordered a thousand circulars announcing his courses in physical culture."[5] He tried writing articles for newspapers and magazines, but they were regularly rejected. Eventually he patented an exercise device but grew bored with the bookkeeping and other details involved in running a business.

Closing down his New York operation, he decided to take the exerciser on the road. He would go to England, where physical fitness was more popular than it was in America. So he embarked for Liverpool. In that city he managed to cut a deal with a sporting goods dealer to supply his exerciser and to send him around the country to promote it. For two years, Macfadden traveled around England giving two-shilling shows. He hired a ticket taker and bought himself a cabinet with a black velvet backdrop against which he would strike poses as various strong men of history, a live version of the photographs he had displayed in New York. After his poses, he gave lectures and demonstrations and handed out folders of his health articles. Thinking these were magazines, people asked for subscriptions.

On his return to America, he began in 1899 to publish his magazine *Physical Culture*, which would continue into the 1940s. The magazine turned out to be the cornerstone of the Macfadden publishing empire—an empire that eventually included *True Story*, the first confessional magazine. *Physical Culture*, however, was the vehicle for Macfadden's theories on health and exercise, and he had lots of them. It would be a mistake to think he was merely selling snake oil or that he was simply a showman. Macfadden genuinely believed what he preached and that his own life and development was the proof. His enthusiasm was persuasive, and the time was right for his message.

The early twentieth century saw the rise of the Progressive movement. There was a great belief in activism in all spheres. Muckrakers like Upton Sinclair, Ida Tarbell, and Lincoln Steffens had exposed the social problems caused by the rapid expansion of industry. Women were fighting for the vote. People thought that society was perfectible, and this notion spilled over into the sphere of personal perfectibility. If the nation could be reformed, so could the individual. And if the individual were perfected, then society would be also.[6]

People were looking for answers, and Macfadden had the confidence to give them unequivocally. Unlike the earlier health reformers, Macfadden had a creed that was entirely secular. He gave God no more credit than he gave the medical establishment. The body was his temple of worship. Or as he himself put it, his crusade was "of far more importance than any religion. It is a religion."[7] Sin was neglecting the body, which included a sedentary life, poor diet, and the use of alcohol and tobacco. One should not fear death, but not because of the promise of an afterlife. Death, on the contrary, after a life considerably lengthened by right living, "is natural, is expected." We are like "autumn leaves that wither, fall and disappear," life having "served its purpose."[8] With a nod to the era's interest in spiritualism, Macfadden affirmed that the "great moments" of a person's life continued to "penetrate the atmosphere" after death.[9] And we also, of course, live on in our children. Marriage and procreation were always important for Macfadden: he fathered five daughters and three sons. With the exception of Helen, their names all reflected Bernarr: Byrne, Byrnece, Beulah, Braunda, Beverly, Berwyn, and Brewster. Another, Byron, died in infancy, possibly because Macfadden refused to call a doctor when the child went into convulsions.[10]

Physical Culture was the essence of both Macfadden the man and his message. In that one magazine was the germ of the many publications that would eventually make up the Macfadden empire. From its inception the magazine trumpeted Macfadden's primary interest, which it reiterated during its many years of publication:

"Lest we forget," let me make it plain that this magazine is leading the fight for a cleaner, purer, nobler manhood and womanhood, that we are working for the complete annihilation of those terrible evils that curse humanity in every civilized community:

1. PRUDISHNESS
2. CORSETS
3. MUSCULAR INACTIVITY
4. GLUTTONY
5. DRUGS
6. ALCOHOL
7. TOBACCO[11]

The magazine itself was more wide ranging than such a creed would lead one to expect. Macfadden came at his ideas in many different forms, and like most successful teachers, he was able to get his point across in many guises. His editorials stated his beliefs, and the articles showed them in various ways. In the early issues, for instance, Macfadden serialized his own novel, *The Athlete's Conquest*. On the first page, the young hero is searching for a bride—"a woman in every sense of the word—physically, mentally and morally." His definition of such a woman included one who did not wear the corsets of the time. "The Chinese woman crushes her feet until there remain only little stumpy, shapeless masses of flesh and bones to serve as a means of locomotion. She hobbles around like a man on crutches . . . is she any worse, or even as bad as the American women who crush the most important organs of the organism into a shapeless mass with bands of steel?" [12]

Macfadden continued to serialize fiction in the magazine, a clever way to keep the reader anxious for the next issue. He published adventure stories by the likes of John Coryell and one very long piece of science fiction by Tyman Currio purported to be a true story, although Macfadden maintained that he had always considered it fiction. Titled "Weird and Wonderful Story of Another World," the story claims to be "the unparalleled experiences of a young scientist who solved the problem of navigation not only of the atmosphere but the heavenly spaces outside it—claims Jupiter to be peopled by a superb race of men and women who live physical culture lives of the highest order and who in themselves prove the magnificent possibilities of physical culture principles." These alien physical culturists are entirely unselfconscious nudists who are able to transmit "a current of life" to the young scientist and to each other by grasping hands. [13]

Here on earth, Macfadden found ample examples of the athletic life to cover. Numerous articles featured successful Ivy League football, baseball, swimming, and crew teams. To his credit he also featured women's sports teams from Smith and Wellesley. Every issue included articles on stretching, bending, and strength building for men and women. In its step-by-step explanations and serial pictures, it anticipated today's fitness magazine. He also featured strength-building exercises for boys and girls, and even a series for babies, illustrated by photographs of Macfadden himself putting a naked baby through its paces. Ranging farther afield, his writers produced such articles as "Athletic Horsemanship of the Wild West and Far East," featuring Arabs, Cossacks, Native Americans, and cowboys. Sometimes the contests described were historical, such as "Boxing among the Ancients." Macfadden illustrated his magazines with photographs of nude classical statues and nineteenth-century paintings of mythological scenes in which the principals were usually naked. The reader could also buy reproductions of Macfadden himself, photographed in his classic strongman poses against the black velvet curtain that had always been a staple of his shows. He also liked to feature "children of nature," such as the White Mountain Apaches. Apaches lived the natural life: they ate when they were hungry, slept when night fell, and as a result lived long and healthy lives—or they did until the white man gave them his diseases.

Every issue contained recipes. Most were vegetarian because Macfadden considered this diet to be the healthiest. One recipe for Christmas dinner outdid modern mavens of culinary complexity like Martha Stewart in its recipe for Mixed Nut Turkey, written by Macfadden's then-wife Marguerite.

> Two cups mixed nuts; two cups boiled rice; two cups tomato, the thick part of the can (the liquid if strained off will serve for spaghetti or macaroni sauce for supper); two small onions; three eggs; pepper, salt, and sage to taste. Beat up lightly your three eggs and stir them in, then season, and put all on the fire to heat through very thoroughly, indeed long enough to cook the eggs (stirring constantly). Then remove from the fire and let stand until slightly cooled so that it can be handled. Now mould into the shape of a turkey, using macaroni for bones, for legs and wings. When all is formed press over with a thin layer of boiled rice; dust with cracker crumbs, pat tiny piece of butter over top and place in moderate oven to brown. Serve with hot cranberry sauce.[14]

Not surprisingly, Macfadden was much impressed by Upton Sinclair's *The Jungle*. An early *Physical Culture* editorial announced that "every meat eater owes a debt of gratitude to Upton St. Clair [*sic*], the author of 'The Jungle.' He has laid bare the filthy secrets of the Meat Trust. . . . Nuts, fruits and cereals are, indeed, inviting in comparison with food such as this. . . . Meat is bad enough at its best, but, when the greed for gain induces the Meat Trust to turn every old filthy carcass into human food, it is about time to call a halt." [15] Thereafter, he published a number of excerpts from the novel and offered a copy of it as a premium with a subscription to *Physical Culture*.

Macfadden argued for a restricted as well as a vegetarian diet because he believed Americans ate too much. He advocated two meals a day and regular fasting to rid the body of toxins. All disease, according to Macfadden, was caused by the body's efforts to rid itself of these toxins.

Macfadden had no respect for medical doctors, who he felt promoted disease for profit. He blasted appendectomy in an article titled "Surgical Butchery under the Name of Appendectomy." Even worse were the medical fakirs, whom Macfadden regularly exposed in a feature called "Rounding Up the Quacks," to which readers were invited to contribute their experiences. Macfadden always involved his readers, publishing their letters, comments, and recipes and sponsoring contests with generous cash prizes for the best vacation suggestion, the largest family, or the most beautiful physical culture baby. Babies were important to Macfadden, and indeed he had a plan to adopt a number of orphan babies and raise them according to physical culture principals.

Nor were the arts neglected. Interviews with actresses who subscribed to physical culture were common. The well-known anarchist Voltairine de Cleyre, friend to Emma Goldman and the Modern School movement, contributed an article on sandals. She allowed that her own were made by a renowned violinist who "realizes the William Morris ideal that an all-round man must work with his hands as well as with his head." She also described a lecture she gave in London at the Pharos Club, a left-wing association of which George Bernard Shaw was a member, where she "had occasion to remark the many pairs of shapely, sandaled feet, quiet testimony that in the multitude of reforms and reformers, the foundation [that is, healthy feet] has not been neglected." [16]

Besides doctors, Macfadden inveighed against patent medicine, most of which, as he pointed out, depended heavily on alcohol. He supported Edward Bok, editor of the *Ladies' Home Journal*, in his campaign against them. On a more controversial topic, he spoke out against the practice of vaccination in another regular feature, the "Anti-Vaccination Department."

The rhetoric is typical of Macfadden: "people are beginning to assert their rights as human beings against being made the victims of a hideous and filthy medical superstition which exists only to satisfy the greed of a class of grafters who do not hesitate to sacrifice the health or in some cases even the lives of others for the sake of contingent fees." [17]

Macfadden also waged war on prudery, and in particular on Anthony Comstock, secretary and leading crusader of the New York Society for the Suppression of Vice. In October 1905, as Macfadden advertised his second Madison Square Garden Physical Culture Exhibition with posters of women in white union suits and men in breech cloths, Comstock, accompanied by police, ransacked the offices of *Physical Culture*, confiscated posters, and arrested Macfadden. The effect of the raid was the opposite of what Comstock might have hoped, however. In fact, "advance publicity and the news of Macfadden's arrest drew a large and boisterous crowd of 20,000 to Madison Square Garden when the show opened on October 9." [18] Macfadden was found guilty of violating New York State obscenity law but received a suspended sentence. He never forgot or forgave. From that time on, Anthony Comstock was for him the embodiment of prudery. He ran articles with titles such as "Comstock King of the Prudes" and quoted George Bernard Shaw's remark in a 1905 letter to the *New York Times* that "Comstockery is the world's standing joke at the expense of the United States. Europe likes to hear such things." [19]

The back pages of *Physical Culture* were devoted to advertising, and Macfadden was not above promoting his own products. These included his line of health books, the Macfadden combined Massage-Exerciser, and something called the Pole-Air, a hood apparatus hooked up to a window by something resembling a vacuum cleaner hose. The user would put the hood over his or her head and thus be able to breathe "fresh, cold air." Advertising revenue grew steadily.

With the success of *Physical Culture*, Macfadden was busy. He worked to set up Physical Culture organizations all over the country. In 1901, he opened the first of his penny restaurants in New York City. Specials like pea soup, steamed hominy, and whole wheat bread cost from one to five cents to prove that wholesome food didn't have to be expensive. In 1902, he rented the Grand Opera House in New York City, where he spoke to an audience of about three thousand on "The Religion of Health." Macfadden continued to give these talks, which were more like theater pieces, with full orchestra and male and female models in revealing costumes. By 1903, *Physical Culture* had a sister magazine for women called *Beauty and Health*. He also ran a sanatorium, which he called a cooperative health home, in Highland, New York, and in 1905 he opened the Bernarr Macfadden Institute of Physical Culture in New York. The purpose of his institute, laudable enough, was to train health directors for schools and colleges. Macfadden believed that children should spend an hour playing actively for every hour of studying. A strong population would make a strong country. For Macfadden, the body drove the mind. Forty-week courses were given "in anatomy, physiology, the theory and practice of physical education, and Macfadden's curative methods which he called physcultopathy." [20] And Macfadden dreamed of creating a cooperative community based on his principles of health reasonably close to New York City.

In the August 1904 issue of his magazine, Macfadden addressed his readers on the subject of his city.

> Because I have failed to give much space in recent issues to matter relating to the Physical Culture City, it need not be inferred that I have lessened my efforts with a view of finding a suitable location. . . . I am now considering several plots of land which have been submitted to me. If any of my friends know of a thousand acres within an hour of New York that can be purchased at a reasonable price, I would be pleased to have him write me. It is not necessary that a station be near the land, provided a railroad runs near a part of it. In locating my business in such a place, it is, of course, necessary to have complete railroad facilities. This will also be of special importance to insure the future commercial success of the city. [21]

In 1905, he found the plot he wanted, buying 1,900 acres in Outcalt, New Jersey, halfway between Helmetta and Spotswood, thirteen miles northeast of Princeton. New York was thirty-nine miles away, Philadelphia fifty-one. Here Macfadden would create a new Eden called Physical Culture City.

> The path to social perfection may lead backward, be a return to Eden; but more commonly it has stretched toward the future, to a civilization redesigned to accommodate nature. Most hygiene reformers have acknowledged physiological, and moral, amenities of industrial society, and have sought to preserve these while casting aside the insults of luxurious diet, sedentary habits, and nerve-jangling pace. The kingdom of health has been a city not a garden.[22]

In fact it was neither. Rather, it was a flat section of pineland that included an artificial lake, part of the Manalapan River, a section of track of the Amboy division of the Pennsylvania Railroad, and one building, which apparently was a hominy mill. For Macfadden's purposes, it was perfect. Interestingly, part of the property had been owned by a German munitions company, which had planned to build and operate a gun powder plant on the land. This plan had not come to pass but perhaps something of an explosive karma remained.

Macfadden pronounced Outcalt a seat of health because of the salutary air of the pines and because the lakeside mud contained sulfur, a prime ingredient of mud baths.[23] Here Macfadden hoped for a city of 30,000, with libraries, schoolhouses, and a restaurant. In the end, Macfadden's city attracted only about two hundred settlers, and most of the planned buildings were never built. He did construct a large publishing plant, a gymnasium, a restaurant, and a health home. One observer remarked that "many people so crippled and ailing who came to Outcalt, had to be carried off the train. In no time these people could be seen walking around."[24]

Macfadden had identified "six great curses" of his age: corsets, sexual ignorance, inactivity, overeating, drugs and alcohol, and tobacco. None of these would he permit in Physical Culture City. It would be a place not of impressive buildings and parks but of impressively healthy human bodies, an object lesson for the country and the world. Macfadden as a planner was nothing if not grandiose. In April 1905, one of *Physical Culture*'s writers described the projected city:

> Physical Culture City will be a city *in* the country and *of* the country; and as such will be possessed of pure air, scenes to delight the eye, the smell of flowers and wholesome earth, the sound of bird note to please the ear, stretches of greenery whereon the children may gambol without danger of speeding cars and corrupting influences, and uncramped spaces wherein no house jostles its neighbor, and every house has its individual owner—a city of true homes, in which the health-making and brain-strengthening and bank-account prospering principles of physical culture shall take practical form and expression.[25]

This description was contained in a two-part article on home industries for physical culture residents. Suggestions for such employment included truck gardening, small-scale poultry farming and fruit raising, beekeeping, and the breeding of silkworms. These proposals seem unlikely to prosper anyone's bank account, but they do suggest a country life.

Macfadden persuaded the Pennsylvania Railroad to build a station about midway between the eastern and western boundaries of the property, but the railroad refused to use the name Physical Culture City, a name they considered absurd. However, "the name Outcalt called on the train from Trenton or New York was the signal for windows to go up and heads to pop out for a glimpse of the possessors of bodies beautiful."[26]

Early in 1905, Macfadden described the site in glowing terms. It was, he said,

> a little over five miles in length and two miles in width. Lake Marguerite [named for his then-wife], a noble sheet of water, seventy acres in extent, is one of the many beneficial attractions of the city's site. The water is limpid and supplied by the Manalapan river, which, outside of the lake, runs for four miles through the property. . . . The mildness and salubrity of the climate of New Jersey are proverbial. Also,

the city lies in the same pine-belt as does Lakewood, the celebrated health resort.[27]

Two years before Macfadden bought the property, a dam had been built to provide the hominy mill with more waterpower—enough, as it turned out, to power Macfadden's printing presses. The building, 224 feet long by 48 feet wide, contained, according to Macfadden, 22,000 cubic feet of floor space. Here, Macfadden exulted, he would be able to improve *Physical Culture* editorially and typographically. His plans for the colony included libraries and "an assembly hall, a place in which that healthful and enjoyable exercise, dancing, can be indulged in under proper conditions." Athletic grounds were necessary, of course—the plans would be approved by the physical education directors of the colleges that he featured in his magazine. Because he believed the soil was sandy enough to drain well and could, with the addition of topsoil, be adapted to small-scale farming, he would provide "depots and stores" within the city to sell these homegrown foods. A restaurant would be run by the Physical Culture Restaurant Company. Eventually, schools would be set up on physical culture principles, although initially children would have to be sent to schools in nearby towns. Central to the city would be a sanitarium "in which health will be restored through physical culture methods, and by physical culture appliances and principles." There would also be a "summer camp" or "tent colony" for physical culture vacationers. Eventually, he expected the city to have "shops, stores and businesses of all kinds." [28]

Macfadden was clear about what he did and didn't want in his city. Prohibited were saloons, tobacco and drug stores, opium joints, and whorehouses. No medical doctor, or any practitioner who used drugs in his practice, could lease a home or office. No medicine, meat, corsets, or high-heel shoes could be sold in the city.[29] "Applications for building lots and plots are pouring in upon us by every mail," Macfadden exulted in *Physical Culture*. He went on to explain carefully the way the ninety-nine-year leaseholds would be handled: "The terms of purchase will be made so easy that the man or woman of most moderate means can secure a building site at Physical Culture City. Indeed, lots may be had from $15.00 each, and one or more acres can be secured for $50.00 per acre and upward. Lakefront lots cost from $75.00 to $100.00 each." [30] Furthermore, he explained, the lots were double the size of ordinary city lots and could be had on easy payment terms. He also planned to create building and loan associations for this purpose.

Macfadden decided to lease rather than sell the property in order to retain control of his city. He had been warned that if he sold the property, his restrictions would be much harder to enforce. These circumstances were quite different from the leasehold situation of Free Acres, where the land was leased from an association and run essentially democratically. If Bolton Hall was the deist's great watchmaker, then Macfadden was Jehovah, handing down his tablet of commandments. Unlike Jehovah, however, he was not prepared to delegate.

Applicants didn't seem to mind. Physical culturists came from all over the United States and from Canada, South America, Cuba, and even Africa. Freddy Welsh, "an up-and-coming lightweight boxer . . . made the city his training camp." [31] No matter that Physical Culture City, in that first summer, was largely a dream in the mind of its creator, there were plenty of other dreamers ready to join him in the city in the country.

One of the arrivals was the peripatetic poet Harry Kemp, just back from a long tramp to the South Seas. A reader of the magazine and a believer in physical culture, Kemp arrived in what he described as "the mosquito-infested pine woods of New Jersey," a less lyrical description than Macfadden's. But Kemp admired the teachings of Stephen Barton, as he renamed Macfadden in his autobiography, *Tramping on Life*.

[When] I heard of his planning to built a city out in the open country, where people could congregate according to his teachings, I enrolled myself ardently as one of his first followers and disciples. . . . We began the building of the city. We laid out the streets through the pines . . . many of us went clad in trunks . . . or in nothing . . . as we surveyed and drove stakes. The play of the sun and the wind on the naked skin—there is nothing pleasanter, what though one has to slap away horseflies and mosquitoes. . . . the vistas through the pines were glorious. I saw in my mind's eye a world of the physically perfect![32]

Kemp also had a pretty good eye for the flawed present.

> As the laying out of the sites and streets progressed, dwellers came to join with us . . . fanatics . . . "nuts" of every description. . . . There was a little brown woman like the shriveled inside of an old walnut, who believed that you should imbibe no fluid other than that found in the eating of fruits . . . when she wanted a drink, she never went to the pitcher, bucket or well . . . instead she sucked oranges or ate some watermelon. There was a man from Philadelphia who ate nothing but raw meat. He had eruptions all over his body from the diet but still persisted in it. There were several young Italian nature-folk who ate nothing but vegetables and fruit raw. If appearances prove anything, theirs was the theory nearest right. They were like two fine, sleek animals. . . . As they swam off the dam they looked like two strong seals.[33]

He also noted that everyone had his or her own way of exercising by bending, jumping, and flexing, and that it was done lying, sitting, or standing. Children ran naked, as did almost everyone in the seclusion of the deep woods. Kemp was lucky. The wife of a bishop who had come early in the season to be treated for cancer had left to consult regular doctors, ceding Kemp her tent and the rest of her lease on a lakefront plot—good until Christmas.

Macfadden himself did not live among the tents and shacks but in a big house nearby. This, Kemp thought, was at the insistence of his wife, Marguerite, whom Kemp described as "a terror." Soon after Kemp's arrival, Macfadden went on his two-week annual fast, during which, Kemp claimed, Marguerite would taunt him by putting food under his nose. When she moved among the settlers, she would "imply all sorts of mean, insinuating things about her reformer husband." She carried her new baby with her and cooed over it so much that it was the joke of the colony. Marguerite Macfadden wrote a regular column on baby care in *Physical Culture*, in which she refers to the theories of Froebel. She appears to have been more educated than her husband, whom Kemp described as a "strange, strong-minded, ignorant man." [34]

Physical Culture City was problematic from the start and not just because of the mosquitoes. At the beginning, the majority of the city residents were students of Macfadden's Physical Culture Institute who worked for bed and board and their diplomas. They had to put in some ten hours of hard labor daily, for which they were paid fifteen cents in cash. If they could stick this out, they would receive a diploma in about five and a half years. Some of the more subversive of them suggested that by then Macfadden would have his boulevards and parkways, his gardens and truck farms, and a pretty going concern. At the health home, patients, who paid eighteen dollars a week for treatment, were sometimes dissatisfied when they were told on arrival that they would immediately be starting a week's fast.

As well as grumblings among the residents, there were the neighbors to consider. Macfadden's property may have been huge, but there wasn't much else going on in those rural parts and so the locals often visited. In fact, Harry Kemp remembered that "townspeople from neighboring small towns and other country folk used to come from miles about, Sundays, to watch us swim and exercise." [35] They were shocked and fascinated by women wearing men's one-piece bathing suits and men clad simply in trunks. Kemp himself wore a G-string until Macfadden took him aside to say that although he himself didn't object, others did. One Sunday afternoon, a young woman slipped out of her clothes in full view of the onlookers. A shout of amazement went up from the banks, but she merely stepped unselfconsciously into her bathing suit. Another young woman, apparently, liked to row on the lake naked to the waist. When local policemen started arresting Physical Culture City dwellers for walking into town in their bathing suits, Macfadden called a meeting to urge caution and to suggest that everyone go deeper into the woods, despite mosquitoes and sand flies, for the nude sunbaths he recommended.

Macfadden's problems with the local authorities were not confined to such issues of public morality. Physical Culture City needed its own post office, in part because Macfadden had to pay the Spotswood post office about $1,200 a month to handle his large volume of mail. The Spotswood postmaster, however, had received a raise in salary as a result of this increase, which he was loath to lose, so he used political influence to thwart Macfadden's request for a separate facility.

Macfadden found it wasn't easy to run his publishing enterprise and the colony and keep up with his exercises, his rowing on the lake, and his swimming. Staffing also caused difficulties. His cook at the physical culture restaurant was a Scotsman whom Kemp calls, rather predictably, MacGregor. MacGregor was a literary sort of Scot who had memorized most of Robert Burns' poetry as well as much of the lesser-known works of J. M. Barrie. Since the restaurant had to accommodate "outsiders" who worked in the publishing plant, MacGregor had to cook other than nature food for them, even meat. When MacGregor quit, Macfadden asked Harry Kemp to pinch-hit. Even though MacGregor stayed an extra week to train him, Kemp was a failure in the health kitchen. He then had a falling out with Macfadden, who wanted to evict him from his prize tent location and sent one of the colony strongmen to accomplish the job. The feisty Kemp beat him up and jumped exuberantly naked into the lake. In the end, Kemp and Macfadden had a long talk in which Macfadden bared his soul and Kemp "saw his real greatness and was moved greatly." But even more important, Kemp left Physical Culture City to return to school in the fall a changed man. "I was in fine physical condition, better than ever before in my life . . . I felt a confidence in myself I had never known before." [36]

There was no doubt that for someone already reasonably healthy, Macfadden's methods worked. Still, to most people they looked pretty strange, and Macfadden was quick to defend them. In 1906, he wrote an article in *Physical Culture* in which he discussed the criticism of the colony. He was particularly annoyed by the tabloids the *New York Journal* and the *New York World*, which sent reporters to Outcalt to gather lurid stories. Macfadden took them to task in his article for describing Physical Culture City as a nudist colony. Macfadden admitted his belief in "air baths," or nude sun-bathing, but he insisted that the residents had open topped tents with sides intended for that purpose. They did not lie around the banks of Lake Marguerite naked. "To be sure," he said, "we do not wear any more clothes out here than we have to . . . many residents go about a large part of the time in abbreviated swimming trunks, covering the body from the thighs to the waist. The women wear the usual bathing suit, minus stockings and a skirt." It was also not true that the residents of the surrounding towns had objected to the city, although they might have been shocked at first. Macfadden continued that "newspaper reporters delight in sensational stories, and the mind of the average prudish reader is quickly aroused to intense interest whenever any reference is made to the unclothed human body. We believe out here in the sacredness of the human body. We believe that the filthy attitude of the average prude towards the human body is sacrilegious and we take pleasure in ignoring those so-called 'conventional laws' which have a generally deteriorating influence upon mind and body." [37]

As usual, Macfadden escalated the argument. If his colonists are the "crazy fanatics" they are made out to be, if that "fanaticism builds the highest degree of mental and moral health, enables one to secure the best there is in life, and completely annihilates all evil and destructive influences, it is well worth cultivating." Macfadden provoked always produced high rhetoric, the cry of the prophet in the wilderness of modern civilization. "We are what is termed 'queer and peculiar,' because we do not believe in drinking all sorts of poisonous liquors; because we have some respect for our stomachs; because we believe in exercise and plenty of air; because we believe in leading a clean, normal healthful life from every stand point." [38]

Macfadden may have lectured the newspapers on their search for "immorality," but he himself gave his followers fodder for gossip. Saddled with the unsympathetic Marguerite, Macfadden looked for comfort elsewhere and found it in his secretary, Susie Wood. Wood, according to Kemp, was a "beautiful, gentle, large eyed girl," [39] the polar opposite of Macfadden's wife. She and Bernarr would take long walks in the pines, returning hand in hand as long as they thought no one was watching. People did watch, however, and it upset some of the residents to see that their moral god had feet of clay. Most believe that Helen, Macfadden's second daughter, was in fact Susie's child. Macfadden claimed that she was the daughter of a dying health home patient and persuaded Mary, his second wife, to take the child, then about six, and bring her up as one of her own. Susie continued to work on Macfadden publications.

Gradually, the city with its lettered avenues and shoreline boulevards began to take shape, albeit a flimsy one. The health home was constructed as "a 56 room building with baths serving every 2 rooms. It was steam heated, a 40 foot well and boiler room was on the east side of the building. There was a porch around this large building, and to walk around it four times covered one fourth of a mile. This was done four times a day."[40] Men and women in trunks and bloomers walked through the woods barefoot early in the morning, as Macfadden thought the dew was curative. Then there was the sulfur-containing mud: the uninitiated were startled "to come upon bodiless heads sticking up out of the mud of the peaceful woodland but were reassured when the heads emerged with the normal complement of body."[41] Nude sunbaths took place in the topless tents. As patients improved, they could enjoy swimming and water sports or games on the athletic field.

Ever a showman, Macfadden did not neglect entertainment for his followers. Pageants, parades, and events on the lake, such as the water spectacle "A Venetian Night," were regular occurrences, along with group sings on the shore. In all, the experience was like that of a rigorous summer camp, and many people used it as that, leaving the tent colony once the leaves of the oaks and maples began to turn and the healthful air of the pines grew cold. Others who had built somewhat more substantial "cottages" stayed on. Still, it was a place where even a public building like the central store was "a flimsy looking edifice surrounded by several old picnic tables [that] resembled nothing more than a hot dog stand."[42]

Macfadden was committed to a year-round community. For him, utopia was not just a summer place, and so he set out to build himself a glass house, or, as he dubbed it, a "physical culture house." Macfadden intended to break away from architects belonging to the "sheep family." (Macfadden was prone to describe the non–physical culturists who made up the bulk of the American population as "sheep.") Hygiene, he maintained, was ignored in the building of the average home: "Sunlight and air are absolutely essential to the enjoyment of vigorous health. In the typical home of today these health-building influences are compelled to creep in through crevices instead of being given free access to the interior of the rooms. During the winter months, at which time even the crevices alluded to are often hermetically sealed, the stagnant condition of the enclosed air can be readily imagined." [43]

This sort of house would not do for Macfadden—he would build his of glass. In fact, the edifice would be constructed much like a greenhouse. There would be a wooden structure, but between the supports the walls would be made of glass, as would the roof. In the winter, the glass roof would ensure that even shaded parts of the house would remain at least sixty-five degrees. "This," Macfadden pointed out, "indicates a method of saving coal which will be of much interest to the economical housekeeper." Solar heat, in other words. Of course, in a New Jersey summer, a glass roof would not be pleasant, so a canvas would be hung over the exterior of the roof, and interior "rolling screens or blinds of Japanese matting or other material" would be installed. There would also be large curtains "similar to those used in a photograph gallery" to shut out the sunlight from different parts of the rooms. Curtains like these formed the backdrop for Macfadden's famous poses, so perhaps they could serve a dual purpose. Curtains and blinds were also necessary for privacy, although that might have been more of a concern to Marguerite than to Bernarr, who in later years was known to stride naked through his house to the discomfort of plumbers and other workmen. Pictures of the house accompany the *Physical Culture* article, so presumably it was built and occupied, although no trace of anything so fragile as a glass house exists today. [44]

Yet even as Macfadden planned and built for the future, time was running out for his city in the pines. In October 1906, *Physical Culture* began serializing a story written by one of Macfadden's star writers, John Coryell—the same John Coryell of socialist/anarchist leanings who became a frequent visitor to Upton Sinclair's Helicon Home Colony. "Growing to Manhood in Civilized (?) Society" was the confessional story of a teenaged son of wealthy, syphilitic parents who had failed to tell him the facts of life. Persuaded by lowlife companions that sex would make a man of him, he drank, read obscene books, slept around, got venereal disease, went insane, and had himself cremated alive. After six installments, in March 1907, Bernarr Macfadden was arrested for violating a federal obscenity law by sending such materials through the mail to a sixteen-year-old minor. He was indicted by the New Jersey federal grand jury on charges that the story contained obscene, lewd, and lascivious material. After a trial and brief deliberation, the trial jury found him guilty. He was sentenced to two years at hard labor and fined $2,000.

Macfadden was completely dumbfounded. In *Is It a Crime to Expose a Crime?* a pamphlet bound into the December 1907 issue of *Physical Culture,* he thundered that the story was aimed at the "elevation of mankind by shedding light upon the vicious conditions that existed practically everywhere."[45] Convinced of his high moral purpose, as always, Macfadden mounted appeal after appeal, all the way up to the Supreme Court, which refused to hear the case on the grounds that no constitutional question was at stake. Macfadden went around the country on lecture tours to put his case before the people, and he printed blank petitions in his magazine to be signed by supporters. He also began a letter-writing campaign. So many letters and telegrams poured into the White House that in 1909 he was pardoned by President William Howard Taft, although the fine was not remitted. Macfadden, who wanted to be cleared entirely, was infuriated.

The trial had consumed his time, energy, and money, and he had neglected his city. At least once during this period, he called a meeting in the gymnasium, where he denounced traitors and backbiters among his disciples and told those who were not with him to get out. Gradually they did. The property was disposed of. Due to the lack of a post office, the offices of the publishing company were sold at a loss, and Macfadden moved his operations back to New York City. Macfadden's stock in the Physical Culture City Land Company was bought out, but the company tried to develop the city as a summer resort. An ad in *Physical Culture* in June 1908 invited people to invest in this future summer colony. "Go Back to Nature," the headline read.

There is no other resort anywhere where you can obtain the same freedom. The object of summer vacation is to build up increased health and strength—to commune with nature—to go back to nature, to make yourself a natural man and a natural woman. Of what value are "swell" hotels or fashionable watering places for this purpose? They simply represent a continuation of the usual performance.[46]

At Physical Culture City, the ad went on, you could erect a tent or a hut on your own plot—presumably without Macfadden's original restrictions. Macfadden had sold his stock because he couldn't give proper attention to the enterprise, but apparently the new owners would. "Physical Culture City will be a monumental success in the near future." The health home, now called the Galatian Sanatorium, also advertised; it promised that "the Macfadden Treatment will be strictly followed." One Frank Koester advertised a tent colony in which one could rent a cot in a tent for $2.00 a week or the whole tent for $4.00. "There are restaurants and grocery stores and other conveniences on the grounds." A number of Macfadden's followers thus attempted to keep their city going in some form.

Unfortunately, soon after Macfadden's departure, a caretaker neglected to open the locks at Lake Marguerite when the spring thaws came, and the banks of the lake were washed away with the ice flow. The lake disappeared, leaving a mossy hollow, which is all that remains today. According to a brief history of Outcalt published in 1963, Macfadden often returned to stand on the bridge and look over his old territory. "My heart is still here," he would say.[47]

As much as his perfect city meant to him, Macfadden was not one to keep all his eggs in one basket, and well before he was forced to sell out Physical Culture City, he had opened his health home in Battle Creek, Michigan, where he was no doubt convinced that he could outdo the Posts and the Kelloggs. He reminded those who could not travel all the way to Battle Creek of the health home at Physical Culture City. "The accommodations at Physical Culture City are, of course, not so modern as those found at Battle Creek and the facilities of treatment are not so varied, but the ability to go out [in] an absolutely unconventional attire without causing comment or being annoyed, is worth considerable to one who is striving for health." [48]

A reader of *Physical Culture* who sold enough subscriptions would be rewarded with a vacation or medical stay at either place. Battle Creek, however, did not work out well for Macfadden. He had particularly wanted a location in Battle Creek because he had invented his own breakfast cereal, Strengtho, but Strengtho turned rancid faster than Macfadden could sell it. The Battle Creek health home followed Macfadden's principles—no meat, deep breathing, and exercise—and Macfadden himself could be seen on the streets of Battle Creek "striding along, barefoot, in shorts, long hair streaming, inhaling and exhaling rhythmically." [49] He still gave Friday evening lectures, which included his poses, his body nearly nude and dusted with white powder, in front of a black velvet curtain. By this time, Macfadden had become something of a caricature of himself—always fodder for a news story. One winter night, he knocked at the door of his Battle Creek health home, dressed "in a Davy Crockett cap . . . bearskin coat, wristlets, gauntlets and carrying a hot Chinese stove in each hand." [50] Not recognizing him, his staff threw him out into a snow bank. Soon after that came the obscenity indictment, and although he claimed it would not affect the Battle Creek health home, the home closed down. In 1909, he moved his establishment to Chicago's South Side and entrusted its future to the reliable Susie Wood. She ran it faithfully until after World War I.

In 1912, after temporarily resigning as president of his publishing company, Macfadden went to England on a lecture tour. There he sponsored a contest for the most perfect woman and married its winner, Mary Williamson. He was forty-five; she was nineteen. The marriage produced seven children, although eventually it ended in divorce. Mary Macfadden's portrait of her husband in her autobiography, *Dumbbells and Carrot Strips*, is generally unflattering. When the Macfaddens returned to America, Bernarr, as planned, resumed control of the Physical Culture Publishing Company, which was renamed Macfadden Publications some years later.

Bernarr Macfadden is remembered for his impact on magazine publishing, rather than his physical culture theories. His publications blazed the trail for magazines as we know them today. *True Story*, a spinoff of *Physical*

Culture magazine, is one example. Macfadden was fascinated by the letters he received from readers confessing their problems and asking for help, and he became convinced that "true" stories like these would make interesting reading. His wife Mary, however, who also read the correspondence, always claimed the magazine was her idea.[51] With a borrowed million dollars, Macfadden had *True Story* on the newsstands in May 1919. By 1926, the publication had a readership of over two million. With its recountings by ordinary girls of their "missteps" or of challenges to their innocence overcome, *True* Story was right for the times. A revolution in manners and morals had swept up the younger generation of the 1920s. The war had produced a heightened "eat drink and be merry" attitude, and Freud had been discovered by America. In this atmosphere, a magazine full of stories with titles such as "I Wanted Love and So—," "His Neighbor's Wife," and "Let My Husband Alone" found a ready audience. That these stories all had moral endings made them no less titillating. From *True Story,* Macfadden went on to *True Romances* and *True Detective*. From these, it was only a step to the *New York Evening Graphic*, a newspaper Macfadden hoped would provide the publicity necessity for his growing yen for a political career. The *Graphic* added a new wrinkle to the tabloid by inventing the "composograph," basically a method of putting faces of real people on the bodies of posed models—a trick that, luckily, papers such as the *New York World* did not have when they were writing about Physical Culture City.

In 1929, Macfadden moved his family from an estate in Nyack, New York, to an even larger estate in Englewood, New Jersey. Once again, genteel, well-off Englewood was home to utopia—even if it was only Macfadden's domestic utopia, or, perhaps, dystopia.

> There was scarcely a minute of their leisure time when the publisher, his wife, and the children were not swimming (in their own pool), skating, throwing dumbbells back and forth, wrestling, or dancing nude on the lawn. The estate at Englewood was heavily booby-trapped with chinning bars, swings, tennis courts, rowing machines, and other apparatus. Macfadden advocated working out in the raw if

possible, and if not, in as scant a costume as could be managed with the family still retaining a skeleton domestic staff.[52]

Macfadden continued to follow his ambitions throughout the rest of his life. He made and lost fortunes, and owned health homes and spa resorts all over the country. At some point he even owned a military school. He continued to have political ambitions. He would have liked to have run for president but settled on running for governor of Florida. He remained committed to his first physical culture tenets and to the importance of living simply in the natural world—even though he himself no longer did. He supported Franklin D. Roosevelt for president in 1932 and took particular interest in the New Deal Resettlement Administration. At the onset of the Depression, he had advocated placing unemployed workers on subsistence farms. He maintained that two to ten acres would produce enough food to feed a family through the winter and that such a life would be "an immeasurable improvement" over impoverished city life. He was a member of the National Advisory Committee for Subsistence Homesteads, set up in 1933, and was present at a number of conferences with Rexford Tugwell and other Resettlement figures. He wrote "back to the land" editorials for *Liberty*, the family magazine he had acquired in 1931.

First send those with families out in the country and supply them with all the land they can individually work. Give them credit for whatever is necessary to erect a small house, to buy a cow, and chickens and the implements necessary to work the land. They will no longer be subjects for charity. The family could operate this little farm and raise practically everything they want to eat, and with milk and eggs and chickens they could live on the fat of the land from their own labor.[53]

Liberty was a lot more conservative than *True Story*, although it featured movie star gossip and stories of European royalty. In it Macfadden serialized work by Agatha Christie, Ernest Thompson Seton, Will James, and Theodore Dreiser among others. Konrard Bercovici contributed often to

Liberty's pages, sometimes stories, sometimes tales of Romanian royalty. Surprisingly, Macfadden allowed advertisements for Camels, Chesterfields, and Lucky Strike cigarettes as well as for Coca-Cola. Despite the demise of his "city in the country," Macfadden continued to believe in the natural world as the foundation for a new society and often referred to himself as a Huckleberry Finn, that is, someone trying to stay ahead of "sivilization," the "bound boy" who found his health and his calling on the farm.

Time has vindicated Macfadden's views of civilization's ills. Tobacco does cause heart disease and cancer. Corsets are no longer worn. Physical exercise is seen as a major key to health; isometric exercise, which he popularized as "dynamic tension," is a part of most exercise programs. As the "obesity epidemic" makes clear, Americans do indeed eat too much. White bread provides no nutrition. Prudishness is long gone, although our headlong rush in the opposite direction may come from the same unhealthy set of attitudes. Obviously, we do rely on drugs and doctors, but a growing mistrust of modern medicine has created a considerable interest in all forms of alternative medicine from massage to acupuncture to yoga to Chinese herbalism. Some also question vaccination, linking it to the rise of autism in children. Macfadden would have been on their side. He was also an early proponent of solar heat, and he decried stagnant air, especially in office buildings. He also anticipated the office gym by giving his employees breaks for desk-side exercise. Macfadden's attitude toward women was more problematic. He championed their freedom to wear practical clothes and gain strength through athletics, but he still saw reproduction as their major function. He deplored abortion and "abortive remedies" and included sermons to be preached against them in the pages of *Physical Culture*.[54]

Toward the end of his life, Macfadden's eccentricities, including parachute jumping in his eighties, marrying another much younger wife and then trying to get her to pretend pregnancy with a pillow, striding around in toeless shoes to retain contact with the earth, and standing on his head in public places, got in the way of his often valid ideas. Macfadden never considered Physical Culture City a disaster, but he never tried to build that kind of utopia again. As he wrote in an editorial in *Physical Culture* magazine in March 1909: "I had many glorious dreams of what would be accomplished in a community of our own, in which we would be free from all the evils with which we come in contact in all large cities. It was a beautiful dream. It was one of those dreams that will undoubtedly be a reality some day, but from my own experience in building up this community, I am inclined to admit that the time is not yet here." [55]

In 1910 Harry Kemp, on his way to pay his fateful visit to Upton Sinclair, who, after the experiment of "Parnassus Palace" (Helicon Hall) was living in the single-tax colony of Arden, Delaware, went out to camp at "Perfection City," his name for Physical Culture City. "Perfection City," he complained, "was no longer the place of ideals it had been . . . it was now a locality where the poorer bourgeoisie sent their wives and children for an inexpensive summer outing." [56] Unlike Bolton Hall, the cool intellectual who set Free Acres in motion as a social experiment and got out of the way, Bernarr Macfadden was a despot, if a somewhat benevolent one. He admired strong leaders like Teddy Roosevelt and Franklin D. Roosevelt. He was even impressed by Benito Mussolini, whom he visited in Italy and who endorsed the principles of physical culture. Physical Culture City could not survive without its leader.

The Self Master Colony
A Home for the Homeless

I am on the parkway again, headed for Union. This time the exit is simple, none of the baroque twists and switchbacks I have come to dread, just a road that tunnels under Route 22 and climbs past the Connecticut Farms Presbyterian Church and Cemetery. It's an old brick and stone church, reminiscent of ones I've seen in southeastern Pennsylvania, although, as the name suggests, Union's first settlers came from Connecticut. At the top of the hill, a modern wooden sign announces Union.

I turn right at the Rite Aid drugstore onto a street of small, fifties suburban houses. I turn again and, after about a block, am at my destination: Friberger Park. To my right is the firehouse, with two engines outside being fussed over by their crews. Ahead is the brick, colonial-style municipal building that houses the public library. I have been told that I can park in the library lot. As I turn into the driveway, I see ahead of me a little wooden house surrounded by trees, the last building left of the Self Master Colony.

This stretch of open ground, dominated by tall trees, bare on this December day, was once the heart of Andress and Lillian Floyd's community. The municipal complex stands on the site of the big house, a white-columned Greek Revival mansion, whose porch was a gathering spot for colony members. The other community buildings—dormitories, print shop, weaving room—were scattered over the original fifty acres.

Most were designed and built by the residents themselves. This last one left standing is a small green-shingled cottage with pale yellow trim. The carved squirrels on the wooden shutters seem appropriate, as the real thing scrambles around in the tall trees. The cottage sits on a foundation of uneven-looking blocks. I imagine that these are the concrete building blocks that were one of the staples of the colony economy. The homeless men whom the Floyds took in made blocks and wove rugs. They also printed pamphlets and books. According to one source, they even raised purebred collies, which sets me to wondering whether Andress Floyd had any dealings with his contemporary, Albert Payson Terhune, hero of my childhood.

I walk around the cottage, trying to ignore the nearby children's playground with its swings and climbing frames in garish primary colors. It isn't really until I look at it from a window of the library, which neatly blocks everything else out, that I can almost imagine the cottage as it was—one of several such buildings, surrounded by the trees and meadows of the Floyds' farm, which produced food for the colony and some surplus, sold locally from a horse-drawn wagon.

If the landscape has changed, the ghosts of the Floyds' homeless men seem still to be here. When I go down to the lower level of the library to use the bathroom, a man is sprawled asleep in one of the chairs. Black trash bags surround him. No one bothers him. I take a walk and stop in a coffee shop. As I wait for my coffee, a disheveled old man comes in. He comments on the weather, and the proprietor hands him a free cup of coffee and a bagel. This is clearly a morning ritual. He sits down, cradles the coffee. Outside, the day is bitterly cold.

The town of Union is relatively quiet for north central New Jersey. Its center reflects the magisterial architecture of the twenties and thirties, giving it the feel of a small town rather than the suburb it has become. When the Floyds arrived, the township would have been largely rural.

I get in the car and drive down Self Master Parkway to Andress Terrace, Olive Terrace, and Lillian Terrace. Like modern developers, Floyd named them for himself, his daughter, and his wife. Floyd speculated in real estate in the 1920s, building numbers of houses. It is hard to see the original bungalows under eighty-some years' worth of changes. The house in Friberger Park is now the clubhouse of the local Girl Scout troop. I make arrangements to come back and see the inside when they are there.

On my return visit, the weekend before Valentine's Day, the Scout troop is in residence. The door is open. I enter an outer foyer or mudroom, with two small rooms at either side of it. I knock on the door to the main room ahead of me and am welcomed in. This room is long and narrow, with new linoleum on the floor and wood paneling on the walls. There is a brick fireplace, which apparently is no longer functional since it houses a dusty arrangement of artificial flowers. Along the wall are storage benches. On one wall is a space heater; the building has no central heat. I wonder how the earlier residents managed with just a fireplace. Maybe they had a woodstove. The main room has been set up like a schoolroom with a blackboard on the wall and long green tables. At one of these, about ten little African American girls are giggling over the valentines they are making. Off the main room is a kitchen, and, off that, a bathroom. The Scout leader pulls up a piece of carpet to show me a grill over the crawl space underneath.

The entrance foyer and the two rooms off it are essentially untouched, with board floors and wide-board walls. Each room has a window, with one looking into the kitchen and one into the main room. Were these rooms originally individual sleeping quarters or was the main room a bunk room? The house is a roughly built but adequate shelter—far better than the streets. It's hard to superimpose a bunch of homeless men, recovering alcoholics, parolees, on this room with its glass cabinet of dolls dressed in the Girl Scout uniforms of various countries and a party of little girls making valentines.

Sprawled over 10 acres of mud and scrub . . . are the unimposing remains of a once flourishing cooperative colony of reformed derelicts. SELF-MASTERS COLONY, *patterned after Elbert Hubbard's Roycrofters of East Aurora, N.Y., was founded in 1908 and led by Andress S. Floyd. Here, on 50 acres, approximately 40 hoboes, drunks, and dope fiends lived and worked, desperately trying to make good. During the boom years the men left for outside jobs; the camp failed in 1929, leaving the ruins of a print shop, a weaving place, and two dilapidated frame buildings. Michael Moore, a tall, 69-year-old, bewhiskered native, who speaks intelligently and says he's the last of the Mohicans, still holds the fort, weaving silk and cotton rugs and table covers on hand looms.*

WPA GUIDE TO 1930S NEW JERSEY

ot long after 1938, according to Union town history, the "last of the Mohicans" of the Self Master Colony died, and the township bought what was left of Andress Floyd's property. Union is a town with a lot of history. Originally it was called Connecticut Farms because its first settlers were a group of Connecticut natives tired of being told by the Puritans how to live. It was also the site of a major battle in the Revolutionary War. The Presbyterian church on Chestnut Street was rebuilt after British raiders burned the original as well as most of the homes in the village.[1] Hessian soldiers who fell at the battle of Connecticut Farms are buried in the churchyard. The land, fed by the Elizabeth and Rahway rivers, was fertile; in fact, George Washington, passing through, called it "the garden of the state."[2] Once the war was over, the settlers turned again to farming and fruit growing.

When, in 1908, Andress Floyd and his wife, Lillian, moved there from

Rahway, where they had run a small colony along similar lines, Union was a sleepy country town. Floyd chose Union after persuading Charles Ingersoll, millionaire manufacturer of the Ingersoll dollar pocket watch, to buy the old Hoyt estate, a fifty-acre tract of land with a large, white Greek Revival house. He gave the use of it to Floyd, who eventually raised the money to buy it. Here he would establish his Self Master village for the rehabilitation of derelict men. Set with its barns and outbuildings on a wooded hillside above Morris Avenue, surrounded by ample land for small-scale farming or industry, it must have seemed a paradise to men who had been living rough on the streets of nearby Elizabeth, Newark, or New York. Along Morris Avenue ran an interurban streetcar line, making the colony accessible from Elizabeth, which was in turn accessible by Pennsylvania Railroad from New York. It was an ideal situation. On the side of the terrace overlooking the road, the words "Self Master Colony" were spelled out in cobblestones.

Floyd identified seven categories of men, the "prodigal sons," that he would take into his Family at the colony:

First. The man unable to find immediate employment.
Second. The man in middle life who has lost his business.
Third. The intemperate man trying to control himself.
Fourth. The country boy stranded in the city.
Fifth. The rich man's son, wayward, estranged from his family.
Sixth. The man discouraged through domestic troubles.
Seventh. Men run down physically and mentally—needing a permanent home.[3]

Andress Floyd was born in Saco, Maine on June 7, 1873, graduated from Thornton Academy, and went on to study law. As a young man convalescing from an unspecified illness,[4] he apparently had literary ambitions, sending some of his work to the famous Maine writer Sarah Orne Jewett. In one of her letters of reply, dated November 22, 1894, Jewett is kind but blunt.

I have read your short story and the chapter and the verses and I do not think that they are by any means as good work as you with your experience of life ought to do. The verses have so much simplicity and dramatic touch that they interested me a good deal, especially in your sense of fine art in the way you used the refrain. But they lack finish—the rhyme and sometimes the metre are not well worked out. The short story is not so good as the chapter. I find it boyish and crude in its plot, which may be good but should not have been turned upon so serious a subject as the hero's affection! Don't you see what I mean?

I am sure that one should always try to write of great things in a great way and with at least 'imaginative realism.' There is nothing so good in what you have sent me as the scene between the hero of your novel and the little girl with the books and patchwork—you have done a beautiful thing there![5]

Perhaps discouraged by Jewett's criticism, Floyd dropped the literary life and went back to the law. From 1898 to 1900 he was a partner with Charles E. Sawyer in their law firm of Sawyer and Floyd, in Haverhill, Massachusetts. On June 7, 1899, he married Alice Downing Hart and went to live with her, her mother, and stepfather, Charles P. Farnsworth, in Lincoln, Massachusetts. There his only child, a daughter, Olive Beatrice Floyd, was born on February 14, 1901. The marriage ended in divorce around 1907.

Charles E. Sawyer eventually became a judge on the Massachusetts Supreme Court, but Floyd left the law for business. With his friend Frank B. Crawford, Floyd became a "tourist broker" in Boston, arranging what would now be called package tours of Europe and other places. In the summer of 1900, Floyd and Crawford managed what became known as the "disastrous Christian Endeavor excursion to Europe" in which hundreds of travelers were left stranded abroad when hotels and other businesses refused to honor coupons for board and transportation issued by the Boston firm.[6] At the time, Floyd and Crawford explained that they had had to suspend payment on the coupons after the burning of four north German Lloyd liners in the Hoboken pier fire of June 30, 1900. In any case, Floyd and Crawford left the travel business and moved on to Wall Street, where they ran Floyd, Crawford and Co., which, according to the *New York Times* of May 10, 1904, was "one of the largest wirehouses in the country with offices in sixty cities."

In 1904, the firm of Floyd, Crawford and Co. was suspended by the Consolidated Exchange Board and the Chicago Board of Trade for "obvious fraud and false pretenses." When, the following morning, demands were made at the firm for the transfer of accounts to other brokers or for payment of funds, neither of the principals could be found. Frank Crawford was said to have left the Algonquin Hotel, where he was staying, for a trip out of town, and Andress Floyd had no known New York address. Because neither man appeared before the Consolidated Exchange Board to answer the charges against them, the firm was expelled. Floyd, Crawford and Co. was bankrupt.

Floyd eventually gave a rather arrogant statement to the *New York Times* in which he suggested a dubious reason for his suspension:

> I believe that my suspension was due solely to the fact that my customers did not lose enough money on the floor of the Consolidated Exchange. The officials of the Exchange, who are floor traders, are always sore when a firm's customers don't lose money to them. When I was summoned this afternoon, I saw that it was useless for me to offer any further explanation, as they had already examined my books for six hours two weeks ago and had found them in perfect order.[7]

All, however, apparently was not in perfect order. Crawford and Floyd admitted bankruptcy two weeks later. The proposed settlement, agreed to by 31 percent of their creditors, provided for 10 percent of the amount owed to be paid in cash and a "series of nine notes for the balance maturing from thirty days to twenty-eight months from the date of the first payment."[8]

How much of the settlement was ever paid is not clear, but Floyd, having gained and lost a fortune, left Wall Street and dropped out of sight for four years. When he reappeared on the New York scene, it was to give a public lecture at Carnegie Hall on his work at the Self Master Colony. A reporter from the *New York Times* journeyed out to Union to find out if this Andress Floyd was the same Andress Floyd of Floyd, Crawford and Co., to which

Floyd, discovered on the verandah of the main house, replied dramatically, "I am that man." In the exchange that followed, he provided an explanation for the sea change his life had undergone.

> "I look back with a great many regrets upon my past," he said, "especially my Wall Street experience in which I not only ruined myself financially but brought heavy cares to men whom I felt to be my friends. The suffering that was caused through that financial failure, determined me to try to live a constructive rather than a destructive life and finally [seeing] how difficult it was for me to get on my feet. I thought how much more difficult for a man without business experience or friends to gain a footing."[9]

Floyd went on to explain that he believed a man could "restore himself to the confidence of good people by clean and unselfish living and by honest industry." Acting on this theory, Floyd had taken several young alcoholics into his home to help them. As word spread and the work grew, he moved to Rahway, New Jersey, and then, because he needed a farm, to the property in Union. As he explained to the reporter, all the people who had helped him in his work knew of his past and the Wall Street debacle. The two talked until dusk, when Floyd showed the reporter a quotation from Tolstoy to be printed in the next *Self Master* magazine. Once again the sage of Yasnaya Polyana had provided support for utopia.

> People often say to me if you think there is no reasonable life outside the teachings of Christ and if you love a reasonable life, why do you not fulfill the Christian precepts? I am guilty and blameworthy and contemptible because I do not fulfill them but at the same time I say— not in justification but in explanation of my inconsistency—compare my previous life with the life I am now living and you will see what I am trying to fulfill. I have not, it is true, fulfilled one eighty-thousandth part and I am to blame for it, but it is not because I do not wish to fulfill all but because I am unable. Teach me how to extricate myself from the meshes of temptation in which I am entangled, help

me and I will fulfill all. Condemn me if you choose—I do that myself—but condemn me and not the path which I am following, and which I point out to those who ask me where, in my opinion, the path is.[10]

❊   ❊   ❊

Andress Floyd of the failed "bucket shop" was a complex character. Handsome and dapper, he looked every inch the Wall Street businessman. Even seated in a rocker on the columned porch of his house at Union, he was always dressed for the Street not the farm. Yet Floyd clearly had a mystical side not restricted to quotations from Tolstoy. The logo he chose for his colony was adapted from the Egyptian sign Abraxas, which he interpreted as the Gnostic symbol of self-mastery.[11] As he explained it, the priests of Huzat represented the most powerful and democratic order of the seven schools of Gnostic thought. In their temple, freed slaves, many of whom had been enslaved during war, "carried the symbol as a sign of their redemption and freedom." Their motto, "Men who have wept are victors," was adopted as the motto of the colony. "The strong straight line in the symbol indicates life; the bar at the top forming half of the Syric word Iao means strength; the Egyptian sign of Death forms the base, while the circle designates unity of life and death—the victory over slavery and sin—the spiritual goal of the Self Master!"[12]

It is not surprising that Gnosticism, with its emphasis on duality—light and dark, spiritual and material, good and evil, the eon and the demi-urge—appealed to Floyd. Only self-mastery could hold the evil in the individual at bay. He clearly knew from his own experience that the material world could conquer the spiritual.

The world that Floyd created on the farm in Union was assuredly not like any that Floyd's "fellows," as he referred to them, had known, at least in their recent lives. Meals were provided in the big house; the men slept in dormitory-style bungalows built around the property. A man could choose his occupation from a number that the colony provided: weaving rugs, creating copper ornaments, making concrete masonry blocks, or working in the print shop, where *Self Master* magazine and other works pertaining to the colony, as well as outside commissions, were printed. Then there was the farm itself, where vegetables were grown for the table and the surplus was sold by horse and cart. Of course, there was always work in the kitchen, and also in the Self Master teashop catering to "autoists." In summer, corn was sold from a roadside stand. This was a world in which no matter who you were, you could choose what you did. It is no accident that Floyd often referred to his colony as a village, since it was modeled more on the past than the future, on a world of arts and crafts. As such, it undoubtedly owed something to William Morris and, closer to home, to the example of Elbert Hubbard and his Roycroft Community at East Aurora, New York.

Elbert Hubbard also began his career as a businessman: he was an extremely successful salesman for the Larkin Soap Company of Buffalo, New York. At thirty-six, in September 1893, he left the business world to enter Harvard University as a special student but withdrew in December of the same year. Harvard found him underprepared, and he reacted with bitterness toward the university's intellectual establishment. Hubbard then left for a walking tour of England, tramping over the territory of literary greats Scott and Wordsworth and Dickens as though he were searching out their ghosts to compensate for the dry criticism he had encountered in Cambridge. He did, however, quite by accident, meet the utopian socialist William Morris in the flesh, when he heard Morris lecture to a small group of workingmen on the effects of color in house decoration on human character.[13] Hubbard later described Morris as "big, bold and shaggy," but the encounter changed Hubbard's life. He returned to East Aurora "with ideas about fine book publishing, arts and crafts in home furnishing, and benevolent paternalism in industry that were to kick up a lot of dust."[14]

In 1895, he began publishing his magazine the *Philistine*, so called because it countered the literary establishment that Hubbard so disliked. His Roycroft Press began to print fine books, and soon Hubbard was producing furniture, pottery, hammered copper, wrought iron, tooled leather goods, rugs, baskets, stained-glass lamps and windows, as well as preserves and maple sugar candy. After its first success, the *Philistine* printed an invitation to all good Philistines to visit East Aurora. And come they did. Soon it was clear that such a number of pilgrims could not be accommodated in

Hubbard's house, so he built an inn with rooms named for writers and phi-losophers. Roycroft became a quasi-communal village of skilled workers and guests who could be given simpler work to do. Hubbard and his com-munity embraced a kind of Morris-inspired medievalism that equated the publishing of hand-lettered books with monasticism. Hubbard was known as Fra Elbertus. Sculptor-in-residence Jerome Connor was known as Saint Jerome. And like the monastery of old, Roycroft invited the pilgrim into its community.

Harry Kemp, that colony traveler, put in his time at Roycroft, arriving hobo style by boxcar, where he had been set upon and beaten by three fel-low tramps. They took his clothes, so he arrived at "Eos," as he renamed Roycroft in his autobiography, in rags. Hubbard (Spalton, in Kemp's ac-count) had no problem taking him in and putting him straight to work chopping wood. Guests and workers all ate together in the dining hall that night, and by the next morning he was at work in the bindery, gluing spines on books. He described his fellow pilgrims as "derelicts, freaks, 'nuts' . . . with poses that outnumbered the silver eyes in the peacock's tail in multi-tude . . . and yet there was to be found in them a sincerity, a firmness, and a genuine feeling for humanity that 'regular' folks never achieve—perhaps because of their very 'regularness.'"[15] Kemp lasted until he had a final dis-agreement with Hubbard, who wanted to print his poems as the work of the anonymous "poet of Eos."

There are obvious parallels between Roycroft and Self Master in the production of crafts, the printing and binding of fine books, and the open door to the wandering pilgrim. Like Hubbard, Floyd used the monastic id-iom, referring to his "fellows," his "prodigal sons," also as his "Monks of Vagabondia," a fanciful title that could have come out of William Morris's works—or the Fra's.

Unlike either Roycroft or Morris's Kelmscott, however, Self Master vil-lage catered only to men. There were no married couples save for Andress and Lillian Floyd themselves, while Lillian and her Italian maid, Katrina, were the only women. In fact, women seem to have been considered an-other temptation, like drink. And whereas Hubbard was producing very successful commercial art and creating a flamboyant persona doing it, Floyd was in the business of saving souls and was the keeper, after his Wall Street days, of a very low profile. In one issue of the *Self Master* magazine, his editorial explains:

> Several friends have belabored me of late for being too modest. If true, it is a grievous fault and my apology will appear in my honest endeavor to correct it.
>
> "Do not work—I am advised—so hard to build up your Village for your Up-against-it-boys—but write about it often and long. Then the enterprise will gain friends who will lift the burden with you."
>
> The idea—as I understand it—is to have a snap-shot taken when in the performance of a kind act and have it enlarged.
>
> Personally, I don't care much for the enlargement of Kodak pictures. We had one made of a favorite Aunt of mine and her good points suffered frightfully. No more does a kind act lend itself to a photographic skill.
>
> A picture of myself giving a hungry man a bowl of beef stew wouldn't prove much, maybe the stew might not be up to standard quality. I know of a ruffian who struck a blind man with a brick and the shock gave the man back his vision. Perhaps that was a kind act, but it wouldn't appeal to me as a movie feature.[16]

In this, as in much of Floyd's writing for his magazine, there's a whiff of the Yankee contrarian.

The *Self Master* magazine, itself printed in the colony's print shop, was a small, pamphlet-sized publication of about twenty pages. It contained editorials and small essays by Floyd and occasionally pieces by visitors to the village that told stories of the prodigal sons. There were ads for village products and appeals for needed items such as a truck, print shop supplies, plate or window glass for the concrete-block houses, and clothing. And of course there were requests for money to keep up the good work and to construct an administration building "to be built in the MONASTIC STYLE of our concrete blocks and stuccoed." A drawing shows a building rather like one of California's Spanish missions, complete with palm trees that probably would not have survived in Union, New Jersey. Letters were printed from readers such as Bolton Hall and the secretary to Mrs. Wilson, wife of the U.S. president, who had sent a contribution. The typesetting, colophons, and illustrations were done by the colonists themselves. One of the colonists, who had been a printer in his former life, was happy to teach others to use the presses. Every issue contained quotations from scripture and directions for reaching the colony, in case it fell into needy hands.

Floyd seems to have been a religious freelancer, more a mystic than a churchgoer. His idea of salvation was the control of self, not the intervention of any other Being, and in this he was something like a Bernarr Macfadden of the spirit. Although he quoted from the Gospels and Proverbs, his view of humanity was much closer to that of the Gnostics. In 1914 a guest writer for *American Magazine* called him a Greek mystic, despite his New England roots.[17] In fact, the Gnostic view of the world as a place of duality accords well with the New England of writers such as Nathaniel Hawthorne. The young Salem minister in Hawthorne's story "Young Goodman Brown" is changed forever by the vision he has in the woods of his parishioners' dark side. Add to that the Yankee idea of self-reliance as preached by Emerson and others and you get self-mastery, a way to control the darkness within.

When a man came to the colony, he was fed and provided with a place to sleep and the possibility of "honest labor"—but it was up to him to make a choice, to take the opportunity, and then to overcome whatever had brought him down, whether it was circumstance or alcohol or depression.

The idea is "Master yourself." But Floyd doesn't preach it to the alcoholics and drug fiends and other pieces of human debris who inhabit his home; in fact says scarcely a word about it. Rather, he tries to live it, and depends upon the intangible influence of his own calm, self-controlled life to breed a spirit of self-mastery among the eighty men his home can accommodate. He is the Self Master![18]

Across the road from Floyd's colony was Riley's, a country saloon, and one can imagine that Floyd did not consider this situation a drawback. For the alcoholic, learning to avoid Riley's,[19] being able to watch the comings and goings of its patrons without having to join them, was a true test of self-mastery. In fact, when such a man first arrived, Floyd did not insist on immediate cold turkey. Instead, Floyd would tell him that if he really needed a drink, he could go to Lillian and she would provide it. The man had to decide to turn away from drink himself, without external prohibition.

Although Floyd often notes that he could not have run the colony without Lillian, this instance is one of the few clear references to her role. She seems to have acted as a sort of matron, handing out whatever the men needed. At mealtimes, there was a hierarchy of tables. Those who had mastered themselves the best sat at the Floyds' table, with Andress at the head and Lillian at the foot. She once described the place as a kindergarten and was quoted as saying that the most glorious achievement in the world was restoring life and self-respect to "dead" men.[20] It seems that the two of them were perfect parents to their band of boys.

In 1913, the Self Master Press produced a little book by Andress Floyd titled *My Monks of Vagabondia*, a collection of the various stories of the men who had come to the village. He seems to have taken to heart Sarah Orne Jewett's advice to his younger self: write about real life. According to the book's introduction, the "writer has received his facts for his stories direct from a life-experience with outcast men." He also announces his greater hope that the "day approaches when broken men shall have beautiful, though simple, homes of their own making, modeled after the group idea of The Self Master Colony. They will be established outside of the different cities of the world, and opened hospitably to all men who come in their hour of need or weakness, seeking Self Mastery and the peace that accompanies it."[21]

In a pamphlet titled *The Making of Our Book,* Floyd contended that "fifty men, selected at random, possess all the necessary qualities to carry out any conceivable enterprise. They only need a proper leader to whom they are willing to give service."[22] Indeed, it turned out that the colony had in residence a typesetter, a binder, and an artist who produced the title page, initials, and tail pieces.

Andress Floyd was an admirer of the Western writer Bret Harte and seems to have found his literary model in Harte's chronicles of life in the mining camps of gold rush California, another all-male world. Harte wrote about drinkers, gamblers, thieves, and other outlaws, men who were running away from various problems back East. Gold mining, like the stock market, was a speculative business, dependent on luck as much as skill:

> in such a comfortless, temporary, hazardous and reckless wilderness world where seeking gold was the chief occupation, where making a big strike which would get you out was the chief hope, and gambling and betting the chief amusement, and where former beliefs and moralities lost their power all too rapidly, chance or luck, whether good or bad did become the deepest and most constant concern. It *did* assume, that is, something like the consequence the great Greek tragedians gave it under the name of Fate, or in the form of the arbitrary and interfering activities of the gods.[23]

Luck or fate is crucial to Harte's stories, as, for example, the snowstorm that traps the travelers in "The Outcasts of Poker Flat," but there is also an element of Christian redemption. In Harte's arguably most famous story, "The Luck of Roaring Camp," he paints a community somewhat analogous to that of the Self Master Colony. The denizens of Roaring Camp are a rough group of men, probably rougher than Floyd's down-and-outers. Like Harte's gold rush men, however, Floyd's villagers came from many different backgrounds. In one issue of *Self Master,* Floyd described current members of the colony: a young man who, while in government service in China, had became addicted to drugs; an alcoholic Yale graduate; a printer who had lost his job; a recent prison inmate; a vagrant; the former amanuensis to a "famous New England writer"; an agricultural worker out of a job for the winter; an actor; a skilled mechanic; an aging career waiter; and a couple of young runaways. Some of Floyd's fellows, like some of Harte's characters, were secretive about their names and pasts.

Like the characters in Harte's stories, Floyd's fellows were often known by names that arose from some peculiarity or characteristic. In Harte, "these appellatives were derived from some distinctiveness of dress, as in the case of Dungaree Jack, or for some peculiarity of habit, as shown in Saleratus Bill, so called from an undue proportion of that chemical in his daily bread, or from some unlucky slip, as exhibited in The Iron Pirate, a mild inoffensive man, who earned that baleful title by his unfortunate mispronunciation of the term 'iron pyrites.'" [24] At Self Master there was Slippery Jim and Happy Holland and Delmonico Bill, Lakewood Tom, Ulster Mike, Big Jean and Little Jean, Corduroy Tom, and Paddy the Turk.

In "The Luck of Roaring Camp," Harte describes Roaring Camp as a "a city of refuge." Of its denizens, "one or two . . . were actual fugitives from justice, some were criminal and all were reckless." When a prostitute named Cherokee Sal gives birth to a baby at the camp and promptly dies, the men must cope with the new arrival. They vote to adopt him and name him for that elusive element, Luck. "And so the work of regeneration began in Roaring Camp. Almost imperceptibly a change came over the settlement. The cabin assigned to Tommy Luck, or The Luck, as he was more frequently called, first showed signs of improvement. It was kept scrupulously clean and whitewashed." [25]

Stumpy, with whom "The Luck" lives, insists that any visitors be themselves clean and washed. No profanity is allowed near the baby, and the usual shouting and yelling of the camp ceases so that The Luck can get his sleep. He is carried out to the gulch where the men are panning for gold on summer days. They bring him wildflowers, "suddenly awakened to the fact that there were beauty and significance in these trifles which they had so long trodden carelessly beneath their feet." [26]

Floyd tells a similar story in *My Monks of Vagabondia*. One year, near Christmas, a young mother and baby appear at the colony door, exhausted, cold, and hungry. "If anyone comes to us hungry," Floyd writes, "we like to give them something more edible than a card to a professional charity." And so mother and baby are taken in. Like the men of Roaring Camp, the fellows of Self Master wanted to keep the baby. The mother is put to work helping in the kitchen while the "boys themselves made two wooden beds and fitted up a room for the Baby." The men are very interested in the baby, taking turns playing with her and arguing about the best things for her to eat. "To see rough homeless men sing lullabies to an infant-in-arms, congratulating themselves when she falls asleep soothed by the monotonous humming of some cradle song that they themselves thought they had forgotten long ago, might renew one's faith in the kindly humanity that lives in every heart." [27] This baby has, in fact, a father. Soon a job is found for him, and the little family, reunited, can leave the colony. Like most of Floyd's stories, and unlike Bret Harte's, this one has a happy ending. In all the stories, Floyd comes across as a wise and distant presence, quoting the Bible and the Vedas, a model of calm and understanding. He has no reproach for those like Lakewood Tom who spend their winters in the village but, with spring, go back on the road as hoboes.

> "Adieu," said Lakewood Tom, taking up his staff, "when the snow falls next year I may visit your Monastery again with your permission, if by happy chance I am on this earth. If not, I'll meet you some Christmas day on the planet Mars, for I never forget a friend. Good cheer! Adieu."
>
> "Much privation has crazed the old man," said a comrade who, with me, watched the old vagabond walking slowly down the drive.
>
> "I do not know," I said. [28]

Floyd's vagabonds are a literate lot, prone to quoting Shakespeare and the Bible, and most seem eager and quick to reform. There were, of course, failures who slid back into drink or other problems. And some like Lakewood Tom could not completely foreswear the call of the open road. Floyd was a great believer in the ability of a man to change, and it certainly seemed that he had changed—or as his magazine put it, "Andress Floyd capitalized his personality not for dollars, but in exchange for stock, in the big corporation of mankind." [29] By the 1920s, Floyd had earned a national reputation and presented his work at many speaking engagements. Yet ironically, Floyd himself did not completely change.

The Coolidge years, from 1924 to 1928, were years of great prosperity for the country. The businessman, particularly the salesman, was king—or perhaps God. In *Only Yesterday: An Informal History of the 1920s*, Frederick Lewis Allen calls "the association of business with religion . . . one of the most significant phenomena of the day. . . . Under the beneficent influence of Coolidge prosperity, business had become almost the national religion of America."[30] It certainly beckoned again to Andress Floyd.

World War I changed life in Union. The war had created a housing shortage, and Union, which was close to major cities but still had plenty of land for building, attracted both people and industry. Bus lines were established, and the good economic times meant that more people had automobiles. The Rahway Valley and Lehigh Valley railroads built branch lines into the town to attract industry. From 1920 to 1930, the town's population quadrupled.[31] The real estate boom that would really accelerate after World War II was beginning.

If Floyd had warned his fellows to stay away from past companions who had led them into trouble, he seems to have ignored his own advice: he returned to his old partnership with Frank Crawford, who by then had become, fortuitously, a builder. Floyd owned a lot of property, not all of it necessary for the workings of the colony, so he and Crawford formed several companies to develop sections of the Floyd property in Union. Eventually, the two were involved in a number of different real estate companies and were buying lots beyond the boundaries of the colony. They built bungalows and Tudors and colonials and some two-family homes on roads like Self Master Parkway, Floyd Terrace, Andress Terrace, and Lillian Terrace, making Floyd an early proponent of tract housing. Floyd's corporations were responsible for building more than 250 units, which he justified with the dictum that a "job that pays and the home a man owns are the two foundation stones upon which the nation stands."[32] It seems that he had moved away from his design of cooperative colonies like Self Master, to be built on the outskirts of many cities, and toward plans for single-family suburban houses. Perhaps the two were meant to coexist. In any case, Floyd invested heavily in real estate that was not always easy to sell. He kept his prices reasonable, but many of his developments were on unimproved roads, without the suburban infrastructure that would be built several decades later. Floyd also went back to investing in the stock market.

Around this time, some people came to believe that Floyd's work at Self Master might not be entirely altruistic. After all, his vagabonds made the cement construction blocks that Floyd and Crawford used to build most of their houses. Was he exploiting his fellows? Harry Kemp had made a similar charge about Elbert Hubbard at Roycroft.

> Working in the bindery, I began to find out things about the community of Eos that were not as ideal as might be . . . most of the illumination of the books was done by girls, even by children in after school hours. . . . In each department, hidden behind the gorgeous, flowing curtains, were time-clocks, on which employees rang up when they came to work, and when they left.[33]

Hubbard, like Floyd, was a businessman, and, as Kemp also pointed out, every piece of pottery and furniture in the community had a price tag on it. Neither he nor Floyd was a friend of socialism or anarchy. Hubbard vilified Upton Sinclair and other muckrakers in the *Philistine*, or as he said: "I believe in Big Business and more of it."[34] Floyd, in a chapter of *My Monks of Vagabondia* titled "Our Friend, The Anarchist," told the story of a German immigrant who came to the colony. Floyd recounts the reformation of this character, a hater of capitalism, who had been prepared to throw bombs before seeing the men of Self Master turn their lives around within the system.

As the town of Union grew and more services were needed, taxes naturally increased. Floyd found himself facing bigger tax bills for his unsold properties. When, in 1929, the stock market crashed, Floyd once more went from riches to rags.

On August 17, 1929, Floyd put up for sale ninety-five commercial and residential lots at the intersection of Morris and Stuyvesant avenues in the heart of Union and next to the Self Master Colony. The lots were to be bisected by Self Master Parkway, which would connect them with State Highway 29, "the direct route between New York and Philadelphia." In his prospectus for the auction, Floyd describes Self Master village and asserts that 100,000 men were helped as "handmade articles were sold from the little art shops until [the men] became self supporting from their own efforts." Obviously the Self Master village helped a good many people, but 100,000 seems an exaggeration. He further attempts to make the sale look less like an act of desperation and more like a novel undertaking:

> Then again the Floyds turned [to] their organizing genius and nearly 1,000 houses sprang up in three years until it [Union] is rapidly becoming the state's most youthful city and is today the pulse and center of highways leading to every spot worthwhile. Now choice business frontages are being released but Mr. and Mrs. Floyd reserved the old mansion with all of its romances and true stories and make it one of the beauty spots of the city they helped to build.[35]

Floyd even took out a full-page advertisement in the local paper to counter rumors that he was "quitting." As he put it, "there is a time the trees shed their blossoms and begin to produce fruits. We think our Self Master Village has passed out of one stage and on into another and higher stage of growth. . . . The sale is just another step in the program of work we have marked out as our contribution."[36]

This time, however, Floyd could not pull out of his financial morass. The sale did not raise enough money to meet his tax bill, and the remainder of his village was taken by the town for back taxes. Most of the colony bungalows were eventually pulled down to make way for more housing. Andress and Lillian continued to live on the property, taking in boarders to make ends meet. Despite their penniless state, they apparently continued to walk around town as well dressed as ever.[37]

According to his obituary in the *New York Times*, Andress Floyd died in his sleep on January 9, 1933, of heart disease. The article goes on to detail his work at Self Master and to mention his Wall Street days, but it says nothing about his Union real estate development. Floyd was buried in Saco, Maine, his birthplace. Lillian, perhaps despondent over their finances, had attempted suicide in December 1932 and was hospitalized at the newly built Marlboro State Psychiatric Hospital in Marlboro, New Jersey. The colony, or those few individuals who were left, struggled on for another five years after Floyd's death, until the last of the Mohicans died in 1938.

Lillian died at Marlboro Hospital in 1940. Marlboro has been closed for some years now, and the small cemetery on a hillside outside the gates has become an overgrown meadow, its numbered markers almost hidden in the long grass. In a small rotunda, with a tattered flag and rusting metal chair, beneath straggling cedars, a bronze screed matches names to the numbers. Lillian Floyd is not buried there.

Surviving were a brother and Floyd's only child, his daughter, Olive Beatrice, for whom he named Olive Terrace in Union. Olive Floyd lived a life of privilege in Lincoln, Massachusetts, in the home of her step grandfather, Charles Farnsworth: private schools, camps on Cape Cod, trips to Europe, and Bryn Mawr College, from which she graduated magna cum laude. She taught French and Spanish at the Westover School, a girls' boarding school in Connecticut, for a couple of years and then made her way as a writer and lecturer, traveling all over the world in the process. Her papers, left to the Schlesinger Library in Cambridge, Massachusetts, at her death in 1985, include scrapbooks of travel photographs and diaries, collections of programs from plays and musical events, and a list of all the books she ever read. Of her father there is almost no mention. A few postcards sent to the child Olive from Wall Street, New York, are clearly from him although they bear no message. Her main interest in her father seems to be his ancestry, which allowed her to claim Mayflower descent. In a diary she notes a genealogical foray to Saco, Maine, in August 1940: "visited the old Floyd house on Hill St., Saco and Laurel Hill Cemetery where grandparents and Andress Small Floyd are buried." [38] She also published the Jewett letters to her father in the *Yale Review* in 1936, three years after her father's death, after having carefully removed anything she found too personal. She had some success with writing herself, including a novel, *Doctora in Mexico*, which was made into a radio play starring Irene Dunne for NBC's *DuPont Cavalcade Theater*. She continued to live in Lincoln when she wasn't traveling. She enjoyed a number of summers at Eaton's Ranch in Wyoming and proved herself her father's daughter when she wrote of the cowboys: "the friendship and love of those boys for each other—the only love they have—are perfect." [39] Clearly the divorce and the trouble on Wall Street had made Floyd persona non grata in the comfortable world of her step grandfather. It is intriguing to wonder whether Olive ever saw her father again.

Andress Floyd remains an enigmatic character. As the *Union Register* wrote in his obituary, "citizens of Union knew very little about the existence of Mr. and Mrs. Floyd because they took no part in the social, political, or business life of the community."[40] In fact, the writer went on to say that Mrs. Floyd, then at Marlboro Psychiatric Hospital, was "said to be staying with friends." The irony is obvious. The preacher of self-mastery could not, in the end, master himself. The lure of a material fortune proved too strong. It seems, however, that it was he, and the equally enigmatic Lillian, who paid the price. The hundreds of men he helped during the twenty years of his colony's existence were not the losers.

Woodbine
Immigrants on the Land

South Jersey farmland is flat. The drive inland from Cape May reveals a landscape of broad fields fringed by trees, both pine and deciduous. Lakes appear around curves in the road. Stretches of woods are preserved habitat for wildlife. When the Jewish farmers first came here to Alliance, at the end of the nineteenth century, it was a wilderness. There were no motel cabins by the lakes then, and few cleared fields. On the map, the first colonies cluster close to Vineland and Millville. I follow the order of the road.

Carmel is at the crossroads of Routes 634 and 552. Houses are strung along 552, shaded by established trees—maple, holly, dogwood—and one so immense and ivy-covered that it must be a survivor of the earlier settlements. Most of the houses are meager, narrow, and shabby, built to provide only the most basic roof for a family. A new school proclaims itself Pinelands Elementary. Streets of newer houses run off to the north.

To the east of the intersection is a small strip mall featuring a discount liquor store and a beauty supply business. Across from that, at the intersection of 552 and 608, is Big Daddy's Sports Haven, selling dirt bikes, paintball supplies, and archery equipment. Traffic is heavy and the sidewalks intermittent. The area is not pedestrian friendly. Nor does much here proclaim it the hotbed of radical thought that was its reputation with the other colonies of the region.

Rosenhayn is another crossroads by train tracks. Weinstein's General Store is being rehabbed. There's a U.M.E. church. I turn onto Landis Avenue past Speranza's Deli and gas stations, heading for Norma. I am out in farmland again, passing a Pentecostal church and billboards for Harley Davidson and Dunkin Donuts.

A turn on Gershel Avenue brings me into Norma. Old houses, with their typical back ells, stand amid new ranches. The landscape remains, but little is left of the human settlement save the street names: Isaac Avenue, Steinfeld Avenue, Rosenfeld Avenue, Gershel Avenue. Yards sport red canna lilies. I pass Ron's Animal Shelter and a feed and grain store. Between Norma and Brotmanville, fields are lush with timothy. A flock of wild turkeys feeds. There's an apple orchard at the corner of Schiff Avenue and an overgrown tree farm. A garage and Morgan's grocery store seem to make up the village of Brotmanville. Alliance is a dot on the map, where, in spring, paint horses graze in a pasture speckled with buttercups.

On a second trip, in fall, I find Alliance's one remaining synagogue, Tifereth Israel, at the corner of Schiff and Gershel avenues. Across Schiff Avenue are cornfields; across Gershel, the woods are reclaiming a handsome brick house. The synagogue, a white frame building, looks like a farmhouse until you notice the long windows and the circular blue plaque above them with Hebrew letters painted in gold. Beneath the windows are hydrangeas, faded an end-of-summer pink. Behind the synagogue, the mown lawn holds the tangled woods at bay. The door is locked; a sign advertises electronic protection. New concrete steps lead up to the main door, and a typed sheet announces services for Rosh Hashanah and Yom Kippur, just passed.

Down Gershel Avenue, across from a cluster of small houses and a derelict trailer, a grove of trees marks the boundary of the Alliance Cemetery. Beyond them a small brick building proclaims itself a museum, open on occasional weekends and holidays. Just beyond are the brick gates to the cemetery itself.

I come upon another set of gates; the plaque there reads:

> IN MEMORY OF THE FIRST COLONISTS WHO MIGRATED
> FROM RUSSIA TO THE WOODLANDS OF SOUTH JERSEY
> AND ON MAY 9, 1882, FOUNDED ALLIANCE, THE FIRST
> JEWISH FARM COLONY IN THE UNITED STATES

Beyond these gates, the gravestones are old, recording deaths in 1893, 1894—memorials to hard times of one kind or another in those early years. The inscriptions are often in Hebrew. A narrow paved road leads from the main gate down an avenue of sycamores, between two rows of gravestones. It ends in a grassy circle around a flagpole, where the American flag is flying. Plantings of daylilies flank four benches where one can sit on this cool, overcast day. Around the cemetery are pine woods and, on one side, open fields. Like the synagogue, it is tidy and well kept, silent except for birdsong. In the distance, two other people peer at a stone; one has a camera slung over his shoulder. Tourists? Descendants?

A marker, a stone tree trunk with limbs cut off, reminds us:

> IN LASTING MEMORY OF THE SIX MILLION JEWISH MARTYRS
> OF THE HOLOCAUST DURING WORLD WAR II

On it, people have left pebbles.

I walk to the other side of the cemetery, through newer graves—1995, 1997—pebbles left on these stones show that there are still living friends and relatives to remember these dead. A breeze moves the branches of a large holly and a long-needled pine. I reach the cemetery office, a cement bunker of a building. Beyond it are more graves and beyond that fields with paths where, obviously, more will be buried.

Suddenly, I am in front of a circular brick wall with three entrances. A bronze plaque explains that I am standing under an archway representing the "infamous gateways to a life of torture, slave labor and starvation at the innumerable concentration camps throughout Germany and its occupied territories." Over the gate: REMEMBER NOT TO FORGET.

Inside the brick wall is an inner circle of brick columns that represent the crematoria chimneys of the gas chambers. I walk through the archway and around the circle between the wall and the pillars. At the center is a sculpture of three hands reaching upward from stones set atop a Jewish star; they are bronze hands holding a piece of opalescent glass, "the flame of hope: never again." Set into the walls and pillars are memorial plaques. Here too stones have been left.

On the wall behind the six pillars are the stark names of concentration camps: the famous ones like Dachau and Auschwitz, Treblinka and Buchenwald; others less known like Ponar and Chelmno and Majdanek and Malthausen. All these are more than what's usually remembered, more even than most of the world knows. This memorial summons up the farthest reaching pogrom of them all and the catalyst for another wave of immigration.

To get to Woodbine, one heads back toward Cape May—quite a distance from the cluster of early colonies. Route 47 provides vistas of marshes now and frequent signs for Belleplain State Forest. Woodbine, always bigger than the others, has neither disappeared nor devolved into a crossroads hamlet. Driving up narrow, wooded Route 611, one swings right, and the road opens out onto Woodbine's tree-lined Main Street. Like its model, Vineland, it looks planned. The houses here are bigger. Many are the typical South Jersey frame house, peaked eaves echoed in peaked windows, maybe a little shabby, but set back from the street, with big side yards, plots that were intended, in colony days, for vegetable gardens, even a few chickens. Now they are lawns with shrubs and ornamental trees, giving the town its open feeling. Avenues are named for U.S. presidents: Washington, Adams, Jefferson; side streets for poets: Longfellow, Bryant. All are broad and tree shaded. The sky here seems big and open, as it does in much of the Pinelands. There are no hills to obscure it, and one could believe in falling off the edge of a flat earth.

I first came to Woodbine in spring, when the woods around it were a tapestry of foliage. It's easy to see how insistent those woods are: on the outskirts, they encroach on rundown houses. In the town, it was the time of dogwood and huge clumps of purple lilac. As with archaeological sites, where the turf retains the imprint of an abbey or a fortification, here you can still see the imprint of utopian Woodbine. The colony was laid out on the model of a medieval village, with pasturage on the outskirts, then farms, and then the town itself, with factories, gone now, along with the shops that once made Woodbine the shopping hub of Cape May County. Especially on Sundays, when other towns closed down, people came by carriage, then automobile, for bakeries and kosher butcher shops, general stores and clothing stores, outlets, probably, of the factories.

The shops are gone on Adams Street now. Washington Street is the only commercial street. There's not much here. However, the legacy of the early settlers who went to New York to buy bric-a-brac and resell it remains in a couple of "antique" malls. On this October day, I wander through them, noting the usual collection of glass and china, clothes, souvenirs, and beanie babies. In one, I find a section of old tools and kitchenware. I look at the heavy, rusted scythes and axes hanging on the wall and imagine the toil of clearing these woods, rife with wild grapevine and poison ivy. Old pots, washboards, and flat-irons are reminders of what must have been the endless cooking and washing and ironing, the kettle always steaming on the wood stove. Outside, stacked "campfire wood," presumably for use at campsites in Belleplain State Forest, recalls the cordwood chopped by the settlers to supplement their income and stacked on street corners to be taken to Philadelphia.

It's a warm, golden day as I wander down Washington Street. One house, with storefront windows, announces its reincarnation as Whispers of Serenity: Center for Massage, Relaxation, and Personal Growth. Another bears the sign Woodbine Wellness Center. At the end of Washington Street, at the junction with Route 550, on the site of the old Roosevelt Hotel, is the Woodbine municipal building, low and modern and heavily planted with marigolds.

I have lunch, homemade lima bean soup, at the Dionysus Restaurant. The building has been fronted with the fake stone beloved of Greek diners. Inside, photographs of Greek archeological sites cover the wall, along with a fresco of Dionysus himself, downing grapes with several scantily clad maenads.

Out on State Route 550, heading east toward the coast, are Woodbine's two main present-day employers, the Sea Isle Ice Company and the Woodbine Developmental Center. The latter occupies some of the red brick buildings of the former Baron de Hirsch Agricultural School. I drive in, past greenhouses and gardens being irrigated by sprayers, and rows of topiary, most of them, ironically, shaped as chickens. Beyond the buildings are wide grassy fields. A barbecue is taking place near one of the houses.

The most beautiful building in Woodbine is the Woodbine Brotherhood Synagogue. Built in 1896 of red brick, made by the colonists themselves, it stands on Washington Avenue, surrounded by cropped lawns and next to the squat, modern post office. It is restored now as the Sam Azeez Museum of Woodbine Heritage. You enter at the basement level, where the brotherhood meeting rooms once were. The large room houses panels of text and pictures that trace the town's history.

Upstairs, the synagogue is airy and light, painted a pale spring leaf green and white. Sitting in the pews, you look out through tall Palladian windows into the canopy of the trees. Only occasional services are held here now. Other faiths dominate in Woodbine: Catholic, Baptist, Jehovah's Witness. If you pass by the elementary school at the end of the day, you can see the demographic change. African Americans and Puerto Ricans came here as agricultural and factory workers and stayed. Woodbine, one of the eight Pinelands towns, protected as part of the region's heritage, is still an immigrant town. It is still a place where substantial houses are affordable, a place to begin.

≺–≺––≻–≻

Adam was placed in the garden of Eden not to trade or peddle therein, but to till it and to keep it, and the greatest of lawgivers, kings and prophets in Israel came not from merchants, but from the rural population of farmers.
  ⊸ RABBI BERNARD L. LEVINTHAL ↜
dedication of a new classroom building at Baron de Hirsch School, 1900

Haste to yonder woodbine bower
The turf with rural dainties shall be crowned,
While opening blooms diffuse their sweets around
  ⊸ ALEXANDER POPE ↜
"Spring," in Pastorals

oodbine, New Jersey, in Cape May County, had been romantically named for the woodbine, or wild honeysuckle, that grew there in profusion. Honeysuckle is not particular about soil, and the soil of Woodbine and the other Jewish agricultural colonies was the thin, sandy soil of the Jersey Pinelands, yet these colonies outlasted by many years similar attempts to settle Jewish immigrants in Texas, Arkansas, the Dakotas, Louisiana, Oregon, and Colorado.

Woodbine, along with Alliance, Carmel, Norma, Rosenhayn, Brotmanville, and other smaller settlements, was the result of efforts by several Jewish philanthropic organizations to rescue their fellow Jews from the Russian pogroms of the late nineteenth century. In so doing, they also planned to rehabilitate the image of the Jew as urban and parasitic, the Shylock of the popular imagination.

At the end of the nineteenth century, most of Russia's Jewish population were forced to live in one area known as the Pale of Settlement comprised of Lithuania, Ukraine, Belorussia, Crimea, and part of Poland. "Only a privileged few, who were considered most useful to the state, were permitted to move about within the Russian interior to practice their trade or profession. Inside the crowded Pale, hundreds of thousands of impoverished people struggled for economic survival mainly as small retailers, artisans and peddlers."[1] Most Jews were not allowed to live in certain cities within the Pale, such as Kiev, Sebastopol, and Yalta. A very few who had served in the imperial army could own land, but for most this was impossible. They were heavily taxed and often harassed by the Russian police.

The assassination of Czar Alexander II, in St. Petersburg in March 1881, after two previously failed attempts, was an excuse for violence against the "Christ killers" as Jews were called. Although the assassin was a Christian Pole, several Jews were implicated in the plot. When Czar Alexander III ascended the throne, he instituted a period of repression of all minorities. The country was in a state of chaos and near revolution, making minorities, particularly Jews, convenient scapegoats. Pogroms against Jews were sanctioned by the state.

The Russian word *pogrom* means "devastation" or "destruction." To the illiterate Russian peasant, whose own life was narrow and miserable, it was gratifying to have such a scapegoat, to be able to harass, torture, and kill. Jewish homes were pillaged, girls and women raped, and many Jews were murdered. Bluma Bayuk, daughter of one of the founders of Alliance, Moses Bayuk, tells the story of her own mother, the only child of poor Jews outside Odessa. One night the drunken peasants came. Her father told her that no matter what she heard downstairs, she was to climb out of the window and run to a nearby tavern, whose Russian owners were friends to her parents. "When she heard the door burst open downstairs, and the ear splitting shrieks that followed, she had run away sobbing and dazed, through the fields away from the cobbled streets and up to the back door of the tavern."[2]

The May laws of 1882 further restricted Jews to urban areas within the Pale; those who lived in rural areas had to move to towns, or "townlets," known as shtetls, on their outskirts. The shtetl was centered on the synagogue and the marketplace. Life in the shtetl, however, produced great good. The shtetl Jews devised *tzedakah* (Hebrew for "justice"), a system of charity that provided food, clothing, medical treatment, and other necessities for indigent Jews. Also, the study of the Torah reemerged. The idea of helping one's people was crucial to the future of Jewish immigrants—or, in the words of Rabbi Hillel: "Do not separate thyself from thy people," and "If I am for myself alone, what am I?" Both of these traditions would contribute to community life in the new country of America.

Even in this period, however, members of the Jewish intelligentsia still attended universities and had the right to reside anywhere in Russia. Christian and Jewish university students were not segregated, and their relations had always been friendly. After the assassination of Czar Alexander II and a number of high officials, however, Christian students and professors also began to blame the Jews. The idea of the pogrom had entered the university, and Christian students began to organize. In autumn 1881, a group of Jewish students, the law student H. L. Sabsovich of Odessa University among them, organized a self-defense league, gathering ordinary young Jewish workers and collecting any tools or weapons they could use against their enemies.

On the fifth day of Passover, the first of Easter, the pogrom began. Sabsovich and the others rushed to the defense of the victims. The young organizers of the self-defense league were arrested, but they were ultimately released because they came from influential families. It was this group that became the core of the movement that would be known as Am Olam, "the Eternal People."[3]

The Am Olam movement had two aims: to help Jews emigrate from Russia, and to foster a back-to-the-land movement for Jews that would show the world Jews could be independent farmers rather than traders and peddlers. Members of the group subscribed to the Tolstoyan view of the noble life on the land, as Levin in *Anna Karenina* muses: "The simplicity, the purity, the sanity of this life he felt clearly, and he was convinced he would find in it the content, the peace, and the dignity, of the lack of which he was so miserably conscious."[4] Had not the Jews of the Old Testament been farmers? Sabsovich and his Am Olam comrades discussed emigration and decided on America as the best choice. Appeals were made to Jewish organizations in Poland, Austria, France, and England. Funds were provided that allowed hundreds to emigrate, some carrying the flag of Am Olam, emblazoned with the symbols of a plow and the Ten Commandments and the words "Arise from the dust, throw off the contempt of nations, for thy time has come." Sabsovich studied law for one more year and then decided to go to Switzerland to study agriculture and become an agronomist, so that he could lead his people "back to the soil."[5]

*　*　*

Vineland, New Jersey, began as another kind of utopian dream of a young Philadelphia lawyer named Charles K. Landis. Landis wanted "to found a place which . . . might be the abode of happy, prosperous and beautiful homes; to first lay it out on a plan conductive to beauty and convenience and in order to insure its success, establish the best of schools . . . manu-factories . . . industries and churches of different denominations."[6] Landis looked at tracts of land in the American West and in other parts of New Jersey, but he settled on South Jersey for its climate and soil, which he be-lieved would be suitable for growing fruit and grapes, easier crops for small farmers than stock or grain. He bought about 20,000 acres and, envisioning vineyards, named his town Vineland.

Vineland was laid out in a one-mile-square grid, with Landis Avenue, one hundred feet wide, at its center and shade trees carefully planted at even intervals. Landis advertised his Garden of Eden in newspapers across the country. He advertised also in the first Italian-language newspaper in New York and sent flyers to Italy. Italians were there in force by 1878, growing grapes, and Charles E. Welch had begun creating his grape juice.[7] South Jersey needed immigrant labor, so the New Jersey Bureau of Statistics sent off flyers to southern and eastern Europe in which it compared the South Jersey climate to that of the south of France or the shores of the Mediterranean.[8]

Vineland was not yet prosperous in the 1880s, but it was here that the leaders of Alliance, the first Jewish agricultural colony in South Jersey, came looking for land in May 1882. They were shown a wedge-shaped tract of

1,000 acres, about five miles northwest of Vineland itself, owned by Leach Brothers, a lumber firm. Eli Stavitsky and Moses Bayuk, the latter a lawyer and well-known Talmudic scholar, chose the land because the Jersey Central Railroad ran right through it. The railroad's proximity would be helpful in "marketing produce, but also in bringing relatives from Philadelphia and New York for visits; in bringing a few 'pleasureniks' to board for the summer."[9] Sponsored by the Hebrew Emigrant Aid Society of New York and the French Alliance Israelite Universelle, after which Bayuk named the young colony, about twenty-five families arrived to clear the land.

They were dropped, "dumped off" as they put it, by the train at a flag station, where they were at first housed in tents lent by the U.S. army. By summer, three barracks had been built on a hill overlooking the Maurice River, called by the settlers Castle Gardens after the infamous immigrant landing depot in New York that preceded Ellis Island. The rooms were tiny, like steamer cabins, but an observer from Philadelphia remarked on the bouquets of swamp flowers on almost every table.[10] Those swamps produced not only flowers but hordes of mosquitoes, and clearing the land of trees was a hard job for city people.

Houses were built with the aid of the Leach brothers, and Landis himself assured Vinelanders of his confidence in the immigrants' ability to make "the wilderness blossom as the rose."[11] Settlers got their twelve- to fifteen-acre plots by lottery; houses were built with two rooms, one up, one down, and a cellar. There was no indoor plumbing. In the first year, colonists survived economically by hiring themselves out as pickers working on local fruit farms or in the cranberry bogs. Some cut corn in Palatine and Deerfield; others made bricks in Vineland or worked in the glass factory in Millville.

In that same year, the Hebrew Emigrant Aid Society established an "overflow" colony of six families in nearby Rosenhayn. The immigrants worked hard, but the lack of money, poor soil, and an epidemic of a kind of lung fever ended the project. In 1887, however, with improvement in the local economy, a number of families returned. Rosenhayn was never an exclusively Jewish community, and by 1909 its farmers were doing well with lima beans, sweet potatoes, and strawberries. Rosenhayn's proximity to lakes also made it a popular destination for the "pleasureniks," which helped bring in money.

Three miles south of Rosenhayn, at a place called Beaver Dam, one W. H. Miller had settled German immigrant families from Philadelphia on his land. Eventually, they abandoned their holdings and fled back to the city. Michael Heilprin saw a chance for his Jewish brothers. Beaver Dam became Carmel, named for the mountains in Israel known by the prophets Elijah and Elisha. Heilprin enlisted the help of philanthropists such as Jacob Schiff, and the first colonists arrived in the 1882, the year of the founding of both Alliance and Rosenhayn. Heilprin, a scholar, author, philanthropist, and idealist, was a native of Russian Poland. He and his family had fled to Hungary in 1842 to escape czarist persecution. Heilprin joined the Hungarian independence movement, and it was the Hungarian nationalist leader Louis Kossuth who advised him to go to America. Arriving in Philadelphia in 1856, he became involved in the antislavery movement and wrote for the *Nation*. He also worked with the Hebrew Emigrant Aid Society to help provide for the new influx of Russian Jews. When Heilprin died suddenly in 1888, the Carmel dwellers were devastated. Their cause, however, was taken up by Sabato Morais, the influential Sephardic rabbi in Philadelphia, and leading Jewish Philadelphians took over the colony's affairs. The farmers of Carmel raised rye, buckwheat, corn and other vegetables, as well as some cattle and poultry, but the majority also depended on tailoring, making shirts for contractors in Philadelphia. "After all, the 'farming tailors' had large families to support as well as rental or mortgage payments on their homes, for in 1889, W. H. Miller . . . still owned many of the homes in addition to the synagogue, post office, library, school and butcher shop." [12] The "farming tailors" were known as the most radical of the settlers, embracing Russian nihilism, atheism, and even, it was said, free love.

As Alliance grew, several smaller communities appeared on its outskirts. At the southeastern end was Norma, which, by the 1890s had achieved a reputation as the poorest and dirtiest of the Jewish colonies. Vineland residents on their way to lake resorts complained about the slovenliness of the main street. Norma, however, came under the care of philanthropist Maurice Fels, of the Fels Naptha soap fortune. Fels established a model farm in

Norma to serve all the Jewish colonies, where asparagus, sweet potatoes, and various fruits were grown to instruct the would-be farmers. In 1901, Fels founded the Allvine Canning Company to make use of local produce.

At the northeast corner of Alliance was Brotmanville, developed by a New Yorker, Abraham Brotman, whose plan included both farms and a big factory. "Lighted by electricity generated on the premises and powered by steam, the modern factory seemed to symbolize Brotmanville's betrayal of the agrarian ideal, or, at least so it appeared to the farmers of Alliance." [13] Other smaller communities sprang up, among them Garton Road, Six Points, Estellville, Hebron, Mizpah, and Zion. Most did not last long.

Around the same time, the late 1880s, when Jews in Russia were suffering a new outbreak of persecution, a German Jewish railroad magnate and philanthropist, Baron Maurice de Hirsch, carried on negotiations with the czar's government in which he promised to pay for educating his "fellow-Jews in agricultural and mechanical pursuits, providing the government would repeal the harsh and discriminatory legislation denying the Jews a position of equality in the Russian Empire." [14] Eventually, when de Hirsch realized that the Russian government had no interest in improving the position of the Jews, negotiations broke down. Emigration looked like the only solution. He too had a Tolstoyan belief in agriculture: "The poor Jew, who until now has been hated as an outcast, will win for himself peace and independence, love for the ground he tills and for freedom; and he will become a patriotic citizen of his new homeland." [15] The baron supported colonies in Argentina, and in the United States he created the Baron de Hirsch Fund. A group of prominent Jews in New York were asked to form a central committee to determine the uses of the money that the de Hirsch Fund would provide.

The Baron de Hirsch Fund was not simply interested in creating Jewish farmers. The fund's main goal was to help Jewish immigrants to adjust to their new homes by whatever means seemed viable. In later years, the fund would turn over all agricultural responsibilities to the Jewish Agricultural and Industrial Aid Society, which eventually became the Jewish Agricultural Society. But in 1891, the fund took on the development of Woodbine. [16]

When H. L. Sabsovich of Odessa arrived in New York, he found his

Am Olam friends working in sweatshops. After a year of hand-to-mouth jobs, he got a place on the staff of an agricultural experiment station in Fort Collins, Colorado. He was then offered a post as head of the department of Agricultural Chemistry at Wyoming College. But the trustees of the de Hirsch Fund, whose names read like a "who's who" of American Jewry,[17] wanted him to be superintendent of the new colony that de Hirsch would subsidize, and he complied. Several parcels of land were available. Sabsovich and three other board members visited them, deciding finally on 5,300 acres in Dennis Township of Cape May County, in southern New Jersey, originally the estate of one Judge Moore. The site became known as the Woodbine tract. The property was bought on August 11, 1891.

The reasons for choosing this particular spot were that it was only twenty-two miles south of Vineland, where, along with Alliance, Carmel, and the other settlements, Jews were already in residence and accepted by their neighbors, and fifty-six miles southeast of Philadelphia. Markets for agricultural produce existed there, as well as in coastal Sea Isle City some eight miles to the east and Cape May another twenty-three miles to the southeast. The West Jersey Railroad passed through the tract, providing transportation. Although the land was covered with South Jersey's typical growth of scrub oak and pine, farms nearby proved that the soil could be adapted to truck farming and fruit growing. Catherine Sabsovich recounts, in her biography of her husband H. L. Sabsovich, that "my husband told me that although there were undoubtedly better localities insofar as marketing facilities went, and richer soils, the Committee would rather spend the difference in preparing the land for the future farmer, enriching it according to modern scientific methods."[18]

Sabsovich handpicked twelve "pioneers," bought them hats and overalls, and set out with them for the Woodbine tract. At the time, Woodbine consisted of "a railroad station, one house owned by an old couple and a shanty across the track. All this was so thickly surrounded by woods as far as the eye could see that I remember we always feared the children might stray away and become lost therein. A single track of the West Jersey Railroad passed through, and the main occupation of those who lived nearby was wood chopping, although there was an occasional farmer."[19]

Two six-room houses were hastily built. During those first weeks, Sabsovich and his twelve pioneers slept all together in one of them, on the floor with blankets.[20] By November and December the colony had grown to sixty men; most had families and had been picked from residents of the southern Pale, who were considered more likely to succeed at farming. The Jews in the northwestern Pale were more concentrated in cities, whereas those in the southern Pale often lived in rural areas and, because there were fewer of them, they were better assimilated.[21] The other house was given to a widow with children. She would provide food and lodging for anyone who wanted to board with her. A big barn was built as temporary housing for the sixty men, who presumably arrived before their families. A large stove was installed, although it only really warmed those who sat close to it.[22]

Each settler was to be allotted thirty acres, which he was to clear himself, a house, a cow, and some chickens, seeds, and tools. The debt was to be repaid in twelve years. "Their Russian costume," announced *Frank Leslie's Weekly* of April 7, 1892, "has in most cases been laid aside. Some of the older men, however, cling to the astrakhan cap and the long coat with astrakhan trimmings." Clearing the land was hard for these men. Even though Jews in the South Pale may have lived in rural areas and had some acquaintance with agriculture, most were small merchants, for whom "this work of chopping down trees and pulling up tree-stumps . . . seemed . . . as difficult as tearing down the pyramids" and must have made them feel like the slaves of Egypt.[23]

David Ludins came to America in 1891, after a chance conversation in an Odessa café with the sister of H. L. Sabsovich. Ludins wanted to settle on the soil "even as my idol Tolstoi had done in the later days of his life. But this could not be done in the country of my birth. Jews could not buy or rent land."[24] Ludins had wanted to emigrate to Palestine, but the Turkish government was barring Jews, so he took the woman's advice that Woodbine would be a good place for him to live out his farming dream and went to New York. At the first meeting between Ludins and H. L. Sabsovich, the latter was dubious. Ludins was single, and the colony needed big families because some "in the family will have to work in shops, while the others make the land ready for farming. The locality of our enterprise is wooded land. It isn't like the Ukraine where you can begin to plow at once." He invited Ludins to Woodbine, however, and Ludins traveled down on the train to inspect this new land he had come to. "There was nothing striking in the landscape I saw from the windows of the train to Woodbine. Flat land, poor vegetation, yards of advertisements on boards offering bargains with all kinds of inducements. Here and there an unpainted farmhouse, a barn with a caved-in roof, broken carriage wheels, and a horse, a cow or two, pasturing between dwarf trees." [25]

Things were not much better when he got there. In the tiny office of the Baron de Hirsch Fund, Professor Sabsovich introduced him to one Fred Schmidt, "an agriculturalist and the manager . . . a big red-bearded, red-cheeked man with a loud voice." Schmidt, who was referred to as "the Prussian," was in charge of all the farmers-in-training. He agreed to lend the newcomer an axe, although the fund's rule was that everyone should have his own tools. The first trial was the mosquitoes.

> In the Ukraine, with hundreds of miles of steppe, there were no mosquitoes. Here they were everywhere: in my ears, nose, mouth, and even in my eyes. Unable to drive them away, I walked close to the trees with the leaves of the lower limbs as a protection. I looked at Goldberg. He, too, suffered from the mosquitoes; only Schmidt was walking erect, and not once did he drive away the mosquitoes. I wondered: either his blood wasn't "kosher" or his lifetime in the woods had made him immune to mosquito bites.[26]

In the course of a morning chopping down trees, Ludins meets two of the other pioneers in a scene straight out of a Russian novel. One of them, Goldberg, has nothing good to say about the colony.

> Can you, a learned young man, tell me why I am here? There in my Bessarabia, I drank wine instead of water. There I ate fresh *mamaliga*—puffy and hot, right from the oven. I was a respected member of the synagogue. . . . In this country, I am "Hey, old man!" Can you explain all this to me? Listen: to drink just water instead of wine; to

eat wood shavings—they call it "cornflakes"—with cold milk instead of hot mamaliga; and listen to that accursed Prussian Schmidt,
with his, "Do this, do that!"—for what? Thirty acres of land. Land!
Look at the corn here. A chicken can jump over it without even using its wings. There, in our Bessarabia, corn is corn, you have to
use a stepladder to reach the upper ears. . . . I don't want thirty acres
of land. What for? Half an acre is enough for me—and enough for
everyone![27]

Not long after, Jacob Lipman comes to bring Ludins water. He is an intense young man with the opposite point of view.

There are six of us besides my parents. We were tired of New York
tenement life without sunshine and no room to move around. The opportunity to change to country life with open horizons fascinated my
mother especially. Besides, we come from Libau where I attended the
gymnasium and my major subject was chemistry. Professor Sabsovich is a chemist. The Baron de Hirsch fund is going to build an agricultural school; so you see the future for us seems very bright.[28]

Like the hero of a Russian novel, Ludins is left with "sudden nostalgia . . . for
the open steppe, for flocks of bleating sheep, even for the squeaking sound
of marmots under the blazing sun, and most of all, for the horizon where
the blue sky meets the warm black earth."[29]

Woodbine was not Ukraine, nor the fertile ground of Pope's poem. The
sandy soil produced meager crops. The tract had no lakes or creeks. Ice
had to be bought from flooded cranberry bogs in nearby Steelmantown and
stored for summer use. The water table was very near the surface, causing
occasional flooding. "The combination of high water tables and sandy soils
with an extremely thin crust of topsoil ensured that farming would be a
marginal existence in the early years. There was no way that the farmers
could compete with the naturally rich farmland of the Midwest or the established nearby farms."[30]

According to Catherine Sabsovich, however, Woodbine in May 1892 was a "veritable bee hive." Mrs. Lipman was running her boardinghouse, and a grocery store had opened.

> The people on the trains passing to the watering-places and re-sorts—Cape May and Ocean City—during the summer months of this year could hardly believe the testimony of their eyes. What had been a short time before, a stretch of barren, desolate pines, was changed and enlivened so that they did not recognize it. For, when they reached Woodbine, the monotonous scene blossomed into new houses, brightly painted outbuildings, surrounded, where the pines had been cut away, with crops and young orchards. Inquiring, they would be informed that the wealth of the philanthropist, Baron de Hirsch, had made all this possible.[31]

In its early days, the Woodbine experiment attracted many distinguished visitors. Among them were the anarchist Voltairine de Cleyre and the Russian writer and activist Vladimir Korolenko. Korolenko was much impressed, writing in 1893:

> I came here expecting only a caricature of a colony, not a real enter-prise. The two days' visit proved me wrong. . . . Here a group of peo-ple were organized who love the earth soaked with their sweat. . . . In this new Palestine, the forest covering the entire area only two years ago has been cut down, uprooted, the area has been cleared and built up by the citizens of Woodbine . . . our Jews. Men and women show me their farms near the forest, growing melons, making ready to gather their crops of potatoes and cabbages. Corn covered entire fields . . . orchards planted with trees. In their new town, wide streets and boulevards, telegraph station, post office, electric lanterns . . . all proof of a good future for Woodbine.[32]

Despite all this activity, including the building of houses for the farm-ers, as designed by New York architects, the smallest with four rooms, the largest seven, the trustees of the fund realized that the farms would take several years to produce a living and that it might take even longer for the inexperienced immigrants to become successful farmers. To make it possible for the farmers to work on their land and still earn a living, the trustees persuaded various manufacturers to move plants from urban areas into Woodbine. Companies were offered incentives such as free rent, light and power for the factory, and housing for the factory's necessary employees. "Thus factories were built, with great lofts and large windows close to one another, so different from the dirty, dark sweatshops of New York and Philadelphia."[33]

Charles Landis made his Vineland plans available to the Woodbine developers, and as a result Woodbine's grid system of wide streets is similar to that of Vineland. Woodbine, however, was also laid out on the plan of medieval English communities. Lots in the center of town, each of which included a house and a large side lot for a garden, were surrounded by the thirty-acre farms, and beyond them land was reserved for pasturage. By the summer of 1893, a staggering amount of work had been completed. The agent for the New Jersey State Board of Agriculture reported that

> Six hundred and fifty acres of farmland had been cleared, and a hundred miles of farm roads had been built. Farmhouses were erected, and in his opinion, they were as well-built as town houses. They contained the latest features in scientific ventilation and plumbing. The recently established Jonasson Cloak factory was in operation and employed one hundred and fifty people, and other factories for cutlery, knitting and cigars, were soon to be built. Anticipating the demands of a transient trade, a new hotel was built, and the railroad even opened a station at Woodbine to accommodate traffic.[34]

David Ludins watched the same growth with less enthusiasm.

> The factory buzzed with sewing machines. Woodbine was alive with the building of homes and a hotel. Streets were built and electric-light poles with signs, "Washington Ave.," "Jefferson Ave.," "Baron de Hirsch Ave.," and other fine names shone under the elec-

tric lights. However, all this did not warm the hearts of the farmers of Woodbine. There weren't enough farmhouses. Wages were low in the factory. The immigrants from New York—some straight from the steamer—unused to chopping trees sometimes made the mistake against which Schmidt had warned me of taking one's leg for a tree, and accidents increased. There were no doctors in Woodbine. The Dennisville doctor, who served many small communities, had little time and charged fees which the Woodbine farmers could not afford to pay. The growth of misunderstanding between the old and the young, the conservatives and the liberals, also added to the chaos.[35]

Woodbine was ripe for trouble, and it came in 1893, the "Year of the Trouble" as settlers called it. To begin with there was a lack of understanding between the cultivated, Westernized Jews, mostly of German Jewish background, who were running the de Hirsch Fund, and the Russian, Yiddish-speaking immigrants who were working the land in Woodbine. One only has to read the *Jewish Exponent,* the newspaper published in those years for the Philadelphia Jewish community, to understand this gulf. The *Exponent* provides social notes, the proceedings of literary societies and sewing circles, even photographs of debutantes. Lead articles sport titles such as "Moses and Confucius," "Greek and Roman Ideas of the Jew," and "The Jew in English Literature." Advertisements feature clothes, cigars, pianos, and hotels in Atlantic City. There are also articles about the persecution of the Jews in Russia and about the new colonies, particularly about the necessity for more "religious work" among the new settlers, who were seen as not sufficiently observant. This world was light years away from the hardscrabble world of the Woodbine farmer. The attitude of the members of the de Hirsch Fund's committee was that the immigrant was like a child and that his benefactors, most of whom had been very successful in business, knew what was best for him. It was this attitude that underlay the problems leading up to the Year of the Trouble.

The de Hirsch Fund had required a down payment of two hundred dollars from Woodbine's settlers. In the first months of work, settlers had chopped down thousands of dollars worth of cordwood to be sold in the cities. Although they were paid seven dollars per acre for clearing the land, the wood belonged to the Woodbine Land and Improvement Company, the corporation set up by the fund's trustees. The Land and Improvement Company had been directed by the fund to manage the enterprise.

The company hoped that town lots would sell at prices that would eventually reimburse the fund for most of the money advanced to the colonists. In actuality, the settlers struggled under mortgages averaging a little more than a thousand dollars. There was not enough housing, and many families had to depend on their children working in the factories for subsistence. With the opening of Jonasson and Company, a clothing manufacturer, the fund trustees felt that the colony was well established and that the farmers should begin repaying their debt. It had always been de Hirsch's plan that the settlers should become self-sufficient members of their new society as soon as possible.

As David Ludins tells it, when the farmers received their lease agreements and saw that they were expected to pay interest on their loans at once, the rebellion started. In a meeting held in the schoolhouse, the "bankers" were denounced. Women demanded the cows they had been promised. The men scorned the loans for their farms: "If we have to pay for land that produces nothing, we would rather buy old farms with cleared land instead of woods." [36]

In March 1893, Sabsovich had in fact asked the company to advance each of the farmers one hundred dollars for the spring plowing and planting. He explained that although they had made money in the past year, they had had to build houses, invest in their farms, and send money back to Russia to bring family members over, which left them with no savings. "By helping them to improve their farms," he wrote, "we shall sooner free them from our wardship. After all, they are our wards!" [37] But the company disagreed. The money in the fund was depleted, and, with the clothing factory operating, farmers could find work during the slack season, making aid unnecessary.

In fact, it was really too soon to expect the community to stand completely on its own. The trustees "insisted on business standards and individual responsibility, the colonists were deluded by their excessive estimates of philanthropy's capacity . . . some of the immigrant farmers labored under the delusion that their land was an outright gift, with further allowances forthcoming as needed."[38] Although Sabsovich did not entirely agree with the company's position, he supported them. He believed that the company had a duty to the fund.

In January, all but two of the sixty farmers refused to sign their leases. Their anger with the "bankers" extended to Sabsovich. As a Westernized, Swiss-educated professor, he was seen as having more in common with the "enemy." Fires were set in the woods. There were threats on Sabsovich's life and threats to burn down his home. Letters to the press described him as ruling Woodbine like a Russian czar. The farmers sent telegrams to trustees blaming Sabsovich for their plight and claiming that he had Pinkerton men in the woods ready to shoot them. The drama had escalated to the imagining of an American-style pogrom. That spring of 1893, no crops were planted, and most other work was also stopped. Sabsovich worried that the revolt would put "the whole crowd of the Russian Jews of Woodbine in a very bad light."[39] Woodbine's Dennisville neighbors were indeed upset. Never had the volatile foreigners in their midst seemed so foreign. There had already been trouble when a Dennisville barber had refused to cut the hair of Jewish colonists, and the Jews threatened a boycott. The authorities of Dennisville apologized but the Jews found their own barber to open a shop in Woodbine. Now there was agitation against the immigrants, and the immigrants retaliated by threatening to boycott local merchants.[40]

The rift between the colonists and their benefactors was deep—"it's extent was partly indicated by their mutual inability to speak the same language, figuratively and literally."[41] When the trustees spoke to the colonists they spoke in German. Sabsovich himself did not speak Yiddish, only learning it many years later. In the winter of 1893, a recession hit the clothing industry and temporarily closed the factory, exacerbating the economic woes of the Woodbine settlers. An old woman, whose only support was her daughter who worked in the factory, was evicted when she could not, or would not, pay rent on her cottage, which belonged to the Land and Improvement Company. The incident fanned the flames of revolt.

Eventually, an arbitrator was brought in, and Sabsovich persuaded the company to make some concessions: mortgage periods were extended, the basic price of houses was reduced, interest payments were postponed until October 1894, and repairs were made at company expense.[42] However, Sabsovich and the company wanted to make it clear that the company was still in control. The ringleaders were tried at Cape May Courthouse, where company lawyers argued that the company was trying to develop honest citizens, whereas "years of persecution in the countries of Eastern Europe had made *shnorrers* [beggars] of potentially fine human beings." The judge found no "valid excuse" for the farmers' refusal to meet their financial obligations, saying "America was not built on charity."[43] The eight most intractable were evicted and given ten days to leave the colony. They would be reimbursed for any money they had spent and given one hundred dollars to start them on their way. One effect of the decision was "to advertise Woodbine unfavorably" to other immigrants.[44]

The Year of the Trouble had shaken the community. The colonists took stock and began to think about their need for schools and a place of worship. The Woodbine Brotherhood was formed, and work began on the Brotherhood Synagogue. The de Hirsch Fund provided two-thirds of the cost, and the colonists raised the rest. According to the official history, "The enthusiasm was so strong that the whole community once went to work on the road and put their earnings, amounting to about $150, in the Treasury of the Brotherhood."[45] Woodbiners built the impressive building still standing today with their own hands. They worked at night—after a long day on their farms—digging clay, making bricks, and cutting wood. This was the "big shul," a congregation of Orthodox Jews, including the town's intellectuals and industrialists. Factory workers frequented the smaller Tifereth Israel, a converted Baptist church.

Additional factories were moving in as the trustees began looking to a more agricultural/industrial model. Although the troubles of the year had taken a toll on Sabsovich, causing his collapse and necessitating a period of recovery in the Catskills,[46] he, disciple of Am Olam, clung to his dream of Woodbine as an agricultural colony. Before the end of the Year of the Trouble, Sabsovich began his People's University.

The upper floor of a barn was converted to a lecture hall. The ground floor held mechanical shops, and farms 59 and 60 were used for technical demonstrations. Sabsovich taught botany, chemistry, and physiology, while Frederick Schmidt taught poultry raising and dairying. In that first class were Jacob Lipman, who became a renowned soil chemist, and Jacob Kotinsky, who became a famous entomologist. Such was the beginning of the Baron de Hirsch Agricultural School, one of the first agricultural secondary schools in the country.

The school's curriculum continued to expand, and by 1898 it offered a three-year advanced course in both academic and practical subjects. Sixty students were enrolled, and that number soon increased to one hundred, including fifteen girls in a domestic arts program. The fund and the Jewish Colonization Association provided substantial financial support. A large brick school building, dormitories, assembly rooms, and study halls were built. The school had 270 acres under cultivation, stables, and a model dairy herd. Students aged thirteen to eighteen came from Woodbine, from the other colonies around Vineland, from other Jewish farm families, from city tenements, and from orphanages.

Arthur D. Goldhaft, who would become a veterinarian, an expert on poultry farming, and the inventor in 1921 of the fowl pox vaccine, was sent there by his godfather. At the time he was just a boy living in the Philadelphia ghetto. "The way our home was, no matter how valiantly my mother worked, it was a home of worry, of disorder, of constant scrambling and scratching to make a life. And so up until then I had been a chip-on-the-shoulder kid because of shame for my father who seemed a ne'er-do-well, and shame altogether for the way we lived." [47]

Goldhaft was not particularly happy to be sent away to school in the country, which he could only imagine as a kind of reform school. What he found was something entirely different.

The farm school was, I suppose, a combination of prep school academy, with even a touch of an orphanage, and it had the before-its-time idea of the work-and-study combination program that is practiced in several colleges today. Only for me, from the first days, Woodbine was something even more. I think the first thing it did for me was to give

me a feeling of self respect, even that it was all right to be a Jew. . . .
The atmosphere of the school, of the town, had an open, warm quality. Despite the fact that it was a free school, with room and board
and clothing provided by the Baron de Hirsch fund, and that many of
the students were from the ghetto and from orphanages, there was no
atmosphere of inferiority, but rather of a good boarding school academy. We had our uniforms and capes, like West Pointers.[48]

As Catherine Sabsovich described it:

The students were trained in practical work including the raising of
crops, caring for the live-stock and working in the dairy, the apiary,
the hothouse, the nursery and the shops. The apiary was a special feature. It was located in the center of the orchard, and the honey which
the bees produced was the finest in New Jersey. In the mechanical
shop, a little of blacksmithing, plumbing, carpentry, medicine and
veterinary surgery were taught. This was designed to make the prospective farmer equal to any need or emergency that might arise on
his farm. Nor was the marketing side of the farmer's work neglected.
In the poultry plant, the students were taught how to use incubators,
and the method of packing poultry for market. The newest of agricultural implements—mechanical ploughs, seeders, reapers and bind-
ers—were used by the boys of the school.[49]

All this sounds idyllic, but in fact the school did not last long, just twenty-
two years, closing its doors in 1917. During those years, neither the town
nor the school was free from strife. "Thus, in the long run, Woodbine's
Agricultural School only reflected the strengths and weaknesses of the
community that furnished its staff, students and support."[50] The de Hirsch
Fund trustees criticized Sabsovich's curriculum as laying too much stress
on academic and scientific subjects; the course was too long and elaborate,
and the graduates too few to justify the expense. The length of training was
eventually cut to two years, and more focus was given to practical work.
Boris D. Bogen, who succeeded Sabsovich as principal, felt that the phi-

lanthropists wanted "a contented Jewish peasantry" on local farms rather than students who were able to go farther afield to jobs in the agricultural laboratories of the U.S. Department of Agriculture.[51] Internal trouble was also caused by student strikes, one apparently begun over the substitution of jam for butter in the dining room and complaints that oatmeal and coffee constituted most of the school diet. The philanthropists thought this behavior was caused by a lack of discipline, whereas Arthur Goldhaft remembers it as the natural boisterousness of the young.

> Strikes were a favorite form of activity in those days. They were more than protests, they were a kind of spiritual action—and assertion of personality. So once when there was no butter in the dining hall due to a mix-up in purchasing, the "firebrands" among us immediately called a strike. Jam was substituted, but still we struck. Professor Sabsovich . . . called a big assembly and told us that he was disappointed in us. But things were never much worse than that.[52]

The school's successes are unquestionable, however. In 1900, it won a silver medal for its agricultural exhibits and a grand prix in secondary education at the Paris Exposition, as well as medals at the St. Louis Exposition of 1904.[53] The school could also claim a number of successful alumni, including the previously mentioned Jacob Lipman, who became the first dean of the State Agricultural College at Rutgers; two well-known entomologists, David Fink and Jacob Kotinsky; Samuel Goldberg, who became an animal pathologist at Cornell; and Arthur Goldhaft, who founded the Vineland Poultry Labs.

Some of the unrest in Woodbine's factories possibly rubbed off on the agricultural school students. The Baron de Hirsch Fund, learning from the experience of earlier colonies, had always intended to have an economy based on manufacturing as well as agriculture. A large three-story shirt factory had been built as part of the original plan, but because this industry was vulnerable to business cycles, the factory went through a number of owners, ending up in the hands of Daniels and Blumenthal, a manufacturer of children's clothing. The second largest firm in town was the Quaker

City Knitting Company, for whom the fund built a factory in 1901. There were also a number of smaller firms producing hats, machinery, paper boxes, metal ware, cigars, and baskets woven with local willows and sold to Wanamaker's in Philadelphia. The town's location remained a problem and made it hard for the factories to compete with those in urban areas; thus wages were low in Woodbine, and dissatisfaction eventually erupted in a series of strikes, the first major one being against Daniels and Blumenthal in 1903. Instability in the needle trades exacerbated the situation, causing wage cuts and layoffs. The local workingmen's association became more and more militant. In 1908, Woodbine workers presented a petition to the Baron de Hirsch Fund. Their rights, they maintained, were being violated. Wages were much lower than those of city garment workers, plus they had to pay a $25 security deposit to retain their jobs and give four weeks' notice if they wanted to leave. "Would not the distinguished trustees protect them from these management abuses?"[54]

The fact was that the trustees also heard countercomplaints from the Woodbine companies, which threatened to move their operations to Philadelphia or other cities where there were a greater number of more cooperative workers. Woodbine's location created heavy freight costs for their products. The companies constantly asked the fund for financial help. In 1909, workers struck the Woodbine Hat Company after it announced that "those not reporting for work by 7:10 would be locked out for the day."[55] By 1911, the United Garment Workers union, which was well established in Woodbine, was mandating a fifty-eight-hour workweek, with only eight hours of work on Friday and no work on Saturday (the Sabbath), piece rates for tailors alone, and the introduction of an arbitration board. In the years that followed, 1911 to 1914, Woodbine's reputation for radicalism made it hard to attract new factories. "A Philadelphia firm claimed that it had been interested in Woodbine but fear of the 'anarchistic-socialistic characteristics of the people coupled with broken pledges . . . and striking on the least provocation'" had kept it away.[56]

In those years leading up to the First World War, life in Woodbine took on its particular color. Despite the strikes and lockouts, the fund's incentives attracted more industries. Real estate values rose, and Woodbiners began to resent Dennis Township for refusing to improve Woodbine roads or give money to its schools. Numerous meetings resulted in a petition to the General Assembly of the State of New Jersey, and in 1903 Woodbine was incorporated as a borough, the first Jewish borough in the country and, according to David Blaustein writing in *Circle* magazine, "the first self governed Jewish community since the fall of Jerusalem."[57] H. L. Sabsovich was elected mayor. Woodbine also had the first kindergarten in the county and one of the first in the state. It had a public school as early as 1894, while the central consolidated grammar school, built in 1905, had electricity, steam heat, and plumbing when many rural schools still used coal stoves and outhouses.[58] On Columbus Day, 1914, the Woodbine High School opened its doors, making Woodbine the first town of its size in the state to have a high school. Education and intellectual activity were of great importance to Woodbiners. There were lots of clubs: Woodbine Mothers, Girl Scouts, Boy Scouts, bands, orchestras, singing groups, drama clubs. Samuel Fleisher, another Philadelphia philanthropist and de Hirsch Fund trustee, was responsible for music programs and an art program at the high school and community center, which would culminate in 1929 in the Cape May Art League, still active today.

Woodbine also had shops that closed on Saturday, the Sabbath, but were open on Sunday, when other area shops were closed. This practice went against state laws, and small fines were levied until the Jews demanded the same privileges as a colony of Seventh-Day Baptists in nearby Shiloh, who had been observing Saturday as the Sabbath long before the Jews arrived.

> Groups of noisy children played in the street. Women wearing shawls and brightly colored kerchiefs gathered in front of their houses chatting loudly together in a language that was strange to me. Old men with beards plodded up and down the streets, heads bowed and hands thrust into the sleeves of their coats like a muff, looking neither to right nor left, speaking to no one. Dogs were everywhere. It was like being in a foreign country.
>
> It seemed that every family that could save a few extra dollars and had room in their home, that they could spare, opened a shop of some

kind. Most of these dealt in clothing, shoes and dry goods although there were some paint, wallpaper and hardware stores. . . . Most of the other shops were a hodge-podge of factory rejects, broken lots, remnants and sale odds and ends bought in New York and brought back to the one room stores to be piled up there without regard to neatness or order. In some part of the room one could generally see an elderly bearded man wearing a skull cap and jacket, who, although he didn't understand a word that was being said, still kept a watchful eye on the proceedings. This was usually a grandfather and he was treated with the deepest respect by every member of the family.[59]

Woodbine's showplace, the Baron de Hirsch Agricultural School, settled in its red brick buildings at the edge of town on Baron de Hirsch Avenue, was threatened as early as 1897 by the creation of other, similar schools, particularly the National Farm School in Doylestown, Pennsylvania. Founded by Rabbi Joseph Krauskopf of Philadelphia, the National Farm School was nonsectarian and soon drew its support from the same benefactors as those who had wanted to help the eastern European immigrants of South Jersey. Not affiliated with any agricultural colony or charitable fund, it offered a "peaceful rural environment, with the nearby Burpee Seed Farm to provide some practical training."[60] It was also only twenty-six miles from Philadelphia. In the *Jewish Exponent* of those years, the National Farm School gets a lot more coverage than does the de Hirsch school. Quite possibly it was more appealing to the settled German Jews of Philadelphia than was the school sited at the unruly eastern European "peasant" colony of Woodbine. Also, agricultural experts took a dim view of the de Hirsch school and the farming potential of Woodbine itself, declaring the site depressing. Professor Charles S. Phelps from Connecticut State Agricultural College remarked on the school's "absence of beautiful scenery" and its "disheartening environment,"[61] although he also included in that judgment the industrial unrest of the town. Others felt that the location, in an area where farming was largely unsuccessful, would not foster a love of agriculture. Of course it was also true that "at the time that a number of Jewish pioneers were attempting their return to the land, the main current of American life was away-from-the-land. In 1860, less than one fifth of the American population had been urban; forty years later, nearly a third was urban." [62]

Julius Rosenwald with Jacob Schiff, one of the original fund trustees who had long been a critic of the school, offered $300,000 to relocate the school to Peekskill, New York, an agriculturally more desirable location. The fund's trustees accepted the offer. The Woodbine settlers were up in arms at the loss of one of the town's major attractions, but their protests were ignored. By the end of the war, in 1919, building costs had raised the estimates for the new school in Peekskill; also the site was discovered to have poor drainage. The money was returned to Schiff and Rosenwald, and the Woodbine Agricultural School property was donated to the state of New Jersey, which established there the State Institution for Feebleminded Males.

The war had given a boost to Woodbine's troubled factories. The demand for clothing for the troops kept the needle trades humming. Employment in Woodbine's factories rose from 240 in 1914 to 700 by 1918. [63] Zelda Meranze, daughter of Joseph Rabinowitz, owner of the Woodbine Children's Clothing Company which had replaced Daniels and Blumenthal, remembered: "Everybody rented out closets for bedrooms. . . . People took in boarders who had never had boarders." [64]

The temporary boom affected all the Jewish colonies. Army tents as well as clothing were made in Brotmanville, Rosenhayn, and Norma. The brief prosperity did not end strikes and labor disputes neither during nor after the war, however. Vineland, Carmel, Rosenhayn, and Brotmanville saw strikes. In postwar Woodbine, imported strikebreakers took part in violence, causing many firms to shut down. By 1919, almost all its factories were closed and unemployment was high. In town, fifty-five houses were vacant. [65] Twenty old settlers and former employees of the Woodbine Children's Clothing Company finally pooled resources to start up a semi-cooperative enterprise, the Woodbine Borough Clothing Company, in the original factory built by the fund. The Woodbine Children's Clothing Company, founded by Joseph Rabinowitz, was still in business, as was the Bradstone

Rubber Company, one of whose cofounders was the son of a Woodbiner. By 1921, however, tired of labor troubles, Rabinowitz moved his family and his operation to Philadelphia.

Uneasy times also brought a resurgence of the Ku Klux Klan in South Jersey. Robed Klansmen paraded down the streets of Vineland on Saturday nights, causing Arthur Goldhaft's young son to ask if he could have "one of those nightshirt ghost uniforms."[66] Prohibition also made stills in the Woodbine woods profitable for a time.

Then, right after the crash of 1929, the harassed de Hirsch Fund decided to sever economic connections with the borough of Woodbine. As part of the process, it sold the power and water plant to outside interests, although the deed provided that "for all time, the plant shall be maintained to provide electric light, water, steam and heating for the manufacturers and the residents."[67]

Woodbiners suffered during the Depression, although farmers generally had an easier time than workers. In the winter of 1937–38, unemployed needleworkers chopped timber to get by. Some of the wood was bought by the Amalgamated Clothing Workers' relief services, which then distributed it to needy union members in Philadelphia. It must have seemed a return to the early days of the colony, when cordwood was chopped for the fund and exported to the city. Then came the New Deal with its subsistence communities that could have been modeled on the old Woodbine. The Resettlement Administration planned those communities in poor, isolated areas as a way to get people out of the cities and onto the land—a sort of American version of Am Olam. Now it was the federal government paying the bills, not the individual philanthropists. The federal government didn't hold on as long. By the beginning of World War II, it was effectively out of the resettlement business, having lasted roughly ten years to the de Hirsch Fund's twenty odd.

The New Deal, however, had provided considerable assistance to Woodbine. The PWA and the WPA helped to rebuild sidewalks and drainage systems, and renovated playgrounds and buildings at the State Institution for Feebleminded Males and in the town. In 1933, a CCC camp was built.[68]

To relate Woodbine's volatile history, however, is to distort the reality of the town as a community. Woodbine had movie theaters, including the Colonial, which advertised itself as "the theater of perfect sound," a roller rink, a bowling alley, and schools that raised the bar for the rest of Cape May County. The de Hirsch Fund had provided money for a community center, under Samuel S. Fleisher's direction. He had worked with underprivileged city youth in the arts, and his hopes and plans for Woodbine were high. He wanted to initiate classes in woodworking, tile making, wrought iron work, and other specialties that would allow Woodbine youth to become craftsmen. Such a skilled worker pool, he thought, would bring in better industries, reducing dependence on the competitive and unstable needle trades. He also planned to teach weaving, so that rug making could become a cottage industry—much the way it had for those who participated, with the help of Ami Mali Hicks, in the Maine island project. On November 11, 1928, a new community clubhouse was dedicated.

For those who attended the opening celebration, it must have become clear that Woodbine's population had diversified. An "Invocation to the Spirit of America" included the singing of not only "The Star-Spangled Banner" but the Jewish, Polish, Italian, and Romanian national anthems as well as Negro melodies. The community center provided music, art, drama, and rhythmic dancing. The new clubhouse unfortunately burned in 1929, but by 1930 "a well-equipped playground, with tennis courts and a children's playhouse, stood on the ruins of the clubhouse site. A cottage which had been used to house Woodbine's out-of-town school teachers was converted into the Center's new headquarters." [69] One has only to read the Woodbine Community Center report for September 1932 to be awed by the distance traveled in less than fifty years from those mosquito-ridden woods. In the preface, the director describes the undertaking as one "fraught with greater peril or benefit to the understanding of life itself by the present and future citizens of the whole community. . . . It attempts to see the whole town and see it clearly. It hopes to help each person grow a little each year toward that complex of interests and application of energies that will gradually make him a helpful, wholesome part of his community." [70]

By the summer of 1933, what resources the de Hirsch Fund had left were needed by a new wave of emigrants from Germany. Funding for the community center was discontinued. The work went on with volunteer help but not on the sort of scale Fleisher and others had envisioned.

Most people will tell you that it was after the war that Woodbine changed. The high school closed in 1944. The town had done so well educating its children that those who left for college did not return. Woodbine was just too isolated. After the war, a new group of immigrants arrived. Survivors of the Holocaust in Europe, they were different. They had their poultry farms on Friedrichstadt Road, on the outskirts of town, but they were there to make a living, not to create a community.

> These people had been through everything. If they had been in the slave camps they survived because of superior strength or cunning. If they had been hidden, they had been through years of silent fear, buried alive in a closet, or a garret, or a space between two floors, half starved. If they had been among the partisans, they had lived as wild hunted things, and killers . . . they were suspicious, selfish, fearful. It was painful to see what the world had done to them.[71]

"A lot of them," said Marjorie Rosenfeld, who married a second-generation Woodbiner, "were well educated. They weren't going to stay."[72]

Like the immigrants before them, they eventually left Woodbine, but Rosenfeld could as well have been talking about the children of the long line of Woodbine's immigrants. Almost all went away, and their places were taken by African Americans and then Hispanics, who came as agricultural or factory workers. There are few Jews in Woodbine now, and few farmers. The biggest employers are the Woodbine Developmental Center, currently home to some six hundred developmentally disabled men and boys, on the old de Hirsch Agricultural School property, and the Sea Isle Ice Company on Route 550. People work in Millville or May's Landing or even Atlantic City, some forty miles away.

Woodbine's agrarian dream is over. In many ways, it was a failure. America had been moving away from the farm toward industrialization, including eventually the industrialization of farming itself. The Jewish farming population was never huge, but with the aid of the well-organized Jewish Agricultural Society, it made an impressive effort to absorb the refugees from Europe's Holocaust. The dream of combining farm and factory—the vision of radicals like Peter Kropotkin—did not survive either.

At a gathering in 1958 for the sixty-fifth anniversary of the Woodbine Brotherhood Synagogue, Zelda Meranze, daughter of clothing manufacturer Joseph Rabinowitz, remembered the old days:

> We were like one big family and we still are. For every big event, every baseball game the high school played, for weddings, funerals, concerts, the fireman's ball, or the arrival of the train on Saturday with the movie—the whole town turned out. During vacations, the boys and girls would go to Sea Isle City, ten miles away by horse and buggy. A gentile farmer from nearby Dennisville remembered those days. "We always knew when the Woodbiners were coming home," he said, "by the singing that just echoed across the field at night." [73]

Woodbiners still come home to tour the San Azeez Museum in the Brotherhood Synagogue; sometimes they come to visit friends and relatives in the big Jewish cemetery out on Belleplain Road or the smaller one on de Hirsch Avenue. Like the Old World shtetl, Woodbine was a community in which everyone knew each other and looked out for each other, but it was also a stepping stone into a new world.

This Woodbine was a far cry from the Woodbine described in the *Philadelphia Inquirer* for October 31, 1977:

> From the steps of the municipal hall here, the view is of a ghostly, burned out factory across the street. Its charred shell is a reminder of this town's demise.
>
> There are other reminders. A few blocks away, old homes stand vacant and abandoned, their windows boarded up. Stores also are empty and the movie house and roller skating rink are memories of another time.

On a nearby sagging porch, two black men sit on rocking chairs. They talk about the lack of jobs. On a nearby corner, unemployed Puerto Ricans hang out.

It could be a scene in Newark or Camden. But this is Woodbine, a small borough in northern Cape May County situated on the edge of the picturesque pine barrens.[74]

Woodbine has struggled on, confronting new urban problems at least as difficult as agricultural ones were for the original settlers. Traces of the dream remain in Woodbine: the developmental center is, after all, an attempt to fit a marginalized population into the mainstream. Woodbine is still an immigrant town, absorbing African Americans from the rural South and Hispanics from Puerto Rico. And Woodbine lives, too, in the journeys that began here.

Roosevelt
New Deal Town

Route 571 winds through meadows; it is far enough inland that there are gentle hills, plowed fields, stands of trees, a horse farm. On this spring day, wisteria gone wild is blossoming high in the trees. This corner of the state, near Hightstown and Princeton, is hardly isolated, yet there is still farmland, making it easier to imagine the early farming days of Jersey Homesteads, as Roosevelt was originally called. A project of Franklin D. Roosevelt's New Deal Resettlement Administration, the town changed its name to that of its benefactor in 1945.

I pass a historical marker.

JERSEY HOMESTEADS HISTORIC DISTRICT
ESTABLISHED 1937

I bear right where Route 571 becomes Rochdale Road, named presumably for the Lancashire birthplace of the Co-operative movement.[1] Rochdale Road is Roosevelt's main street, although the only commercial establishment is Mamacita's Pizza/Deli, next to the post office where people still pick up their mail. Roosevelt does not have home delivery.

The deli has a few shelves of essentials, the usual rack of potato chips, popcorn, and pretzels. A number of 1940s metal-topped kitchen tables, with a selection of mismatched chairs for seating, makes for an odd combination of convenience store and shabby chic. The proprietors also provide some homemade Hispanic specialties, along with the pizza.

Coming out of the deli with my cup of coffee, I read the signs tacked up on the community bulletin board, an interesting collection that reminds me of nothing so much as the bulletin board at the health food store in Brattleboro, Vermont, in the late 1960s. There's a cooperative farm bulletin next to a card proclaiming "sewing machines repaired in my home." It seems that the ghost of the old farm and factory dream endures. More contemporary are notices for tai chi and ayurveda—as well as Mary Kay cosmetics. A guitarist is wanted for a local Punk Project. Someone has posted a digital picture of a "strange light" in the woods, alongside a copy of an article in the most recent *New Jersey Monthly* naming Roosevelt "the best place to live in New Jersey," and another about the importance, for children, of outdoor play and the danger of "social isolation" posed by television and computer games. A local resident who is an employee of Micawber Books in Princeton offers to deliver free any books that are ordered.

I have a sense of this place even before I begin to walk around. Of course, I have been here before. Still, it always takes a moment to adjust to Bauhaus architecture in a semi-rural landscape. Building outlines are softened now by trees and shrubs, but it's easy to see how stark those flat-roofed, cement-block boxes would have looked standing in raw earth, when the town had been newly carved out of woods and farmland.

Today, I plan a trip to the old community building, now the Roosevelt school. I am going to look at the famous Ben Shahn mural. I approach the school from South Rochdale Avenue, but this is not where the entrance is located, so I walk around the low, blocky cement building. In a stand of trees to my left is a bronze bust of FDR, sculpted by Shahn's son, Jonathan, and dedicated in 1961 at a ceremony attended by Eleanor Roosevelt and producer Dore Schary. I also pass a sweet gum tree with a plaque announcing its salvation by the class of 1997. The school doors are locked, but someone comes immediately to let me in. She is not surprised that I have come to see the mural; this is clearly a pretty usual event. I write down my name and affiliation; she gives me a badge.

The mural takes up one wall of the lobby. Beginning on the left side of the work, the Jews depart Europe, leaving behind coffined corpses of the Russian pogroms; a sign reads "bei Juden." A crowd of immigrant Jews walks toward the viewer, with Einstein in the forefront. After that come sweatshops and labor organizing, then President Roosevelt and resettlement, and finally the beginnings of Jersey Homesteads—planners with maps at a table, factory and farm in the background. This is the story of the migration of the Jews from an oppressive Europe to America. It is the story of Roosevelt.

There are other reminders: black-and-white photographs of Jersey Homesteads' farms and factories, as taken by famous photographers such as Russell Lee, Dorothea Lange, and Carl Mydens. In June 1936, Jersey Homesteads' potato crop was the second best in three potato-growing counties. The Workers' Aim Co-operative made coats and suits. In another picture, Benjamin Brown, the godfather of Jersey Homesteads, smiles into the camera. Disappointment is yet to come.

This is a school, and from down a corridor come the lively, engaged voices of children. On the walls are pictures they have painted of monarch butterflies and a large paper mural of a dragon. On my way out, I pass the hand-hammered aluminum door panels designed by Otto Wester in 1938. They depict the life of the farm, with animals, sowing, and scything; also garment workers; and, at the bottom of one panel, a huddle of cold-looking people waiting for coats. Near the doors is a stocky, limestone sculpture of a woman at a sewing machine: "Lenore Thomas. *Garment Worker*. Limestone. 1936."

I leave the school building and cross the playground. Like the school playgrounds of my childhood, this one is a big expanse of trampled grass, spreading trees, and no plastic play equipment. Across School Lane are the playing fields. At their edge, the wind moves through a large stand of bamboo, an invasive newcomer that is not symbolic, I hope. A forsythia hedge is in full bloom, and the sun is hot on my shoulders. School Street is very quiet save for birdsong and occasional traffic on Rochdale Avenue. A deer fence around a garden reminds me of the closeness of the woods. I keep walking, turning the corner onto Pine Drive.

The streets of Roosevelt curve in horseshoe shapes, allowing for common areas of grass and trees, some of which, including pink saucer magnolias, are coming into bloom. Just as magnolias and cherries and crabapples have joined the native pines and hollies, residents have changed the old houses. Conversion often involves a peaked roof, which surely is more practical in a climate that brings snow and ice. Many have been re-sided with brick or stone or clapboards. Redwood is a popular choice. It suits the low style of the houses but gives them an oddly California look. In a few cases, additions are in keeping with the original architecture; in others they are simply a jumble of the various elements of the modern "show" house. In one case, one-half of the old double house is original, whereas the other half is a stone and wood suburban dream of gables and Palladian windows.

The yards surrounding many of the old houses, the ones no one has changed, show a pleasant degree of dereliction—old garden furniture, forgotten flowerpots, the detritus of children—unlike the groomed gardenscape around the newly tarted-up ones. It seems these must be the people who posted the article about getting children away from technology into the natural world. Passing one house, I hear the sounds of clarinet practice. In driveways, there's a marked absence of SUVs. I hear wind chimes and neighbors calling. Properties flow into each other without fences, as their planners intended. There are no sidewalks, but in some places dirt paths, in others, rough stones. I stand under a weeping cherry, looking at a yellow house to which a screened porch has been added. A green plaque on the wall facing me reads: "What a wonderful world this could be. Let's end violence."

I sit on a bench inscribed "Jersey Homesteads Park" at the end of one of Roosevelt's curving streets. The town was planned with common spaces like this one and planted with trees now waiting to flower. Later, I drive around, down Farm Lane, which ends appropriately enough in open fields with a vista of distant woods. Here are the pleasant, tawny shingled buildings of the HUD-financed Roosevelt Senior Housing Cooperative, also known as Solar Village. Appealingly set on irregular ground, they have something of the idealized farm about them, a memory of cooperative farm days. Past them, in the woods, are several geodesic domes, left from a time when the factory in town produced them. They blend into the trees, reminding one of a later idealism and also of hobbit houses in Tolkien's threatened utopia.

On the edge of town, the "modern" factory building remains, although now it houses a small packaging company, a gallery, and artists' studios. If you go out Eleanor Drive, named for Eleanor Roosevelt, you reach the cemetery on its quiet hillside. If you live long enough in Roosevelt, you can be buried there.

It's not communism. It's not socialism. It is the new way—the cooperative way.
〜⋊ BENJAMIN BROWN ⋉〜
as quoted in the Saturday Evening Post, *February 5, 1938*

ugwelltown, Tugwellville, the Four Million Dollar Village—
these were some of the names bestowed by the newspapers
of the day on the New Deal town rising on 1,275 acres of
farmland nine miles southeast of Hightstown, New Jersey,
in a place once called Paradise Corners. Rexford Guy Tugwell was the head
of the New Deal Resettlement Administration and thus eventually had responsibility for the project. But Jersey Homesteads, later Roosevelt, really
begins as the dream of another man.

Benjamin Brown was a Jew born near Odessa in Ukraine. Emigrat-
ing to America at sixteen in 1901, Brown, like a number of Jewish immigrants, traveled his new country as a peddler. He settled in the West and
became a farmer, eventually heading a cooperative farming community in
Clarion, Utah. In the 1920s Brown organized a poultry cooperative in Salt
Lake City. Brown's Western States Cooperative supplied the East Coast;
he ran it from an office in New York, and it made him a rich man. In 1927
he went to Palestine on a mission with a representative of Brigham Young
University. In 1928 he was invited back to his homeland by the Soviets as
part of another mission to help organize the federal farm marketing system
for the Jewish Biro-Bidjan settlement, to be established in a section of Siberia near the Chinese boarder. The few settlers who came had to cope with
malarial swamps and harsh winters as part of Stalin's plan to resettle Soviet
Jews away from the center of the country, out of sight, under the guise of

establishing a "Jewish homeland" in the USSR. Another farm expert and mission member was Dr. M. L. Wilson, who was to become chief of the Division of Subsistence Homesteads under Rexford Tugwell and the New Deal.

The idea of a mixed agricultural industrial cooperative community for Jews had always been close to Brown's heart. By the 1930s, he himself lived on a 300-acre farm at Etra, near Hightstown, New Jersey. Monmouth County had a considerable population of Jewish farmers. Nearby Perrineville had had a Jewish congregation since 1910 and had built a synagogue in 1924. In the 1920s and 1930s, Perrineville was also a Jewish summer resort with cottages for rent around Perrineville Lake. Farmingdale and Howell were centers of Jewish poultry farming.[2]

Legend has it that in 1933, when Brown read in the newspaper about Congress's enactment of the subsistence-homestead program, he leapt from his chair and told his wife he was going to Washington to propose that his dream be realized on New Jersey land.

The Division of Subsistence Homesteads was intended "to decentralize industry from congested cities and enable workers to improve their standards of living through subsistence agriculture."[3] This portrayal was in line with Brown's dream as he explained it:

> The purpose of the project is to demonstrate the feasibility of permanently combining subsistence farming with a highly seasonal industry, which readily lends itself to decentralization to make self-sustaining 200 skilled workers and their families who are now partially or totally unemployed and for whom the prospects of future reemployment are very limited because of recent technological improvements in the industry and to demonstrate the practicability of community-owned agricultural and industrial production and marketing enterprises. The project will also serve to demonstrate the extent to which the Jewish people can succeed in farming when combined with industry. . . . Each individual homestead will provide some of the vegetables needed for family use; the community dairy, poultry plant and truck gardens will provide the remainder of the necessary supply. . . . Distribution of

the community-produced agricultural products will be for sale to the homesteaders through the community store.[4]

The idea of Jews as farmers in the New World was, of course, not a novel one. The Am Olam movement of the late nineteenth century had been a movement to get Jews back to the land, and America was the "Golden Medina," the golden country. The South Jersey settlement of Alliance had been financed by the Alliance Israelite Universelle in 1882, and later Woodbine, in 1891, by the Baron de Hirsch Fund. The idea behind Am Olam was similar to the idea behind subsistence homesteads—to get Jewish workers out of crowded soul-destroying cities and back in contact with the land. The Jews of the Bible had, after all, been farmers. It would also show that Jews were not a solely urban people and change the old Shylock stereotype of Jews as parasites on urban society. The mixed agricultural/industrial model had been tried with sporadic success at Woodbine and also at the other South Jersey colonies of Alliance, Norma, Carmel, and Rosenhayn. Brown's vision for Jersey Homesteads, however, was a triple cooperative: farm, factory, and store. This configuration was different from that of other Jewish agricultural colonies, nor had any of the other settlements been federally funded. For Jersey Homesteads, however, this support turned out to be almost more of a curse than a blessing.

At the beginning, Benjamin Brown was in charge. He arranged to acquire local farmland, but he did not tell the farmers with whom he was negotiating what the land was for, aware no doubt of an early attempt by the Baron de Hirsch Fund to settle Jewish refugees near Hightstown. When word of its proposal got out, land prices skyrocketed and the plan had to be abandoned. Brown organized the Provisional Commission for Jewish Farm Settlements in the United States. He held meetings in New York and organized a board of sponsors composed of representatives of leading Jewish charitable societies and members of Jewish labor organizations, as well as famous individuals such as Albert Einstein and Rabbi Jonah M. Wise. The board applied to the Division of Subsistence Homesteads for financing in the amount of $500,000. M. L. Wilson, director of the division and a friend since the Biro-Bidjan experience, sympathized with Brown's ideals and eventually the money was advanced. The board of sponsors became the board of directors of the New Jersey Homesteads Corporation, and power was to be entirely in their hands. The funds were theirs to disburse. Brown bought the land near Hightstown. In January 1934, Max Blitzer was appointed project manager, and Samuel Finkler was put in charge of selecting suitable families for the project. By the fall of 1934, however, there was considerable dissension among the members of Brown's board. For various reasons, within a few months many of the board members resigned, leaving only Brown's friends, such as Albert Einstein. Brown now had full control but without the backing of any large New York group.

Meanwhile, Harold Ickes, Franklin D. Roosevelt's secretary of the interior, had come to believe that the Division of Subsistence Homesteads program should be centralized and under federal control. He was concerned that if policy decisions were being made by several local groups that didn't have direct financial responsibility for the projects, they would not make decisions designed to save the government money—especially if there was no way to keep track of how funds were being spent at the local level.[5] On May 12, 1934, control over all subsistence-homestead projects was placed in the hands of the federal government. Brown's board of directors became once again a board of sponsors. Now officials at some remove from the local project, and with little knowledge of local problems, had to be informed of everything. As long as M. L. Wilson continued as head of the Division of Subsistence Homesteads, Brown had an ally. However, in June 1934 Wilson resigned to become assistant secretary of agriculture and was succeeded by Charles E. Pynchon. Pynchon granted the project an additional $327,000. It is at this point that the famous standoff between Benjamin Brown and David Dubinsky, labor leader and powerful head of the ILGWU, began.

Because the federal government needed assurances that homesteaders would be able to find work in the community once it was built, Brown planned to find a private manufacturer who would set up a garment shop at Jersey Homesteads and employ the homesteaders until they could get their own cooperative factory under way. Several large clothing manufacturers had expressed interest when Dubinsky stepped in and refused to agree to the removal of a private manufacturer from New York City to Jersey Home-steads. Construction, which had only just begun, stopped. The government would not allow construction to continue despite Brown's assurances that the disagreement with Dubinsky would be settled. Dubinsky was firm:

> They came to us and wanted us to allow a jobber to open a shop in Hightstown. They told us that we had to do this because the jobber is not out for the profits . . . but philanthropy. He wants to help real-ize the project of a Jewish cooperative colony. But even if we were ready to believe in the philanthropy of this or the other cloak jobber, I would have a very had task to make the other cloak jobbers believe it. They know from their own experience that one makes a profit from a clothes shop. And they also know that in a shop in Hightstown where they get a finished modern factory and where the expenses in gen-eral are smaller, they will be able to produce cloaks cheaper than New York and they will therefore have objections, that the Union itself has broken the agreement of "limitation of contractors." And when we come to this, it is not a question of the future of a few hundred cloak-makers, but of many thousands.[6]

Desperate, the sponsors sent their star, Professor Albert Einstein, to plead with Dubinsky. "Doctor Einstein is the smartest man in the world and his visit was a great honor," Dubinsky wrote, "but what does he know about coats and suits?"[7]

Meanwhile, the planned cooperative community of Jersey Homesteads had garnered 800 applications for the 200 available places. Dubinsky, who had been in favor of the project when the factory was proposed as a co-operative, had, along with other labor leaders, made it possible to reach thousands of potential settlers through union publications. Yiddish news-papers also carried advertisements. "However, not all participants came to the project through these formal methods. Louis Cohen, the first manager of the farm, arrived at Jersey Homesteads with $4.50 in his pocket after the theater troupe that had brought him to the United States went bankrupt and he took a train as far as he could go; in his case to nearby Hightstown."[8] He had been an assistant prosecuting attorney in Leningrad before the communists decided to send him to Palestine instead of Siberia. At Jersey Homesteads, he became an efficient farm manager.[9]

Cohen's route was unusual. The qualifications for settlers were strict. Of the two hundred families, 85 percent of the household heads had to be skilled garment workers in good standing with the ILGWU. The rest would be "farmers to work on the cooperative farm, carpenters, store clerks and administrative staff to provide necessary support services."[10] To be approved, each settler had to pass a health exam and show evidence of a solid, well-organized home life as well as an understanding of and willingness to take part in the cooperative movement. There was one other very important requirement. Each household had to contribute $500 toward startup costs for the factory. To come up with $500, some settlers cashed in life insurance policies and World War I soldier's benefits. Others had some savings or were able to borrow from family and friends. As Yetta Ostrow, a child of one settler family told Edwin Rosskam, $500 was "a fortune of money."[11] Apparently the desire for a better life, away from the crowded tenements of New York, was incentive enough for her family to find that "fortune of money" somehow.

As settlers were selected, they attended project meetings and cooperative management classes and began to form a group identity. They already had a lot in common: cultural, economic, and social backgrounds as well as their longtime union membership.[12] In the film *Roosevelt, New Jersey: Visions of Utopia*,[13] they are seen, in grainy black and white, picnicking together in the spring of 1936 in the empty fields that will become their town. The problems they would face from the fall of 1934 until the first of them were finally able to move into houses at Jersey Homesteads on July 10, 1936, only served to strengthen this bond. Also, they did not see themselves as recipients of government aid but rather as participants in a unique economic and social experiment. They felt that they had paid their $500 in good faith to the government as a guarantee of a job and that the government should do its part by finishing the town's construction. At every halt in the building of the town, its future residents rallied for their dream.

In April 1935, the Resettlement Administration was established and took over the projects of the Division of Subsistence Homesteads. Rexford G. Tugwell was appointed its director. Brown was now excluded from the administration of the project.

By August, construction had begun on a slab factory at Jersey Homesteads. The concrete slabs it would manufacture were intended for the building of prefabricated houses; entire walls of each house, including door and window frames, would be cast in one piece in huge steel forms. Once again, however, construction ceased because of the continuing debate with Dubinsky and the resulting negative publicity. The Resettlement Administration, on reviewing the Jersey Homesteads project, fired the project manager Max Blitzer as well as Samuel Finkler, the man in charge of settler selection, both of whom were Brown appointees. Construction then resumed, with more trouble to come.

The first concrete slab houses collapsed, but luckily before anyone moved in. An attempt was made to manufacture cinder blocks using the expensive factory buildings and equipment intended to manufacture the slabs, but soon it became evident that cinder blocks could be bought more cheaply than the project could make them.

As the price tag crept from the original estimate of $500,000 into the millions, the various troubles of Jersey Homesteads had become big news. There was much grumbling about taxpayers' money being sunk into a New Jersey mud hole. "Tugwell Hands out $1,800,000 for N.J. Commune" screamed headlines in the *Philadelphia Inquirer*.

> The American taxpayer is putting up $1,800,000 to erect a model of a Russian Soviet Commune halfway between New York and Philadelphia. Dr. Rexford Guy Tugwell, President Roosevelt's favorite Brain Truster, is the power behind this scheme which look today like little more than a mud hole. . . . But by the fall, the muddy streets of "Paradise Corners," as Jersey Homesteads near Hightstown used to be called . . . will be paved. And 200 carefully selected families headed by a Russian-born little Stalin, will be running their cooperative full

blast not 50 miles from the birthplace of Democracy. Flat roofed, one story houses, looking for all the world like pictures from an architects drawing of the modernistic homes in the U.S.S.R.

The writer goes on to quote Brown as saying that "one industrial-farm co-operative will do more than all the talk in the world to convince the American people that this is the type of thing that is coming to this country." She also points out that Boris Drasin, president of the Workers' Aim Co-operative, was also born in Russia. "He was the head of several of the revolutionary-sponsored farm cooperatives in old Russia in 1906 and 1907. . . . All the American people go right on paying their taxes, and then stand by and see $1,800,000 of these hard-earned taxes finance a Red Flag Experiment within the shadow of the Stars and Stripes." [14]

In fact, there was so much negative publicity that, according to an article in the *Asbury Park Press*, "armed guards patrol the grounds with strict orders to allow no one near the little community . . . the uncompleted factory, which cost $200,000 is surrounded by foundations for 200 small homes." [15] In fact, the engineering problems of the slab construction plan seem to have been well enough covered up that Edmund De Long, the reporter for the *Sun*, informed his readers that the problem was that the patents on the process belonged to one Simon Lake, engineer and submarine builder. According to De Long, Lake had offered Tugwell and his associates the use of the patents, but by then someone had purchased 100,000 concrete blocks at huge additional cost to the taxpayers. [16]

In December 1935, Alfred Kastner was appointed principal architect. He hired the young Louis I. Kahn as his assistant. Kahn was head of the drafting room on the project, and his design for the town was heavily influenced by the Bauhaus style and also the tightening federal budget. "The materials are generally simple but with elegant details: hardwood parquetry floors and plenty of windows, light, and closet space." [17] They were said to be air conditioned, but those who remember them say they were not. The houses were plain and boxlike, with flat roofs and long windows. As important as the architecture was, the siting of the houses and the layout of the town were possibly even more so.

The planners of Jersey Homesteads were influenced by another utopian thinker, the Englishman Ebenezer Howard (1850–1928), who is usually credited with beginning the Garden City movement, an attempt to counteract the grim, crowded cities spawned by England's industrial revolution. Howard was also much influenced by American Edward Bellamy's utopian novel *Looking Backward* as well as by the economic theories of Henry George.[18] These were supplemented by a number of years Howard spent in Chicago during his youth. The American idea of neighborhoods appears often in his work. In his outline for Letchworth, his first Garden City, Howard recommended "that a ring of agricultural land, five times the area of the center, should lie around it."[19] The houses at Letchworth were also turned on their lots to have the sunniest prospect rather than aligned with the streets, and the streets themselves were not planned in a rigid grid system. If the houses at Jersey Homesteads were linear and stark, their settings were not. Each house sat on approximately one acre of ground on roads that curved, which integrated the structures with communal areas, green spaces of trees and benches, and the surrounding woods. The community might not have had the mansarded coziness of the Letchworth cottages designed by Parker and Unwin, but it made use of similar planning. Almost every housing development today employs the cul-de-sac and the curving street, but in 1935 the ideas were new.

Of course, when the first eight houses were completed and the first seven families moved in on July 10, 1936, in the middle of a steamy thunderstorm, what was there was mud. "That mud is an important part of everyone's remembering. It is always mentioned. And every year it gets deeper."[20] Jersey Homesteads was, at that point, a construction site. There were some paved roads but no sidewalks. Clare Nadler Sacharoff, arriving from the Bronx at age ten, thought it was the ugliest place she had ever seen. It was desolate. She missed the lights and bustle of the city.[21] For others it might have been as Edwin Rosskam suggests:

The immigrant tailors had very different expectations. They were looking forward to their own dream of rural life: cozy cottages, perhaps with scrolled woodwork, gingerbread around gabled roofs, and with primroses climbing up clapboard walls, flanked by green shutters that could be closed and locked.

When the families arrived to take possession, they were rendered acutely uncomfortable by the concrete boxes with their floor-to-ceiling windows and their flat roofs pressing down on rooms that seemed to them unduly cramped compared to their vision of Utopia.[22]

As one settler remembered it: "There were no trees, there was no lawn, the houses really looked like chicken coops, you couldn't tell one from another."[23] Certainly the Kastner/Kahn houses would have had no echoes of any European rural cottages the Jersey Homesteads settlers might have remembered, but they did provide space and light and privacy to whole families that had been living in one or two rooms. Clare Nadler no longer had to share a bedroom with her brother. Helen Barth remembers visiting the Gropius house in Lincoln, Massachusetts, years later and thinking, "I was stepping into my house."[24]

Another settler remembered the strangeness of the silent countryside and its effect on a child:

I don't know whether you can imagine the impact of open space on people who had been born then in the crowded parts of the city. I was acutely uncomfortable in the country. I might have been put on the moon in terms of its visual and feeling impact. I was used to the security of all those packed bodies around me. And so much space, all of a sudden, is just as frightening as sleeping in a room by yourself when you never have. The quiet, the lack of light, the sense that there is nobody packed around you.[25]

❄ ❄ ❄

In many utopian novels, such as Bellamy's *Looking Backward* and William Morris's *The News from Nowhere*, utopia is discovered in a dream or after a period of unconsciousness, when the dreamer awakes in a new world. For the garment workers, Jersey Homesteads must have seemed a lot like that.

If the homesteaders already felt themselves to be a cohesive group, the long delays and tangles of government red tape had only increased that feeling. "Every request the homesteaders made which was not immediately granted became the subject of a further test struggle by people who saw themselves as fighting for an ideal in the face of unsympathetic bureaucrats." The government had promised them houses and jobs by the summer of 1935. As one applicant's daughter wrote of her parents: "they sold their furniture and moved to a furnished room where they are still living. They also borrowed money on insurance policies and have had the $500 ready in the bank since spring. My father almost sold his business, but the children very luckily interfered." [26]

It was clear to a worried Benjamin Brown that the cooperative factory, to which Dubinsky had finally agreed, had to get under way as soon as possible. Expecting a minimum of one hundred houses to be built, he planned to open the cooperative clothing factory, the Workers' Aim Cooperative, in the summer of 1936. The factory building itself had been finished in May of that year. Samples of the product line were made and shown in New York, and orders were taken. But when the time came for operations to begin, the government had completed only 8 houses; the remaining 102 houses would not be completed until January 1937. Tents were considered as a solution but rejected by the government because it feared their use would cause more criticism of the Resettlement Administration for failing to complete construction on time. [27] Housing had to be found locally for a sufficient number of workers to start up the factory operation.

The factory managed to open for business on August 2, 1936, with a ceremony that included a "workers hymn" penned by Mrs. Benjamin Brown:

> Midst field and stream
> Our Jersey homes we found.
> To the hum of the sewing machine
> And the tractor's sound

We sing, we work, hand in hand
And to workers everywhere
A welcome hand extend.
Here we live, we hoe, we sow,
We build, we plant,
Come brothers, celebrate,
Everybody co-operate.[28]

It must have been a heady moment.

The Jersey Homesteads Agricultural Association was organized that same summer of 1936. The farm itself was also to have three divisions: a general farm, a poultry unit, and a dairy unit. The hope was that about twenty-five heads of household would work on the farm. The farm could also employ other workers during slow times at the garment factory. The general farm started up in the fall of 1936, the poultry unit started in the spring of 1937, and the dairy unit later that year. It soon became evident, however, that the farmers and the garment workers did not see eye to eye. The farmers wanted to run a successful operation that made an annual profit (which in fact it did, with tomatoes and potatoes in the 1936 season), whereas the homesteaders simply wanted to be able to buy produce and dairy products at a special price. Nor did the garment workers want to work in the fields for less money than the factory normally paid even during slack times when the factory had no work for them. As a result, the farm had to depend largely on transient labor from outside the community.

The farm was also involved in the attempt to persuade settlers to plant "kitchen gardens" to supplement their household food budgets. Experts came out to give lectures on how to garden, what to plant, and how to can food for the winter. In the first season, the farm cooperative plowed and sowed settlers' gardens for ten dollars apiece, but settlers complained that the service was too expensive and that gardens tilled and planted this way could have no trees or shrubs because they interfered with the tractor's progress. After the first season, the farm cooperative offered only tilling and charged less than two dollars, but some homesteaders still felt the price was too high. Shouldn't the farm cooperative be working for them? The plan for subsistence gardening was never a huge success. Many settlers had vegetable gardens, but some raised only flowers and some nothing at all. "The gardening activities of the homesteaders were important mostly as a symbol of the transition from urban to suburban living, as one moment in the migration 'up' as well as out." [29] The desire for the impractical beauty of flowers and shrubs, or a mixed garden, rather than merely practical rows of vegetables is an example of how the settlers saw their new world: not just bread but also roses.

By January 1937 most of the other 192 houses had been built. As each group of houses was completed, they were assigned by lottery, and one settler remembered his father telling him that Einstein was holding the hat. This, according to George Weller, was the shape of Jersey Homesteads in the spring of that year:

> The Jersey settlers are Jews by birth and American citizens by naturalization. Their political views are Zionist and anti-capitalist, pro-Marx and pro-Roosevelt. Religiously they are about equally divided between orthodox and progressive dogmas. They do their own manufacturing in a bright new factory, especially built and leased to them on mortgage by the United States government. They raise vegetables on land owned by the government and they live in houses built and leased to them on mortgage by the government. For the purchase of goods that come from outside the colony they run their own profit-sharing store. . . . Jersey Homesteads is the only community in America where three kinds of co-operatives can be observed trotting in harness.

Weller went on to describe the landscape of this "promised land" as it existed in 1937:

> On both sides of the roads, set well back to allow for future lawns, were rows of highly modernized one story houses and a few two stories, separated from each other by some fifty yards of broken ground. Beyond the houses lay uninhabited country in every direction, wide

189

fields with cornstalks piled high, slender gray trees and thickets, marsh
and brook and hill.[30]

Weller also mentions the "sticky yellow mud."

Jersey Homesteads' problems did not end with the building of more
houses or the resolution of the struggle with David Dubinsky. There was
more to come. In its first year, the factory failed. Some of the failure could
certainly be attributed to the lack of housing, which had created problems
with an adequate work force. In any case, by December the $60,000 capital
contributed by the first 120 settlers was gone, and the Resettlement Administration had to loan Brown $50,000 to keep the factory going. The second
factory season began in January 1937. Again, it was a failure, with Brown
claiming that the inability to fill all orders in the first year had affected the
market for the factory's products.[31] By Easter, operating funds had again
run out. When the Resettlement Administration refused to grant any more
aid, Brown came up with $50,000 (probably his own money) to organize
"a managerial corporation called Tripod [for the three legs of the Jersey
Homesteads cooperative] to control the operations of the factory and to
develop consumer cooperative retail outlets." [32]

Tripod coats and suits were carried around the country by seven trucks
making scheduled stops at farmers' organizations and holding sales that
lasted several days. Each truck held a complete line of coats, along with
mirrors for the customers' use. This process did not always go smoothly.
"For example, when the Farm Bureau Co-operative of Somerset County,
Pennsylvania, advertised a sale of 200 coats made at the Hightstown Factory, infuriated merchants of the town of Somerset not only protested but
called on their chief of police to enforce an ordinance prohibiting transient
retail business and assessing a $100 fine for each infraction." [33]

By May 1938, the factory was once again out of funds. Brown got a final
loan of $150,000 from the Farm Security Administration. The government
tried to prevent reckless spending by limiting the amount of funds "that
could be invested in finished or unfinished goods." It also planned to accept
new applicants to become members of the community to fill the remaining
ninety-six empty houses. When the $150,000 was gone in less than a year,

the Farm Security Administration refused to provide any more money. In September 1938 it began renting the remaining empty houses to "desirable applicants," Jewish or not. Word of the failures of the clothing factory had spread to New York, and only twenty-two families headed by garment workers moved to Jersey Homesteads between June 1938 and the time that the clothing factory ceased operations in April 1939. The prospect of a non-Jewish population was not well received; the settlers who had bought into the cooperative felt that such outsiders would destroy it.

It also soon became clear that the Agricultural Association's farm could not be run simply for the feeding of so small a community, so the decision was made to operate the cooperative as a commercial enterprise.[34] The poultry section was the most successful part of the farm cooperative, at one point even showing a profit.[35] The dairy section was problematic from the beginning. The homesteaders wanted to buy a nearby private dairy, and they tried to get a government loan for the purpose, but the government refused, suggesting that the community build its own dairy. When bids for construction of the dairy were solicited, the cost was found to be prohibitive because local contractors were aware that federal funds were available. The homesteaders petitioned the government again, and again accused the bureaucrats of trying to sabotage the project.[36] The government finally agreed to the loan, but in about a year the dairy was forced to cease operations with a $15,000 loss. The dairyman in charge had originally been a pharmacist who took a short course at Rutgers and did not much like getting up at four in the morning to milk cows.[37] The dairy farm was then leased to a dairy cooperative.

Edwin Rosskam recounts a story told him by Bernarda Shahn, widow of the artist Ben Shahn, in which a professional dairyman friend of Ben Shahn's went to take a look at the failing dairy operation. He found, he claimed, that the cows were standing knee deep in manure because the manure conveyor belt was stuck in a mountain of manure. When he asked why they didn't carry the manure away once a week, he was told that the cart in which it was carried away had disappeared. When he had them get shovels and shovel the manure away, the cart was found under the manure pile.[38] Although this story may well be apocryphal, it suggests a basic truth. The homesteaders at Jersey Homesteads were not farmers, nor were most of them interested in becoming farmers. Some might grow vegetables for their families, but farm work was alien to them. Again, the Resettlement Project leader had hoped that twenty-five household heads would be employed in the agricultural cooperative; at its peak, the agricultural cooperative could boast only thirteen. After all, "factory workers were accustomed to indoor work and high rates of pay, and were not willing to supplement their earnings, even at a time when their services were bringing in nothing so far as industry was concerned, by accepting lower rates of pay for farm work." [39]

The third segment of the Homesteads cooperative was to be the retail stores, of which there were three. The first, intended to sell clothing manufactured at the factory to the general public, was located in the Britten farmhouse at the edge of the community. The store was tied to the factory, so once that failed, the store could not survive.

The second was a cooperative grocery store and meat market intended to serve the two hundred families of Jersey Homesteads. Each family joined by paying a small fee. Since the store had no local competition, it was more successful than the factory, although at times dissatisfied homesteaders did their shopping in a nearby town. In such a small community, it was difficult to dismiss anyone for inefficiency: when one store clerk who had been fired picketed his former employer, no shopper could look him in the eye and pass on into the store. As a result, all business at the store stopped, and he had to be rehired. In the *Asbury Park Press*, reporters doing a story on the town described the storekeeper as not quite getting "the 'hang' of the gasoline pump. The two Press reporters had to stand guard at the pump to tell him when to stop the machine." [40] Still, the homogeneity of the community worked to the store's advantage. It could purchase "stock easily and cheaply because of a regular demand for certain standard supplies, mostly kosher." [41]

The third retail establishment was that 1930s staple, the tearoom. As early residents describe it, the place was more of an ice cream parlor and over-the-counter drugstore located on the ground floor of one of the houses at the corner of Homestead Lane and Rochdale Road. It also provided refreshments for the many curious visitors to the "governmentally financed social experiment," [42] that is, those who had come to see their taxes at work. The tearoom, like the grocery store, long outlived the factory and the farm.

On May 20, 1938, a strange thing happened: Benjamin Brown disappeared from his Etra farm. Some thought he had gone to Washington, D.C., to confront the authorities or to New York to get more financing. Then sightings were reported in places like Red Bank, New Jersey, and a group of settlers went looking for him. Some two weeks later, a second expedition supposedly found Brown wandering around near either the Holland or the Lincoln Tunnel. He was confused and ill. He came home, where he died of cancer in February 1939, his end almost coinciding with the end of his long-dreamed-of colony.[43]

By 1940, the cooperative dream of Jersey Homesteads was over. Farm and factory, despite a good deal of government aid, had failed. On July 2, 1940, at a public sale, the government bought all the land and most of the equipment of the farm cooperative. The next day, it leased the general farm in equal parts to the five farmers who had originally operated it; the poultry unit was leased in equal parts to the three farmers who had operated that. The dairy had already been leased to an outside cooperative.

There was plenty of blame to go round. Some blamed Dubinsky for refusing to allow an outside manufacturer to operate the factory. Although he eventually agreed to the cooperative, the delay had been so great that the factory was unable to develop relationships with buyers and customers. "This labor person wielded so much power that I believe it bordered on ruthlessness. I also believe that these people [Jersey Homesteads workers and union members] had a sense of loyalty to him and desired to maintain healthy relations. This course of action led to their demise. . . . All the evidence points to his not wanting the factory to succeed. He did throw them into a pool of sharks."[44]

Some blamed Benjamin Brown. Apparently Sears Roebuck had offered, through the Department of Labor, to contract to buy the factory's output. At the meeting to discuss the proposal, Brown threatened to leave the colony if the offer were accepted. The workers idolized Brown as a messiah and were unwilling to go against him.[45]

Then there was the government-delayed construction. Houses were not finished when the factory opened, which created a labor shortage so that the factory couldn't fill its first-year orders. Certainly the project had suffered from classic bureaucratic snafus. The slab construction plan was the most obvious, but not the only, example. For a time, the government had teetered between plans for a garment factory and plans for a cannery that would can the settlers' produce. During construction, "supplies were bought through the system of asking for bids and this frequently took many weeks. When . . . workmen needed materials, it often developed that someone—a higher up or a clerk—had forgotten to ask for bids. Another delay was caused by the WPA rule of employing a man only 130 hours per month. About the time a batch of lumber arrived, all the carpenters had finished their allotted hours and gone on vacation."[46] The disconnect between Washington, D.C., and the actual on-site events is typified by the interior decorator sent from Washington just before the first settlers were to occupy the first eight houses. Sent with a load of furniture, she was to decorate a model home. However, the home was needed for a family, so as soon as the decorator hung the last curtain and left, the model was dismantled and everything put in storage.

Some workers blamed themselves for their own failure to cooperate and believed they had given only lip service to the idea of a cooperative.

A homogeneous group of people, all Jews and all labor union men— it sounds good doesn't it? . . . But the fact is they hated each other. . . . The largest group was the Workman's Circle—a workers' socialist group that contained people like the old Russian revolutionaries— Bundists, who ranged from left-wing socialists to Communists. . . . Then we had the Farband. They were Socialist Zionists . . . and the third group was the IWO. They were Communists who hated everybody else.[47]

You know when there is two hundred bosses, you know what happens. And that's exactly what happened here. There were no Indians. . . . And everybody wanted to put in his two-cents worth. This wants it this way, this wants it that way. And we kept on going that way all the time.[48]

Then there were the lingering economic effects of the Depression, to which an industry like the garment trade was particularly vulnerable.

Hard times came to Jersey Homesteads; the utopian promise of a life in balance with work and nature was apparently dead. It seemed as though the epithets of the press—Hightstown Fiasco, Boondoggle Manor—were more accurate than the names the early settlers used to express their hopes: Promised Land, the Land of Milk and Honey, or even the Golden Medina. The world was spiraling toward war, and 120 families now had to find a way to make things work or leave. Few took the latter option; only three families left at once. The others were "Clinging to Paradise Corners," as a reporter from the *Philadelphia Inquirer* titled his article in *Everybody's Weekly* for August 18, 1940: "A process of readjustment has been going on among them [the settlers] ever since the United States Government closed its clothing factory there last year, because the factory product could not be marketed successfully, withdrew from active participation in the colony, and took the passive role of landlord."

"Readjustment" was a mild word for the loss of a living—most heads of household were garment workers, and now there was no garment factory. Some seasonal labor was still available on the farm, but wages were much lower and the amount of work was erratic; some weeks there was none. And of course each family's expenses remained constant—$14 to $17 rent a month, plus gas, electricity, and heating oil. "They were getting more for their money than they would have in the city, but their earning capacity had almost disappeared, and it looked like the experiment would have to be abandoned."[49]

The very characteristics that may have contributed to the failure of the original plan were those that saved Jersey Homesteads in the end. The settlers were independent and stubborn, and their long battle with the federal government in its hydra-headed forms had given them a solidarity. Handpicked and with an investment of $500 in their dream, they were not about to give up. One woman said she would "sooner live in the Homesteads than double the family income by moving back to New York."[50] Heads of households went far afield to find jobs: to New York, Philadelphia, Perth Amboy, Burlington, and New Brunswick. Helen Barth, who came to as a small child in the second group of families, remembers that her father had to commute two hours to Philadelphia to work in a garment factory there, before eventually finding a job in Freehold. Since he neither drove nor had a car, he carpooled with others who paid a driver.[51] A few of the settlers were employed temporarily as laborers by the Farm Security Administration.[52] People did what they had to do to stay. One small story explains why. Israel Weisman describes his little daughter's first morning at Jersey Homesteads:

"Mama, come here! Come a light! Come a light!" We run in and she's running after the sun. "I got this sun for myself." And she was running, catching the sun. . . . So this alone could give you the idea of . . . the difference between New York at 2nd Avenue and 21st Street, or wherever anyone lived in the downtown area, and you find here open space.[53]

When, in May 1940, the Jersey Homesteads factory was leased to a New York manufacturer, there was immediate rejoicing at the prospect of jobs returning. The rejoicing, however, was premature. Kartiganer and Company was a millinery manufacturer. Millinery required a kind of training that the Homesteads garment workers didn't have. Also, when Kartiganer started operations there were not very many jobs, and most paid beginner's wages. Mayor Phillip Goldstein was optimistic, maintaining that "as our people learn the trade and the factory expands, more and more of us will get jobs. . . . The minimum wage for beginners is forty cents an hour; this factory pays fifty, which means a weekly wage of about $22, enough to live comfortably here."[54]

"Back to capitalism," chortled *Time* magazine on April 22, 1940:

As ill starred a social project as ever drew howls from anti–New Deal columnists is Jersey Homesteads, a settlement of 200 flat-roofed, garage-like homes halfway between New York and Philadelphia and hard by the Revolutionary battlefield of Monmouth. . . . Last week, Jersey Homestead's dead cooperative was buried. Rented for five years was Jersey Homestead's factory. The renter: Manhattan's Karti-

ganer and Co. . . . . Hopeful was many a member of Jersey Homestead's 125 remaining families that private enterprise might provide
jobs where their cooperatives had failed.[55]

Jersey Homesteads had become a borough and also a community. It had
a grade school where both English and Hebrew were taught and a community life that included music and discussion groups. As a cooperative, it
might have failed, but as a community it was remarkably successful. When
the government made the remaining houses available for rent, the majority
of "second-wave" settlers were Jewish working-class families attracted by
a Jewish community with low rents and proximity to New York. Although
there was friction at first with the original settlers who had paid their $500
"entry fee," the newcomers could be assimilated, and the community remained cohesive. Although some saw this change as the beginning of the
end of a utopian social experiment, the fact is that something essential about
Jersey Homesteads survived.

Homesteaders remember vividly that sense of community. They describe Jersey Homesteads as one big family where doors were always open
and neighbors could drop in on each other pretty much any time. If someone got married, the whole town was invited to the wedding. Children
romped in and out of each other's backyards, taking advantage of the way
the properties flowed into each other and of the surrounding woods. There
was the school, started in Jersey Homesteads' earliest days because Mill-
stone Township refused to take the Homesteads children (they were Jews
and possibly communists), and religious services held in the basement of
the Britten farmhouse, the unofficial cultural center of the village. Faced
with some hostility from gentile neighbors, members of the community depended on each other for support and social life. Many were freethinkers,
part of a European radical tradition, and much of the colony's social life
centered on meetings and discussions. There were the groups described by
Morris Chasen. Nearly everyone belonged to some club or other, often several. His wife, Augusta, who in 1937 became the first female fire chief in the
nation, described life in Jersey Homesteads. "You were never lonely. . . .
Everybody would drop in and everybody knew where to drop in. . . . The

social life was great; we would stay up all night and sing songs, and I learned so much Jewish that I didn't know before because they sang so many Jewish songs and they were so beautiful. It was just a great life." [56]

Clubs abounded: a dramatic club, a junior league, a sewing circle, a baseball team, and regular cultural evenings—"in fact the community was almost overorganized, with some meeting occurring almost every night. In 1939 there were only three adult members of the original homesteaders who did not belong to one or another of the community organizations." [57]

Children growing up in those early years made their own entertainment. They played the usual games like tag, monkey-in-the-middle, jacks for girls, but there were also the quiet pursuits of reading, drawing, and just plain talking. Few people had cars, although the Kastner/Kahn houses, built for the modern age, all had garages. Hitchhiking was the accepted mode of transport. There was a corner in town where you stood if you wanted a ride to Hightstown and another in Hightstown for the ride back. The driver would cram in as many people as possible.

The Homesteads school went through the eighth grade; after that the students were bused to Allentown High School and, by the 1950s, to Hightstown. As Clare Nadler Sacharoff remembers it, Allentown High was "not a good school." [58] The Homesteads school was small, and the whole town turned out for eighth grade graduation. At Allentown, the Homesteads kids kept pretty much to themselves. It was hard to make friends because the bus left at the end of the school day, so they couldn't stay for extracurricular events. Nor were their classmates, the children of local farmers, particularly receptive, calling the Roosevelt bus the "Jew bus." The Homesteads students were resented for their academic success, and as city kids they had little in common with farm kids, who left school for months during spring planting. At the time, New Jersey experienced plenty of racial hostility— the Ku Klux Klan was active in Hightstown.

Jersey Homesteads had its own amusements, however, including Sunny Heights Lodge, the nudist colony down the road. It had a pool, beach, and snack bar, besides its other attractions. Carloads of teenagers would drive over on the pretense of wanting to join. The joke was that the Roosevelt store sold the Sunny Heights denizens Saran wrap in chilly weather.

The planning of Jersey Homesteads included a community building, now the Roosevelt elementary school. It was what brought Roosevelt its most famous resident, the artist Ben Shahn. Shahn grew up in a Jewish socialist family in Lithuania (his father was exiled to Siberia for a time) and immigrated to the United States with his parents to escape the pogroms in his native land not long after Benjamin Brown did. He was to become a social activist and a leader in the group of artists known as the Social Realists.

In 1934, Shahn became interested in fresco when he assisted Diego Rivera with the painting of his now notorious mural at Rockefeller Center in New York City. The mural, *Man at the Crossroads,* was a sixty-three-foot-long portrait of workers at the symbolic crossroads of industry, science, socialism, and capitalism. Rivera, a lifelong socialist and communist, had included a portrait of Lenin in the mural, which had angered Rockefeller. When Rivera refused to remove the portrait, he was fired and the mural subsequently destroyed.

Jersey Homesteads' principal architect, Alfred Kastner, in 1936 invited Shahn to paint a mural in the community center—the building that is now the Roosevelt school. The mural has three panels. In the first, emigrants are shown leaving behind the dead of the pogroms. In the second they are arriving in America, wearing numbers and carrying lumpy bags and bundles of possessions. Albert Einstein heads the anonymous parade. They progress to a garment factory with rows of sewing machines; a crowd listens to a labor organizer; others study labor economics in a classroom. The last panel shows the planning of Jersey Homesteads, under a portrait of Franklin Delano Roosevelt, and a farm scene of workers in an orchard. Shahn worked on the mural from 1936 to 1938, and remained in town after the project was finished. Jersey Homesteads was cheap and near New York—a practical choice for an artist. Shahn's presence drew others, and suddenly Jersey Homesteads was not just a workers' town but also a place for artists. Shahn and his wife and collaborator, Bernarda Bryson, would eventually spend the rest of their lives there. Shahn, despite or because of his involvement in the town, was a controversial figure. As Rosskam recounts: "The trouble was, of course, that in a small place any convinced believer in the perfectibility of man had to become a pest. With his scale of sins against the spirit, he was equipped to measure and attack intolerance and meanness with the same furious energy nationally or in the town. Inevitably he antagonized more than he persuaded."[59]

Among the artists who followed were: the former chairman of Pratt Institute's fine arts department, Jacob Landau; painter Gregorio Prestopino with his wife, artist Liz Dauber; graphic artist David Stone Martin; wood engraver Stefan Martin; Edwin Rosskam and his wife, Louise, both photographers; and Sol Libsohn, also a photographer. Jersey Homesteads began to gain a name as a suburban bohemia.

The war years were a time of stasis for most of the country. Jersey Homesteads, like every other town, sent its young to war. When one of its own, singer and Broadway actress Tamara Drasin, who introduced the song "Smoke Gets in Your Eyes" in the musical *Roberta*, was killed in a plane crash in 1943 en route to entertain the troops, Jersey Homesteads memorialized her by naming a street Tamara Drive. (This was the same plane crash that badly injured singer Jane Froman, subject of the 1952 movie *With a Song in My Heart*.) During the war, tensions with the federal government returned. In 1943, the Federal Public Housing Authority offered to sell the settlers their houses for $2,900 each. The settlers, through their borough council, drew up a counterproposal to which they received no answer. In May 1945, after the death of President Roosevelt, Jersey Homesteads officially changed its name to Roosevelt. Then, in 1946, the government finally announced plans to divest itself of all the subsistence-homestead projects, including Jersey Homesteads. Residents had to buy their houses for $3,900 or leave. Once again, the settlers had to scramble, and once again, most did not want to leave.

Now that anyone could buy, the town began to change. Different kinds of people moved in, yet something essential about Roosevelt did not change. Although many of Roosevelt's children grew up and left the town, given greater opportunity by their parents' insistence on education, many also came back to raise their own families. A synagogue was built in 1956. The excellence of the small Roosevelt elementary school has drawn many families. Roosevelt is also fortunate in that its physical location, in the New

York–Philadelphia economic corridor, meant that jobs were available after the cooperative dream failed. Academics from Rutgers and Princeton as well as artists were drawn to its historic charm, and more workers discovered it as industrial areas along the New Jersey Turnpike and Route 287 expanded. Its residents may no longer be one big family, but it is a place were people still say hello. Everyone still picks up mail at the post office. People are still involved in the town's government. When a controversial issue comes up, they still crowd into town meeting at the borough hall. The borough hall is also the usual venue for the Roosevelt Arts Project. Founded in 1986, the RAP specialized in bringing artists from different disciplines—painters, writers, musicians—together in collaborative events. The town still feels manageable, and the old spirit is almost palpable.

Roosevelt is now a National Historic District, but, as Dr. Rodham Tullos tells me, it's not because of Louis Kahn's houses or Ben Shahn's mural. Roosevelt's distinction is its site plan. As Tullos, a retired engineer and pre-eminent mycologist, explains it, Roosevelt is the "first example of lower income housing built on a wetland that is ecologically sound." The streets are curvilinear because they run between streams. He agrees that the town also owes a lot to the Garden City movement: all the houses have random setbacks, and front doors "originally faced away from the street. Communication in the town was to be on foot," so houses should face the footpaths.[60]

Luckily for Roosevelt, the state's Assunpink Wildlife Management Area protects the town on the south, but that leaves a lot of farmland to tempt developers. After a couple of close calls that split the town between those who wanted to preserve its history and those, mostly newer, residents who wanted some tax relief, Tullos founded a nonprofit agency in 1999 to protect the greenbelt, and the Fund for Roosevelt was born. After years of tremendously hard work, he can say that all the town's farms are now listed as conserved farmland. Of this land, 93 percent will be farmed; the rest will be open land. And so something essential about utopian Roosevelt has been preserved—the love of those urban refugees for their dearly bought countryside.

Rova Farms
Preserving a Culture

In the summer of 1971, I took a bus from Asbury Park to Philadelphia. As the bus made its way down the coast, I fell asleep. I awoke in the Pinelands to see, rising, like a wayward dream, out of the acres of stunted pines, a gilded onion dome. A minute later we passed a sand lane whose sign clearly read Pushkin Road. Then the bus pulled up to a cluster of buildings at the edge of a lake. My memory, at this distance of time, is that they looked Russian, rustic, and wooden, like a set for *Boris Godunov*. I saw a food pavilion, a hall of some sort, and old people dressed in black walking arm in arm.

"Rova Farms," the driver called out. I don't remember whether anyone descended or boarded, just that we pulled away into the empty expanse of pines.

* * *

I return to Rova years later in winter. The church is still there, gold domed, its mosaic saints showing the flat halos and long, pale faces of icons, exotic and carefully maintained. The *Boris Godunov* buildings, however, are gone. What I think might be the abandoned food pavilion lists morosely at the edge of the lake. The lake itself, its far shore no longer wild but crowded with houses, looks more like a pond. A few disintegrating benches remain on the beach; a sign on the stretch of chain link fence prohibits boating and swimming where once there had been a dock and boats. It is Tuesday, and, as a spray-painted sign proclaims, a flea market is in raggle-taggle progress in the parking lot—trestle tables piled with grubby toys and CDs, and sway-backed racks full of clothes someone would have been glad to get rid of in the 1980s. I notice other hand-lettered signs:

BAR
Sat & Sun 12–11
Wed–Fri 6–11
Happy Hour 5–7
Package Goods

RESTAURANT
Russian and American Cuisine
Sat 12–8
Sun 12–7
Live Entertainment Sunday

PRO WRESTLING

A more businesslike sign announces Beth Zion Messianic Jewish Synagogue every Saturday morning at 10:45 in the Rova Farms Resort Auditorium.

The day is bitterly cold, and I am glad to go inside the Rova Farms Resort Auditorium, also the restaurant, which, happily, is open. This, the old social and banquet hall, is the only secular building still used by Rova. On the wall of the entryway are black-and-white photographs of Rova in the fifties: children on the beach, formal dances, even a Miss Rova wearing a sash and a long white dress. The hall itself is a cavernous space with a stage at one end, its backdrop a large photograph of the lake. In front of the stage, the lights on a leftover Christmas tree blink solemnly. Although the effect is more high school cafeteria than restaurant, a restaurant it is. The round tables have cloths and metal chairs. I order borscht and potato pancakes. When they arrive, they are hot and good. Most of my fellow diners are not young. They nod a friendly hello and return to speaking Russian. Those who are willing to talk to me say that Rova is not what it was. The young people have moved away. There is nothing for them here. I am taken outside by one of them and shown the derelict shingled buildings across Route 571. One was once the manager's office, one the Tolstoy Library, and the third a dormitory. There had been a Russian school for children. At night, there had been singing of old songs on the beach. I look

over toward the lake, where vendors are already taking down tables and packing the leavings into cardboard boxes. It hasn't been much of a flea market day.
Too cold.

Taking my leave, I cross the road and enter Pushkin Park, a triangle of land
between Route 571 and the Cassville–Freehold Road. At the entrance to the
park, a bronze bust of Pushkin rests on a plinth, his dates (1799–1837) incised
below. On the ground, at the base of the plinth, someone has left a spray of
pine branches with plastic ferns and poinsettias. Chickadees call as I make
my way through a tunnel of evergreens. Ahead of me rises a monument to
the persecution at Talerhoff, a World War I concentration camp near Graz in
Austria. When the Austro-Hungarian army invaded Galicia in 1914, a campaign
of terror began against supposed Russian sympathizers. Thousands were sent
to Talerhoff. Many Ukrainian villages have Talerhoff crosses to commemorate
those sent to the camp; this one was erected by Russian Americans in 1964.
Here the park opens out into a grassy space.

SUVs race by on the roads as I cross a sandy path and find the World War
II memorial. Almost Soviet in style, it is dedicated to members of ROOVA (the
Russian Consolidated Mutual Aid Society), sons of members of ROOVA, and
local sons of Jackson Township. At the far boundary of the park, I turn and
walk back. The dome of St. Vladimir's glows through the bare trees.

I drive the mile up Route 571 to St. Mary's Church and Cemetery. When I
get there, the church has an odd, squared off, and distinctly non-Russian look
because both cupolas are down on the ground and workmen are crawling all
over the roof. Rock blasts from a radio.

St. Mary's is painted white, much simpler than St. Vladimir's, but the cemetery is huge and planted with trees and shrubs. A small mausoleum chapel,
known as the Lienz Memorial, or Cossack, Chapel, is dedicated to the Cossacks massacred by the Soviets during the last days of World War II. Near
it are stone benches for sitting. I wander the grassy paths between rows of
headstones, reading the names and distant birthplaces in Russia and Ukraine.
Many have black-and-white photographs set in the stone, something I remember seeing in Italian cemeteries. Flowers, real and artificial, decorate the graves.
The cemetery's perimeter fades into sand and pines, reminding one of what it
took to create the familiar in an alien land.

I get back in the car and return to Thompson's Bridge Road. The section
of the road opposite the banquet hall was once called Pig Road because pigs

were styed there and fed on dining hall scraps. Just beyond the old manager's office, a pale green stucco motel building emerges, then a collection of cabins that look like trailers with slightly pitched roofs, two units apiece, painted in tropical colors: aqua, yellow, peach. They demand palms not pines. These still belong to Rova although they are rented out, mostly to employees of the nearby Six Flags/Great Adventure amusement park. Driving on, I come to Pushkin Road, still unpaved, cutting through the pines to connect Thompson's Bridge with the Cassville–Freehold Road. This road, I know, is the location of the A. S. Pushkin Memorial Home for Aged Russian People, still funded, still functioning, more, I'm told, as a rooming house than a retirement home.

Like so many Pine Barrens sand roads, this one seems to go nowhere, until I come to a spot where the woods are cleared on one side. The Annuity Home, an institutional brick building, sits on a slight rise, fronting a horseshoe driveway. It has no sign. It is shabby, with paint peeling from the portico and sagging iron railings flanking concrete steps. It too appears abandoned, but I know it is not. I drive in the driveway and sit there for a few minutes. No one comes; no one goes. Is there anyone left who once believed in the Rova dream of the old country within the new? I think of those Russian dolls—*matryoshki*—set one inside the other, and how tourists love them.

* ·* *

To return to Rova on two great celebration days of the Russian Orthodox calendar is to return, at least in spirit, to what Rova was in its early days. I come back first to the service on the Sunday after Orthodox Easter. St. Mary's is not very crowded, but it is bright and the air is incense laden. The faithful buy candles and light them. The two priests, one in white, one in black, withdraw from time to time behind the iconostasis, mysterious and magical. When the service ends, we follow the priests outside into the cemetery. People keep coming; the field is filling up with cars. More priests appear from all directions. People come from all over New York, Pennsylvania, and New Jersey because they must go with families to the graveside to swing the censer of incense and give a blessing. I watch families set up tables with picnics. Babies bounce. Small children run around. They have brought picnic coolers and vacuum jugs of coffee, even vodka. Some carry pussy willows, which Russians use on Palm Sunday instead of palms. They bring eggs and bread to leave at the graves. The restaurant, noisy and busy, is open for lunch with food cooked by volunteers. The women filling plates reminisce about Rova in the old days.

I come again on the last Sunday in July, St. Vladimir's Day. It is brutally hot. This time the service is held at St. Vladimir's, named for the Russian prince who brought Christianity to his country. Even inside the stone church, with air conditioning, the heat is stifling. People crowd together; stands of candles burn; the air is thick with incense. The interior walls are completely painted with icons in jewel colors, reminding me of an ancient church I once saw in a village in Romania. People kiss an icon set up for the purpose and light more candles. A boy holds up his little brother. The priests move slowly in vestments stiff with embroidery. The service lasts about three hours, but people come and go. Finally, the priests go outside to process around the church, and the congregation follows. The priests sprinkle holy water. In the heat, it feels pretty good.

Around the outside of the church, booths are set up selling Russian books, tapes, scarves, and dolls. A delegation from a Russian Orthodox monastery in Wayne, West Virginia, sells icons, honey, handmade soap, and oil for vigil lights. There are tables of food and, down in the parking lot, people are setting up picnics.

The illusion which exalts us is dearer to us than ten thousand truths.
ALEXANDER PUSHKIN

ussian diplomats, it is said, went hunting in the Pineland township of Jackson during the Civil War. The Lakehurst Naval Air Station began life as the Czar Nicholas Proving Grounds, a World War I artillery testing range for the Russian Imperial Army. After the Russian Revolution of 1917, a number of White Russians, anticommunist intellectuals, artists, and various other professionals made their way to the Lakewood–Howell area, including a large colony of Don Cossacks. Jackson Township was also home to Stanley Switlik. Switlik, of Polish-Ukrainian extraction, had emigrated to America as a teenager in 1907 and by the 1920s was a successful manufacturer of parachutes. In 1932, he bought the Lahaway Plantation, which had belonged to the reclusive naturalist J. Turner Brakeley. Brakeley's is a romantic story and Lahaway, in descriptions of the times, a romantic place.[1] Switlik bought Lahaway as a summer place for his family, but the wilderness was also a convenient place to build a tower 115 feet high from which to test his parachutes. Amelia Earhart, whose husband was in business with Switlik, made the first public jump from the tower on June 2, 1935. In the same year, plans were made for a "Russian village" in the pines.

The Russian Consolidated Mutual Aid Society was formed in 1926, with national headquarters in Philadelphia. Known as ROOVA, an acronym of its Russian name, the society was made up of small fraternal organizations, called branches or lodges, founded to help Russian immigrants with unemployment, various kinds of insurance, and funeral expenses. Dues paid by the membership supported these programs. ROOVA's broad goals were economic self-help (life insurance, low-cost mortgages, and assistance to the disabled and aged) and cultural enlightenment. As part of this program, particularly the preservation of Russian culture and tradition, the society set out to buy land to establish a place where Russians could come to celebrate and maintain their heritage.

The land they chose was some 1,440 acres of the New Jersey Pine Barrens near the tiny settlement of Cassville in Jackson Township, where John Webb, in 1845, first cultivated the cranberry. Central to the deal was Chester Fedor, a former Russian Cossack officer and real estate broker in Lakewood. The property in question had belonged to the Van Hise family, early settlers of Jackson Township, and included an 1870 farmhouse, a store, and a mill pond created when Pole Brook was dammed for the Van Hise sawmill. Most of the land was wilderness. It was, however, cheap and central, close to major urban areas like New York, Philadelphia, Newark, and other East Coast cities where much of ROOVA's membership was concentrated. It would be a place for people to go, to leave the city tenements for a time. The name became Rova Farms because the sound was more pleasing.

On Sunday, April 15, 1934, a busload of "about forty people" left ROOVA's main office for a tour of the "farm." As the editor reported:

> At this time of year the country anywhere doesn't look at its best . . . and our farm was no exception; the vast stretch of 1400 acres is at this time almost completely covered with bare trees.
>
> The main house near the large lake [mill pond] stands in a clearing just off a highway. It is in this vicinity that ROOVA expects to begin building the nucleus of a future Russian town. The plans at present are for a large club-house (with an auditorium, gymnasium, library, kitchen, lounge rooms etc. etc.) with adjoining fields for sports such as handball, tennis, baseball etc., and a "pier" on the lake (which needs a cleaning).
>
> With the exception of two or three fair-sized clearings the farm is entirely overgrown with forest, very thick and in places impassable.

There will therefore be a demand for much vigorous labor. . . . The general opinion passed on the quality of soil was not very favorable and the tall and thick pines drew many uneasy glances. Each one represents work.[2]

Another journalist with the party was less circumspect:

The start of the tour of inspection was through the only house which was not tilting at an angle of forty-five degrees. Inside we found: twenty-three whiskey bottles (all brands), prehistoric furniture, two beds which must have belonged to Henry the Eighth, the original Bell telephone (with crank)—the kind with which you could listen in on the whole town, statues dating back to the Italian Renaissance, and—well, anyway, all of this, the committee proudly informed us, belonged to us.[3]

He also remarked that the visitors were upset to discover that it was too early in the season to search the woods for mushrooms, those staples of European forests. Clearly, carving a "Russian village" out of the Pine Barrens would be a major undertaking.

Work began at once. Existing structures were converted into administration buildings, and by 1935 a circular social hall, which housed a bar but could also be adapted for funeral services and picnics, was built. The old mill pond was turned into a large, artificial lake that would be central to the resort aspect of the farm, now named Rova Farms Resort. At first, because of the six-day work week, volunteer workers stayed only for the day and overnight accommodations were not necessary; those would come later. ROOVA members threw themselves into the preliminary work and things moved swiftly.

The farm itself was carefully planned to include field crops, chickens, pigs, dairy cattle, mushrooms, and berries. A large orchard and many beehives completed the picture. The products of the farm were intended for the farm's restaurant, with the excess to be sold to resort hotels in Lakewood. Paths were lined with flowers and the birches so dear to Russians to create "a little Russia in the Pines." Within the first ten years, the core of Rova was built: the restaurant/meeting hall, churches, cemetery, Pushkin Park, and the Pushkin Memorial Home for Aged Russian People. Many of ROOVA's members worked in demolition in the cities and were able to salvage much of the material used for the buildings. Rooming houses were built by various ROOVA branches for single members. Philadelphia House, built by the Philadelphia branch, stood at the corner of Route 571; it had a dormitory with separate floors for single men and women. Single- and multifamily bungalows were also built. "Within a year of its establishment, ROVA Farms saw a permanent colony of Russians begin to form around it, as members who had managed to save money bought surrounding parcels, mostly to join the booming poultry business. . . . As the colony grew, it considered the possibility of incorporation as a village, with the name of Pushkinville, but the idea did not seem to garner much support."[4] Eventually other structures were built: a pier and pavilion by the lake and a motel.

Although the economic support ROOVA could provide was obviously important to Russian immigrants, Rova Farms was really about something else—the survival of a spiritual and cultural heritage in a new land. With its flowers and birches, its lake and pavilion, its deep woods, it was intended to re-create a memory or dream of Russia, the best of a country that most ROOVA members had had to flee. That Rova Farms filled a need was obvious from its inception.

> ROOVA members flocked to ROVA Farms from its very first day. They came mostly from the New York City and Philadelphia areas, driving in their own automobiles or taking the bus to Lakewood where they were met by the "Rova taxi," an old farm truck with benches in the back to accommodate passengers. They slept in bungalows, dormitories, tents, out in open fields, or even on the raft in the middle of the lake! Each visitor brought his/her own particular abilities and talents to the project, contributing as farmers, builders, electricians, plumbers, masons, cooks, or other skilled laborers. Some came with only their willingness to work hard and some came each year to per-

form a specific task, such as draining and cleaning the lake, slaughtering and dressing out pigs, or running the children's camp.[5]

As was common practice in summer resorts of the day, women and children came out for the week, while men came on the weekends. Some families would stay a week or two, some the whole summer. One important aspect of Rova Farms was passing on Russian culture to its children. A summer camp was opened, and children were taught the Russian language and folk traditions. Needy children were brought to Rova from the cramped, hot conditions of the cities in a Russian version of the Fresh Air Fund. The Tolstoy Library was filled with Russian books. Music, singing, and dancing were central to life at the farm. In the early days, as many as two thousand people came to Rova in summer.

Two stretches of gabled, one-and-a-half-story cabins were constructed in the stretch between the Cassville–Van Hiseville and Cassville–Freehold roads, along with a community kitchen with rows of stoves and ice boxes so that vacationers could provide meals for themselves. These were never intended to be permanent homes. The Pushkin Memorial Home was built some distance from the resort's center, on a sand road deep in the pines. At the time it had well-kept gardens.

In 1937, the centennial of the Russian poet Alexander Pushkin's death, many Russians felt that there should be a monument in America to the "Russian Shakespeare." In late 1940 and 1941, ROOVA decided that such a monument should be erected at Rova Farms. The foundation was laid on June 1, 1941. A declaration in Russian was read. Those gathered were "yearning to see a symbol of the personification of Russian culture in a foreign land . . . with faith that this monument will serve as a reminder to future generations of the glorious achievements of the Russian people, that it will further strengthen the cultural ties between two great peoples."[6] This declaration, along with the signatures of hundreds of those in attendance, was sealed in a bronze canister within the foundation.

The sculptor chosen to make the bust, Nickolai Dimitrieff, finished the ten-foot monument at the end of that summer. He had based it on the last portrait of the poet painted in his lifetime—a sadder, older Pushkin than the man of more familiar portraits; such an image was suitable perhaps to the melancholy of exile. The unveiling ceremony took place on Labor Day, 1941. Pushkin's poems were read, wreaths were laid, and a huge banquet followed. Writer M. K. Argus, sent to cover the occasion for his Russian-language newspaper, found that the "camp had everything a camp is supposed to have: a swimming pool; a main building with a large dining room; a bar stocked with beer, whisky, and, of course, vodka; bungalows with all modern conveniences (although my [American] wife insisted they were neither modern nor conveniences); a number of trees; a very lovely view." The celebration attracted such a crowd, however, that Argus and his wife eventually had to stay in someone's spare room at a distance and managed to miss the ceremony.[7]

Most of ROOVA's members were ordinary working people for whom the chance to spend a little time away from the cities was a true luxury. As with the earlier Russian agricultural colonies of South Jersey, however, Rova had its share of intellectual mentors. Vladimir Ipatieff (1867–1952), a professor at Northwestern University, a world-famous chemist, and an inventor, came to Rova in the summers, where he lectured and offered help to anyone wanting a career in the sciences. Igor Sikorsky (1889–1972), famous for his helicopter, was actively involved in Rova, where he worked to bring together the two groups of immigrants, workers and intellectuals, to advance the Russian cause, and to fashion a "demonstration against Bolshevism."[8] With his interest in the preservation of Russian culture, he, along with his wife, had started a Russian school in New York. Then there were eccentrics such as Gleb Botkin, son of Dr. Yevgeny Botkin, personal physician to Czar Nicholas II. Dr. Botkin was killed with the royal family at Ekaterinburg. Gleb Botkin lived for thirteen years near Rova, often walking through the woods to the local store to sit at the stove and talk about old times. From Rova, he corresponded with Anna Anderson, who claimed to be the princess Anastasia, who had somehow survived the execution of her family. Botkin and his sister, Tatiana, had been playmates of the royal children and were apparently convinced of Anderson's authenticity. DNA tests, however, have now proven that Anna Anderson was not Anastasia.

The lost princess was not Botkin's only interest; in 1939 he founded a pagan religious sect, calling it the Aphrodite religion.

Rova Farms has two churches. The later of the two, the splendid St. Vladimir's, was built on a rise next to the restaurant and meeting hall. The parcel had been occupied by a Presbyterian church and was sold to ROOVA with the proviso that only a church could be built there. The other, St. Mary's, a mile or so down Route 571, is plainer, although it still has the traditional golden domes and stands at the entrance to St. Vladimir's Russian Orthodox Christian Cemetery, a twenty-acre site. The original section of St. Mary's was built in the 1930s by Rova's men and women: "the women mixed cement while the men laid the blocks."[9] The cemetery also has a chapel, the Cossack chapel, built by survivors of the June 1945 massacre at Lienz, Austria. One section, set aside for Kalmyks of Russian central Asia, contains Buddhist graves.

The two churches, both Russian Orthodox, show how important their religion has always been to Rova Farms' colonists. They also signify a split in the authority of the Russian church, with the congregation of St. Mary's part of the Orthodox Church of America and the congregation of St. Vladimir's part of the Orthodox Church Outside Russia. St. Vladimir's, begun slightly later than St. Mary's and not completely finished until 1985, is the more ornate of the two, with its brilliant external mosaics. It was designed in the style of eleventh-century Novgorod, a center of Christianity in medieval Russia, and named for Saint Vladimir, the Russian prince who brought Christianity to his country. After his conversion, Vladimir had wanted to open all the jails and free everyone. He seems a fitting patron for the immigrants forced to flee from various tyrannies. In July 1988, the Russian Orthodox Millennium, a full week of religious ceremonies took place at Rova Farms. "An estimated 15,000 Russians from around the world took part, including over one hundred hierarchs and clergy."[10] Among them was Grand Duke Vladimir Romanov, putative heir to the Russian throne, along with his wife, daughter, and grandson. July 29, St. Vladimir's Day, would include, as always, the blessing of the waters beside Rova's lake.

The lake was always important to life at Rova. During the winters, ice sculptor Philip Shestakow would go down to the shore and carve an altar in the ice that would be used for special services. Every year it was dyed a different color. When it melted in spring, the water would mix with the lake's flow into streams and eventually into the ocean. People would say that "all the ships in the sea were blessed by sharing the same waters as the altar."[11]

This mystical merging of God and nature explains why much of Rova's wooded acres was not developed, why there was a desire to keep its wildness. Russians love the woods and loved to sing there, until the coming of World War II made such singing seem too German. Helen Zill's memories of Rova are typical:

> It was just a wonderful community existence. It was mostly outdoor living. All people needed was a room with beds. . . . They had a children's camp. The counselors were very gifted ladies who enlisted help from stars in the ballet, the opera, the music world. Since we didn't have heat . . . it was mostly a summer place. Camp lasted eight weeks, and the children's concert at the end was fabulous—but fabulous. Those who wanted to learn Russian were taught Russian Music. All the talent the children possessed was brought forth—and some went on to become rather famous ballerinas or musicians or the heads of music departments in college. Athletic abilities were brought out, too. Non-Russian children were permitted to attend the camp, primarily if the mother was ill or one parent was missing.[12]

Almost everyone remembers the evening bonfires by the lake and the communal dancing and singing.

> Friday night was a very big night because the fathers arrived from the city that night. We'd have an accordionist who was wonderful. We'd have a big campfire by the lake. Everybody would gather. The children, the fathers, the mothers—everybody would sing and dance. It was very simple except in the case of some of the generals from the Tsarist army who came here, some of whom had lived in France for a while and made their own champagne. One general especially would

grow special grapes and make champagne and cool it in the well and give everybody a taste. It was just the greatest thing.[13]

Martin Hrynick, president of the St. Vladimir's Russian Orthodox Christian Cemetery, remembers one Sunday in 1953 counting thirty-three buses in the parking lot. "You couldn't park," he says, "within half a mile of the place." From the late 1940s to the early 1960s, Rova was the place to be on weekends. Every Friday and Saturday night, dances were held with live music. Once the dance ended, everyone went down to the beach, where singing could go on until four in the morning. It was, Hrynick says, a way to meet members of the opposite sex who shared your background and religion. "I couldn't begin to count the number of marriages that originated at Rova Farms on Friday and Saturday nights."[14]

Rova Farms was a welcoming place not only to Russian immigrants but to others as well. Clare Nadler Sacharoff remembers driving down from Roosevelt to watch the Russian dancing at Rova. GIs from Fort Dix and Lakehurst Naval Air Station would have their going-away parties and picnics at Rova before shipping out to the theaters of war.[15]

Times changed, however, and each successive wave of Russian immigrants changed. First had come workers looking for a better way of life. Then the Bolshevik Revolution of 1917 had brought a more educated wave of White Russians. After World War II, a third wave of displaced persons, or DPs, came from the European camps. People remember weekends at Rova, after the war, so crowded that one could hardly move as displaced persons from all over the East Coast searched desperately for missing family members or friends. "Cassville attracted Russians from each immigration but friction developed between the second wave, commonly referred to as the 'White Russians' because of their anti-Bolshevik views, and the DPs. Some say the White Russians consider the DPs inferior because they didn't leave the Soviet Union when the Communists took control. The DPs, in turn, consider the earlier immigrants snobbish."[16] A one-time president of Rova who had come to America in the first wave of immigration said, "Stalin gave them an education, didn't he? But he took their hearts out."[17]

Some say that the cold war years, especially the era of Senator Joseph McCarthy and the Communist witch hunts, hurt Rova Farms. Fearing for their jobs, a number of Russian Americans dissociated themselves from Rova. Others say that the politics of those years had little effect. Most of the Russians at Rova hated the Communists. When Stalin died in 1953, "the occasion was celebrated with a mammoth vodka party."[18] It came as a shock in 1977 when a Soviet seaman and Rova regular Ivan Rogalsky was arrested for spying, accused of trying to obtain secret documents about the U.S. shuttle program from an engineer at a Princeton Research Center.

For Rova, there were other problems. As was the case among the Russian Jewish communities, children of Rova members tended to pursue an American education and then move all over the country. As early as 1954, the *Russian Herald* was begging the new generation to show "your parents and other faithful members that their efforts and energies shall not have been in vain."[19] Successful and Americanized children didn't need the solace of a Rova Farms, a re-creation of a country they had never known. Like the birch trees that did not survive long in the Pinelands, many members of the next generation disappeared. Rova's population, both permanent and occasional, declined as even the aged decamped for warmer climes.

Consistent leadership has also been a problem. Twelve directors, elected every two years by the shareholders,[20] run the corporation. Turnover is high.[21] As development has changed Jackson Township, taxes have risen. A fire at Great Adventure Amusement Park in 1985 mandated expensive changes to Rova's public buildings. Then there was the famous lawsuit brought by a man who dove into Lake Rova, hit his head on the bottom, and was rendered quadriplegic.[22] Gradually, property has been sold off to pay the bills. The 1,440 acres have shrunk to less than 40. Also, as original members of the community died, their property was often sold to people who had no connection with the Russian community of Rova.

By the late 1970s, Rova was in decline. Whether or not Rova could survive was a convenient subject for articles in local newspapers and magazines through the 1970s, 1980s, and 1990s. Buildings fell into disrepair; some were torn down. The motel and cabins were rented to employees of

Six Flags. The bar and restaurant in the main hall continued to serve vodka, borscht, stuffed cabbage, and other Russian favorites on weekends. The twice-weekly flea market and wrestling contests brought in a little income. More land was sold. Contention among various factions was constant, as even another, smaller group of immigrants arrived after the fall of the Soviet Union. Yet at times, like Easter and St. Vladimir's Day, some of the old Rova came back. Father Petrovsky remembers: "You should have seen it around here on St. Vladimir's Day when I was a child. More than 25,000 people would come to town. Some would come in the spring, knocking on doors, asking people if they would have rooms to rent in July. That's why a lot of people built their homes with big basements. They'd go down there and live in the summer and rent the upper part."[23]

Still, people come back to stand in St. Vladimir's for the three-hour service, to follow the priests around the church and down to the lake, and to buy icons and the like at the booths set up outside. On the Sunday after Easter, they come to the cemetery at St. Mary's to visit the dead. Picnics are held at the grave sites. Orthodox priests from all over the tristate area are pressed into service to go with the families to bless the individual graves.

Lydia Wolniansky would like to save Rova. She reminisces about her years as president of the organization and worries about the future of the community, with its forty remaining acres. The churches and the cemetery are separate from Rova and are not in danger, but the Rova she remembers from the 1950s is almost gone. Even then, she says, the old-timers were beginning to die off. The farm was down to one farmer with a few cows and chickens. But back then—soon after being introduced to Rova, she and her husband moved permanently from New York to Jackson Township—Rova meant a lot to her. As someone who remembers the siege of Leningrad and whose father was sent to Siberia, she does not want to see another loss. She talks with animation about her years as president. She recounts the story of a group of Russian musicians who were stranded at the airport when the jobs they had come to America for fell through. A friend brought them to Rova, and they packed the hall with concerts and spent their spare time helping to clean and fix up around the place. Then there were the Russian children being treated at Deborah Hospital who were given a place to stay at Rova, in the old spirit of community. Corruption and mismanagement, she says, have emptied the coffers, and it may be too late for change.[24]

Helen Zill, at one time Rova's secretary, said before her death in 1986: "There is such beauty here . . . I have seen it from the beginning. It is still here. I won't believe Rova will die, even when I, myself, am lying there on the floor. The spirit of this community lives."[25]

Martin Hrynick sees it another way. Perhaps the time for a place like Rova is over. In the early days of immigration to America, he points out, when you left your country of origin, you left everything: people, places. You knew you would never see them again. People needed a way to connect with other people who had had the same experience and who could connect them to the old culture. Now that you can call home or simply fly home, a Rova is not so necessary.[26]

Still, there is always sadness in assimilation. It is unquestionably a loss. One wishes Rova Farms could remain as it once was, that there could be birch trees and beehives and Russian songs sung by the lake on a summer evening.

CONCLUSION

Most of the communities I have written about in this volume were founded between the last ten years of the nineteenth century and the first fifteen years of the twentieth, a time when utopian communities proliferated in response to the industrialization and urbanization of America, and perhaps the sense that people's lives were no longer in balance with nature and other people. In the words of historian Richard Hofstadter, "From the end of the civil war to the close of the nineteenth century, the physical energies of the American people had been mobilized for a remarkable burst of material development, but their moral energies had lain relatively dormant."[1] "Moral energy" marked all of these colonies, including those like Woodbine and Rova Farms, which were founded in response to events in Europe, especially the pogroms against the Jews in late nineteenth-century Russia.

Although a number of these communities did not outlast the period of their birth, a number did. With the notable exception of Free Acres, the ones that lasted—like Woodbine, Stelton, Roosevelt, and Rova Farms—were established by groups or organizations. Because these communities' existence and well-being were the responsibility of a number of individuals, they weathered the First World War and the Depression. In contrast, colonies founded by individuals, like Helicon, Physical Culture City, and Self Masters, did not outlast the death of, or abandonment by, their founders.

Certain time periods are obviously friendlier to communal endeavors than are others. In periods of intellectual ferment, people look for change and alternative ways of living. Intellectual ferment certainly describes the "modernist" period of the early twentieth century, and also the late 1960s and early 1970s, which saw another counterculture movement and another crop of utopian communities. In between came the 1950s and the cold war. Second World War combat veterans presumably wanted to retreat to the safety of the family unit. They wanted Levittown, not Free Acres. The hysterical fear of Russian communism also made any communal endeavor suspect.

Today, the technological revolution, which lacks the dirt and danger of the industrial one but is just as serious in its consequences, has left us again in a situation much like the one Hofstadter describes. It may not be such a surprise that in 2006 *New Jersey Monthly* magazine voted Roosevelt the best place to live in the state. Not everyone wants to live in nuclear-family isolation in a palatial tract house. We can make connections with all kinds of "intentional communities" on the Internet. The co-housing movement tries to prevent segregation by age. We worry about the environment.

If utopian experiments come in response to historical events, that still leaves the question of why New Jersey? Geography is the simple answer. Ideological movements were born in the intellectual and financial capitals of New York and Philadelphia, but the communities they generated needed land. The cheap and available land, within reach of either city, was in New Jersey, making it quite literally the nearest Eden.

New Jersey's geographical position has led to its historical heterogeneity. Where Massachusetts, for example, has firmly positioned itself as the land of the Puritans and the cradle of the American Revolution, New Jersey has never made much of its more extensive Revolutionary history. New Jersey has in effect moved on, becoming a palimpsest of the country's past rather than one definitive image. The danger here is that palimpsests are hard to decipher. I want to remember these places before even the remaining street names become as meaningless as a forgotten language.

These experiments matter. Government and society are too slow and cumbersome for most social experiments. The sponsorship of the federal government, for instance, almost sank Roosevelt. Change is possible on a small scale, change that can later be incorporated into larger institutions. The Self Master Colony anticipated welfare. Physical Culture City anticipated much of our current understanding of health and physical fitness.

Helicon, to some extent, anticipated the emancipation of women. Many of the educational reforms of the Stelton Modern School are now standard. And all of these communities, by stressing the importance of the natural world, anticipated the environmental movement. Some are still thriving, albeit in modified form, but none should be forgotten.

NOTES

Helicon Home Colony: A Cooperative Living Colony

1. Upton Sinclair, *The Jungle* (Cambridge, MA: Robert Bentley, Inc., 1946), 4, 148.
2. Ibid., vi.
3. "The roads were either deep with mud or cut with the tracks of sleighs. . . . The cows broke into the pear orchard and stuffed themselves and died; the farmhands brought from the city got drunk and sold the farm produce for their own benefit." Upton Sinclair, *The Autobiography of Upton Sinclair* (New York: Harcourt, Brace and World, 1962), 127.
4. Sinclair, *Jungle*, vi; Sinclair, *Autobiography*, 112.
5. In a letter to Sinclair, Gilman pronounced the novel "unfortunate."
6. Ibid., 279.
7. Edward Bellamy, *Looking Backward* (New York: Bantam Books, 1983), 79.
8. Gilman, *Women and Economics*, 242.
9. *New York Times*, July 16, 1906, 6.
10. Ibid.
11. Charlotte Perkins Gilman, *Concerning Children* (Walnut Creek, CA: Altamira Press, 2002), 236–237.
12. "Tentative Plans Ready for Sinclair Colony," *New York Times*, August 10, 1906, 5 (emphasis mine).
13. Ibid.
14. "Get-Together Meeting of Sinclair Colonists," *New York Times*, August 13, 1906.
15. Lawrence Kaplan, "The Helicon Home Colony, 1906–1907," *American Studies*, Fall 1984, 63–64.
16. Michael Williams, *The Book of the High Romance* (New York: Macmillan, 1928), 143.
17. Undena Eberlein to her sister Davida de Guibert, November 25, 1906, in Laurel Hessing, ed., *Treasures of the Little Cabin*, trans. Laurel Hessing and Sylvia Heerens (Free Acres, NJ: self-published, 1999), 86.

18. Williams, *Book of the High Romance*, 140.

19. D. C. Serber, letter to the editor, "Hebrews at Helicon Hall," *New York Times*, November 12, 1906.

20. John Spargo, "Facts for Mr. Sinclair," *New York Times*, July 22, 1906, 6.

21. Upton Sinclair, *The Brass Check: A Study of American Journalism* (Pasadena, CA: author published, 1920), 63.

22. Ibid., 62.

23. Sinclair Lewis, "Two Yale Men in Utopia," in *The Man from Main Street: Selected Essays and Other Writings, 1904–1950*, ed. Harry E. Maule and Melville H. Cane (New York: Random House, 1953), 62.

24. Ibid., 67.

25. Ibid., 62.

26. Ibid., 67. Lewis may well have found Helicon a place of dreams. He became engaged to Edith Summers Kelly, an engagement she subsequently broke to marry his friend and co-colonist, Allen Updegraff.

27. Sinclair, *Autobiography*, 131.

28. Leon Harris, *Upton Sinclair: American Rebel* (New York: Thomas Y. Crowell, 1975), 96.

29. Undena Eberlein to Davida de Guibert, November 26, 1906, in Hessing, *Treasures of the Little Cabin*, 86–87.

30. Williams, *Book of the High Romance*, 144.

31. Ibid., 147.

32. Ibid., 143.

33. Sinclair, *Autobiography*, 129.

34. Kaplan, "Helicon Home Colony," 69.

35. Sinclair, *Brass Check*, 68.

36. "Fire Wipes Out Helicon Hall," *New York Times*, March 17, 1907.

37. Sinclair, *Autobiography*, 134.

38. Ernest Eberlein to Undena Eberlein, March 17, 1907, in Hessing, *Treasures of the Little Cabin*, 88.

39. Ernest Eberlein, as quoted in Hessing, *Treasures of the Little Cabin*, 135.

40. *Englewood Press*, March 23, 1907.

41. Sinclair, *Autobiography*, 135–136, 138. The sanitarium was Kellogg's.

42. Williams, *Book of the High Romance*, 187.

43. Harold Gilliam and Ann Gilliam, *Creating Carmel* (Layton, UT: Gibbs Smith, 1992), 97.

44. Sinclair, *Autobiography*, 162.

45. Harry Kemp, *Tramping on Life* (New York: Boni and Liveright, 1922), 317, 389.

46. Sinclair proposed state land colonies to absorb the unemployed and allow them to

become self-sufficient, as well as factories where other unemployed people could produce goods for themselves and the land colonists—a version of the farm and factory system.

47. Sinclair, *Brass Check*, 67.
48. Charlotte Perkins Gilman, *The Living of Charlotte Perkins Gilman: An Autobiography* (Madison: University of Wisconsin Press, 1990), 26.

Free Acres: A Single-Tax Colony

Parts of this chapter were originally published as "Utopia, NJ," in *New Jersey Monthly*, October 2005.

1. Konrad Bercovici, *It's the Gypsy in Me* (New York: Prentice Hall, 1941), 1.
2. Emma Goldman, *Living My Life* (New York: Knopf, 1931), 348.
3. Henry George, "The Single Tax: What It Is and Why We Need It," *Christian Advocate*, 1890.
4. Martin Bierbaum, "Free Acres: Bolton Hall's Single-Tax Experimental Community," *New Jersey History*, Spring/Summer 1984, 44.
5. Bolton Hall, "Conclusion," in *Life, Love, and Death* (New York and London: F. Tennyson Neely, 1898), n.p.
6. The single-tax colonies of Fairhope, Alabama, and Arden, Delaware, are also still in existence.
7. Bierbaum, "Free Acres," 44.
8. Isabel Grace Colbron, "Adventures in Home-Making: Free Acres Homes," *Touchstone*, August 1918, 438.
9. Bierbaum, "Free Acres," 44.
10. Colbron, "Adventures in Home-Making." 438–439.
11. Ella Murray, "Free Acres Twentieth Anniversary" (brochure), 1930, 6.
12. Joseph Romano, "Free Acres Single Tax Colony, 1910–1930: An Experiment in Pleasant Living," master's thesis, University of Tennessee, 1972, 20.
13. Laurel Hessing, ed., *Annotated Anthology of Free Acres Writing* (Free Acres, NJ: self-published, 1992), 6.
14. Romano, "Free Acres," 22.
15. One supposes there must have been two horses, since the problem seems to be the choice of carriages.
16. Romano, "Free Acres," 28.
17. Ethel Fischer, as quoted ibid., 27.
18. Mrs. Moore had apparently studied with Alys Bentley of the Ethical Culture School in New York. Bentley worked with children at the school and at her summer camp in the Adirondacks on musical exercises. Her work was described as follows: "Beginning with the large muscle masses and guided by carefully selected

music the child is led to a series of correlated movements, some of them based on the activities of the animal world. Working from the spinal column as the center, the children acquire a freedom of movement and the power of expression through correlated series that extend to every part of the organism. Through this perfected rhythmical body, the student is then led on to express the feeling wakened in him by various musical compositions." 1915 Educational Conference Proceedings, New York, NY.

19. The use of the word *guilds* shows a debt to William Morris.
20. Whiteway, like Free Acres, still exists and functions in a similar way.
21. Benzion Liber, *A Doctor's Apprenticeship* (New York: Rational Living, 1956), 555.
22. Rion Bercovici, "A Radical Childhood," *Scribner's Magazine*, August 1932, 105.
23. Colbron, "Adventures in Home-Making," 438.
24. Undena Eberlein to her mother, Free Acres, NJ, April 12, 1920, in Hessing, *Annotated Anthology*, 22–23.
25. Undena Eberlein to Cora Potter, Free Acres, NJ, March 10, 1920, ibid.
26. Postcard advertising Free Acres, bMS Am 1614(64), Joseph Ishill Collection, by permission of the Houghton Library, Harvard University, Cambridge, MA.
27. Roxanne Eberlein to Laurel Hessing, October 21, 1986, in Hessing, *Annotated Anthology*, 40.
28. Liber, *Doctor's Apprenticeship*, 486.
29. Bolton Hall, 1923, as quoted in Hessing, *Annotated Anthology*, 61.
30. Martin Bierbaum, as quoted ibid.
31. MacKinlay Kantor, "My Most Unforgettable Character," *Reader's Digest*, December 1966, 221.
32. Harry A. Dix to Will Crawford, March 18, 1926, Free Acres Collection, Special Collections and University Archives, Rutgers Libraries, Rutgers University, New Brunswick, NJ.
33. Kantor, "My Most Unforgettable Character," 227.
34. K. Bercovici, *It's the Gypsy in Me*, 78, 81.
35. James Cagney, *Cagney by Cagney* (New York: Doubleday, 1976), 183.
36. Kantor, "My Most Unforgettable Character," 228.
37. Laurel Hessing, in Hessing, *Annotated Anthology*, 53.
38. K. Bercovici, *It's the Gypsy in Me*, 76, 244.
39. Ibid., 79–80.
40. Terry Conner, interview with author, January 15, 2005, Free Acres, NJ.
41. James Thurber, *The Years with Ross* (Boston: Atlantic Monthly Press, 1957), 147–148.
42. K. Bercovici, *It's the Gypsy in Me*, 69.

43. Minutes of Dramatic Guild Meeting, September 25, 1921, as quoted in Hessing, *Annotated Anthology*, 64.
44. Lillian Leon, "A Free Acres Chronicle," unpublished essay (1949), p. 11, Free Acres Collection, Rutgers Libraries.
45. "Things We Hope For," *Free Acres Post Mortem*, March 1933.
46. Letter to the editor, *Town Crier*, July 29, 1933.
47. Frederick Scheff, "The Urgent Need," *Town Crier*, July 29, 1933.
48. Frederick Scheff, "A Letter from Fred Scheff," *Town Crier*, May/June 1934, 54–55.
49. Michael Gold, "In Foggy California," *New Masses*, November 1928, 169.
50. Konrad Bercovici, "Colonies, Campfires and Theories," *New York Times Magazine*, October 21, 1923.
51. Leon, "Free Acres Chronicle," 7.
52. Terry Conner, interview.
53. Laurel Hessing, "Obituary for Billy Kluver," *Free Acres Newsletter*, www.free-acres.org.
54. Sal and Tami Passalacqua, interview with author, January 15, 2005, Free Acres, NJ.
55. Terry Conner, interview.
56. Laurel Hessing, interview with author, April 11, 2006, Free Acres, NJ.
57. Liber, *Doctor's Apprenticeship*, 47.

Stelton: An Experiment in Education

1. Paul Avrich, *The Modern School Movement* (Oakland, CA: AK Press, 2006), 7, Ferrer quoted at 8.
2. Ibid., 39; Goldman, as quoted ibid., 41.
3. Ibid., 189.
4. Ibid., 190–196 (Kelly), 197–199 (Cohen).
5. Boyesen, as quoted ibid., 79.
6. R. Bercovici, "Radical Childhood," 102.
7. K. Bercovici, *It's the Gypsy in Me*, 65.
8. Durant explains that he was converted to vegetarianism in part by the magazine's photographs, interspersed throughout the text, of "splendid women naked to the waist." Will Durant and Ariel Durant, *Dual Autobiography* (New York.: Simon and Schuster, 1977), 33, 37.
9. Peter Kropotkin, "Declaration of the Anarchists Arraigned before the Criminal Court in Lyon," in *No Gods, No Masters*, vol. 1, ed. Daniel Guerin, trans. Paul Sharkey (Edinburgh: AK Press, 1998).

10. Avrich, *Modern School Movement*, 121.
11. Laurence Veysey, *The Communal Experience* (Chicago: University of Chicago Press, 1978), 79–81.
12. Eugene O'Neill is said to have based the character of Hugo Kalmar in *The Iceman Cometh* on Hippolyte Havel; Kalmar periodically denounces "capitalist swine."
13. Avrich, *Modern School Movement*, 150.
14. R. Bercovici, "Radical Childhood," 102.
15. Durant and Durant, *Dual Autobiography*, 42.
16. R. Bercovici, "Radical Childhood," 102.
17. Terry M. Perlin, "Anarchism in New Jersey: The Ferrer Colony at Stelton," *New Jersey History*, Fall 1971, 137.
18. Avrich, *Modern School Movement*, 110.
19. Another ancestor, Charles Dana, had taught at the school at the famous Brook Farm experiment in Massachusetts.
20. *The Story of Fellowship Farm* (pamphlet), 1, in the Twenty-fifth Anniversary of Fellowship Farm and Dedication of Township Park, October 9, 1937, file, Special Collections and University Archives, Rutgers Libraries.
21. Avrich, *Modern School Movement*, 232.
22. Veysey, *Communal Experience*, 113.
23. Ibid., 233.
24. Perlin, "Anarchism in New Jersey," 133.
25. Michael Gold, as quoted in Avrich, *Modern School Movement*, 243.
26. George W. Spayth, *It Was Fun the Hard Way* (Dunellen, NJ: Spayth Press, 1964), 93.
27. Peter Goodman, interview with author, September 16, 2006, Brunswick, NJ.
28. Avrich, *Modern School Movement*, 250.
29. Ibid., 244–248.
30. Henry T. Schnittkind, "The Function of a Modern School," in *The Modern School Twenty-fifth Anniversary Publication*, ed. Abe Gosner (Stelton, NJ: Modern School, 1940), 16; found in the Modern School Collection, Special Collections and Archives, Rutgers Libraries
31. Mary Krimont was Harry Kelly's companion and later his wife; she had been responsible for his original trip to Fellowship Farm, where she was staying.
32. Avrich, *Modern School Movement*, 250.
33. Joan Baez, *Daybreak* (New York: Dial Press, 1968), 24.
34. Michael Gold, as quoted in Avrich, *Modern School Movement*, 252.
35. Peter Goodman, interview.
36. Avrich, *Modern School Movement*, 256.

37. The Oriole Press was named for a family of orioles nesting in the printing shed at Stelton.
38. Sadakichi Hartmann to Joseph Ishill, Ishill Papers, bMS Am 1614(66) by permission of the Houghton Library, Harvard University, Cambridge, MA.
39. David Freedman, interview with author, April 19, 2006, Edison, NJ.
40. Harry Kelly, *The Modern School* (Stelton, NJ: Modern School Association of North America, 1920), found in the Modern School Collection, Special Collections and Archives, Rutgers Libraries.
41. Ray Porter Miller, "My Teachers at Stelton," in Gosner, *Modern School Twenty-fifth Anniversary Publication*, 27.
42. Veysey, *Communal Experience*, 181.
43. Peter Goodman, interview.
44. Ibid.
45. Spayth, *Fun the Hard Way*, 91.
46. Avrich, *Modern School Movement*, 297.
47. Alexis Ferm, Principal's Report, November 4, 1923, Modern School Collection, Special Collections and Archives, Rutgers Libraries.
48. One favorite morning song goes as follows:

> Pretty little dandelion—
> Growing in the grass
> With your hair of shining gold
> Merry little lass.
> When your pretty hair turns white
> Pray what will you do?
> Will you make a hundred more—
> Just as nice as you.
> (Avrich, *Modern School Movement*, 352–353)

49. David Freedman, interview. The Principal's Report of January 4, 1925, mentions Alys Bentley's mental motor rhythmics, a form of dance also popular at Free Acres.
50. Alexis Ferm, Principal's Report, December 2, 1923, Modern School Collection, Special Collections and University Archives, Rutgers Libraries.
51. Leonard Sacharoff, interview, September 16, 2006, New Brunswick, NJ.
52. Avrich, *Modern School Movement*, 63–64. His old drinking buddy Sadakichi Hartmann had died in 1944, after living for six years in a shack he had build on an Indian reservation near Los Angeles.

53. Nearing and his wife, Helen, would eventually retreat to Vermont and then Maine to live a simple, subsistence life.
54. Veysey, *Communal Experience*, 160.
55. David Freedman, interview.
56. Ibid.
57. Elizabeth Ferm, *The Spirit of Freedom in Education* (Stelton, NJ: Modern School, 1919). This is a particularly beautifully designed pamphlet, set by Joseph Ishill with titles by Rockwell Kent. Modern School Collection, Special Collections and University Archives, Rutgers Libraries.
58. Jacob Robins, "Two Persons and an Ideal," *Modern School*, June–July 1919, 8–9, Special Collections and University Archives, Rutgers Libraries.
59. Alexis Ferm, Principal's Reports, 1922–1925 and 1933–1939, Modern School Collection, Special Collections and University Archives, Rutgers Libraries.
60. Jim Dick, as quoted in Avrich, *Modern School Movement*, 341.
61. The Lakewood Modern School ran from 1933 to 1958.
62. Leonard Sacharoff, interview.
63. Peter Goodman, interview.
64. Leonard Sacharoff, interview with author, July 15, 2006, Roosevelt, NJ.
65. David Freedman, interview.
66. Alexis Ferm, Principal's Report, November 3, 1933, Modern School Collection, Special Collections and University Archives, Rutgers Libraries.
67. Spayth, *Fun the Hard Way*, 89.
68. Veysey, *Communal Experience*, 168.
69. This was not the case at the Mohegan Colony in upstate New York, where the communists gained greater control.
70. Veysey, *Communal Experience*, 169.
71. Alexis Ferm, Principal's Report, 1933, Modern School Collection, Special Collections and University Archives, Rutgers Libraries.
72. A. S. Neill, *Summerhill* (New York: Hart Publishing Co., 1960), 103.
73. Peter Goodman, interview.
74. Samuel G. Freedman, "A Requiem for Anarchy," *New Jersey Monthly*, May 2003, 105.
75. Gerda Koch Reidel, "I Like to Remember Stelton," in Gosner, *Modern School Twenty-fifth Anniversary Publication*, 28.

Physical Culture City: The Kingdom of Health
1. Bernarr Macfadden, "The Editor's Personal Experience," *Physical Culture*, October 1899, 237.

2. Clifford Waugh, "Bernarr Macfadden: The Muscular Prophet," Ph.D. dissertation, State University of New York, Buffalo, 1979, 10.

3. By this time McFadden had renamed himself Bernarr Macfadden, a name he felt had a stronger sound.

4. Sinclair, *Autobiography*, 158.

5. Robert Ernst, *Weakness Is a Crime: The Life of Bernarr Macfadden* (Syracuse, NY: Syracuse University Press, 1991), 18.

6. *Physical Culture*, September 1902, 313–314.

7. *Physical Culture*, March 1899, 199.

8. *Physical Culture*, March 1902, supplement E.

9. There is an interesting similarity here with Sadakichi Hartmann's theory of "soul atoms."

10. Mary Macfadden and Emile Gauvreau, *Dumbbells and Carrot Strips* (New York: Henry Holt, 1953), 330–331.

11. *Physical Culture*, August 1904.

12. *Physical Culture*, March 1899, 13.

13. Tyman Currio, "Weird and Wonderful Story of Another World," *Physical Culture Magazine*, January 1906, 38.

14. Marguerite Macfadden, "A Vegetarian Christmas Dinner," *Physical Culture*, December 1905, 362.

15. *Physical Culture*, July 1906, 112.

16. Voltairine de Cleyre, "Return of the Sandal," *Physical Culture*, May 1904, 393.

17. *Physical Culture*, April 1906, 438.

18. Ernst, *Weakness Is a Crime*, 43.

19. "Comstock King of the Prudes," *Physical Culture*, December 1905, 561–563.

20. Ernst, *Weakness Is a Crime*, 36.

21. *Physical Culture*, August 1904, 574.

22. James C. Whorton, *Crusaders for Fitness: The History of American Health Reformers* (Princeton, NJ: Princeton University Press, 1982), 6–7.

23. At the time, the idea that pine woods had a curative effect was common. There were several tuberculosis sanatoriums in the Pinelands.

24. Sadie S. Dougherty, *History of Outcalt, 1905–1963* (pamphlet), 2–3, Spottswood History folder, Spottswood Public Library, Spottswood, NJ.

25. J. W. Smithson, "Home Industries for Physical Culture Residents," *Physical Culture*, April 1905, 223.

26. Federal Writers' Project, *Monroe Township, Middlesex County, New Jersey, 1838–1938* ([New Brunswick, NJ]: Works Progress Administration), 81.

27. "Work and Progress at Physical Culture City," *Physical Culture*, June 1909.

28. *Physical Culture*, June 1905, 472–473.
29. Waugh, "Macfadden," 65.
30. *Physical Culture*, June 1905, 471–473.
31. Waugh, "Macfadden," 66.
32. Kemp, *Tramping on Life*, 165.
33. Ibid., 165–166.
34. Ibid., 167, 166.
35. Ibid., 166.
36. Ibid., 170, 174.
37. Bernarr Macfadden, "Physical Culture City Criticized," *Physical Culture*, August 1906, 215, 217.
38. Ibid., 217–218.
39. Kemp, *Tramping on Life*, 167.
40. Dougherty, *History of Outcalt*, 3.
41. Federal Writers' Project, *Monroe Township*, 81.
42. Waugh, "Macfadden," 67.
43. Bernarr Macfadden, "A Physical Culture House," *Physical Culture*, November 1906, 403.
44. Ibid., 403–406.
45. *Physical Culture* pamphlet, December 1907, 11–12.
46. *Physical Culture* advertising section, June 1908, unpaginated.
47. Dougherty, *History of Outcalt*, 8.
48. "Magnificent Home for Physical Culturists," *Physical Culture*, September 1907, 162.
49. Carson, *Cornflake Crusade*, 186.
50. Ibid., 187.
51. Macfadden and Gauvreau, *Dumbbells and Carrot Strips*, 219.
52. Robert Lewis Taylor, "Physical Culture," *New Yorker*, October 28, 1950, 48–49.
53. Bernarr Macfadden, "Starving Men Want Work," *Liberty*, September 12, 1931.
54. Rev. James G. Evans, "Our Physical Culture Pulpit," *Physical Culture*, May 1903, 428–429.
55. *Physical Culture*, March 1909, 175.
56. Kemp, *Tramping on Life*, 346.

The Self Master Colony: A Home for the Homeless

1. Bret Harte, who would have considerable influence on Andress Floyd's thought and writing, wrote a poem, "Caldwell of Springfield," about the Connecticut Farms minister whose wife was shot by a sniper during the battle.

2. Robert Corey Allen, *Union, Today and Yesterday* (Union, NJ: Union Township Schools), 1962.

3. This list was published as part of the front matter in every *Self Master Magazine*.

4. Possibly the fact that Floyd died of heart disease at fifty-nine had something to do with this unspecified condition.

5. Sarah Orne Jewett to Andress Floyd, November 22, 1894, Jewett Texts, www.public.coe.edu/soj/let/cary2.html.

6. The first Young People's Society of Christian Endeavor was started in 1881, in Portland, Maine, by Dr. Francis E. Clark, a Congregational minister. Begun as a youth group, it soon embraced all ages and many denominations. The group's mission was to deepen spiritual life. *New York Times*, May 26, 1911.

7. *New York Times*, May 10, 1904.

8. *New York Times*, May 24, 1904.

9. *New York Times*, May 26, 1911, 7.

10. Tolstoy, as quoted ibid.

11. Abraxas is in fact a creature of good and evil.

12. Andress Floyd, *The Self Master Magazine* (1924), 1.

13. William Morris, artist, printer, and author of *The News from Nowhere*, a utopian novel, was a leading light of the Arts and Crafts movement in England. He had his own community at Kelmscott in Oxfordshire.

14. Freeman Champney, *Art and Glory: The Story of Elbert Hubbard* (Kent, OH: Kent State University Press, 1983), 50.

15. Kemp, *Tramping on Life*, 190.

16. Floyd, *Self Master Magazine* (1924), 8.

17. Peter Clark Macfarlane, "When Lang Was Six Months from Riley's," *American Magazine*, January 1914, 4.

18. Ibid., 3.

19. However, a later newspaper article refers to the Meeker Inn and claims that the proprietor would not admit any of Floyd's villagers.

20. *Self Master Magazine* (1920–1921), 4.

21. Andress Floyd, *My Monks of Vagabondia* (Union, NJ: Self Master Press, 1913), 13–14.

22. Andress Floyd, *The Making of Our Book* (pamphlet) (Union, NJ: Self Master Press, 1913).

23. Walter Van Tillburg Clark, introduction to *Bret Harte: Stories of the Early West* (New York: Platt and Munk, 1964), 16.

24. Bret Harte, "Tennessee's Partner," in *Stories of the Early West*, 46.

25. Bret Harte, "The Luck of Roaring Camp," in *Stories of the Early West*, 96.

26. Ibid., 99.
27. Floyd, *Monks of Vagabondia*, 28–31.
28. Ibid., 136.
29. *Self Master Magazine* (1920–1921), 4.
30. Frederick Lewis Allen, *Only Yesterday: An Informal History of the 1920s* (New York: Harper and Row Perennial Library, 1964), 150.
31. R. Allen, *Union, Yesterday and Today.*
32. Lou Velter, "Floyd Housed Many Bums Couldn't Sell Other Homes," *Union Leader*, January 14, 1960.
33. Kemp, *Tramping on Life*, 191.
34. Elbert Hubbard, as quoted in Champney, *Art and Glory*, 169.
35. Auction pamphlet for Self Master village, Union, NJ, August 17, 1929, Union Free Public Library, Union, NJ.
36. *Union Leader*, January 14, 1960.
37. Tom Beisler, telephone interview with author, February 14, 2006.
38. Olive Beatrice Floyd, diary (unpaginated), Olive Beatrice Floyd Papers, Schlesinger Library, Radcliffe Institute for Advanced Study, Harvard University, Cambridge, MA.
39. Olive Beatrice Floyd, "A Trip Out West," diary (unpaginated), Olive Beatrice Floyd Papers.
40. Obituary of Andress Floyd, *Union Register*, January 12, 1933.

Woodbine: Immigrants on the Land

1. Joseph Brandes, *Immigrants to Freedom* (Philadelphia: Jewish Publication Society, 1971), 17.
2. Bluma Bayuk Rappoport Purmell and Felice Lewis Rovner, *A Farmer's Daughter: Bluma* (Los Angeles: Havenhurst Publishers, 1981), 11.
3. Catherine Sabsovich, *Adventures in Idealism* (New York: private printing, 1922), 9–11.
4. Leo Tolstoy, *Anna Karenina*, trans. Constance Garnett (New York: Modern Library), 327.
5. Ande Manners, *Poor Cousins* (New York: Coward, McCann and Geohegan, 1972), 192.
6. Charles K. Landis, as quoted in Loren D. Flood, "Charles Kline Landis," *Vineland Historical Magazine*, centennial edition, August 8, 1961, 6.
7. Welch was a staunch Methodist who believed that it was wrong to use wine, an alcoholic beverage, in the sacrament.
8. Manners, *Poor Cousins*, 180.
9. Ibid., 181.

10. Brandes, *Immigrants*, 55.
11. Charles K. Landis, as quoted ibid., 54.
12. Ibid., 63.
13. Ibid., 67.
14. Uri D. Herscher, *Jewish Agricultural Utopias in America, 1880–1910* (Detroit: Wayne State University Press, 1981), 84.
15. Baron de Hirsch, as quoted ibid., 88.
16. Ibid., 89.
17. Among them were Meyer Isaacs, Jacob Schiff, Mayer Sulzberger, and Eugene S. Benjamin.
18. Sabsovich, *Adventures in Idealism*, 57.
19. The family that owned the house had moved out just before the de Hirsch Fund bought the land but would return every fall with their servants and dogs for hunting; the house was never vandalized in their absence. Ibid., 58 (quotation).
20. Ibid.
21. See Ellen Eisenberg, *Jewish Agricultural Colonies in New Jersey, 1882–1920* (Syracuse, NY: Syracuse University Press, 1995).
22. Sabsovich, *Adventures in Idealism*, 59.
23. Ibid.
24. David Ludins, "Memories of Woodbine: 1891–1894," *Jewish Frontier*, June 1960, 7.
25. Ibid., 8.
26. Ibid.
27. Ibid., 9.
28. Ibid., 9–10.
29. Ibid., 10.
30. Olive S. Barry, "Woodbine, New Jersey: Land Use and Social History," unpublished college paper (1975), 18, Cape May Country Library, Cape May Courthouse, Cape May, NJ.
31. Sabsovich, *Adventures in Idealism*, 67.
32. Vladimir Korolenko, as quoted in *Woodbine Centennial Booklet, 1891–1991*, Cape May County Library.
33. Samuel Joseph, *History of the Baron de Hirsch Fund* (Philadelphia: Jewish Publication Society, 1935), 51, 68 (quotation).
34. Herscher, *Jewish Agricultural Utopias*, 93.
35. Ludins, "Memories," 11. Except for Baron de Hirsch Avenue, Woodbine's avenues are named for American presidents. Arthur D. Goldhaft, writing in his autobiography, *The Golden Egg* (New York: Horizon Press, 1957), described the time his little sister Lillian's head was accidentally split open by an ax. His mother and

the other women applied a poultice of sour black bread and took the child from Alliance to Vineland by cart. Lillian recovered completely.

36. Ibid., 12.
37. H. L. Sabsovich, as quoted in Sabsovich, *Adventures in Idealism*, 90.
38. Brandes, *Immigrants*, 116.
39. H. L. Sabsovich, as quoted ibid., 118–119.
40. Brandes, *Immigrants*, 120.
41. Ibid.
42. Ibid., 122.
43. Ludins, "Memories," 14.
44. Joseph, *History of the de Hirsch Fund*, 56.
45. Ibid., 57.
46. Sabsovich, *Adventures in Idealism*, 95 96.
47. Goldhaft, *Golden Egg*, 88.
48. Ibid.
49. Sabsovich, *Adventures in Idealism*, 117–118.
50. Brandes, *Immigrants*, 134.
51. Joseph, *History of the de Hirsch Fund*, 71.
52. Goldhaft, *Golden Egg*, 96.
53. Barry, "Woodbine," 10.
54. Brandes, *Immigrants*, 154.
55. Ibid., 155.
56. Ibid., 158.
57. David Blaustein, "The First Self-Governed Jewish Community since the Fall of Jerusalem," *Circle Magazine*, no. 2 (1907), 138–140.
58. Barry, "Woodbine," 13.
59. Eva M. Hughes, as quoted in Lawrence DeFeo, "The Transformation of a Community: A History of the Development and Education of Woodbine," Ph.D. dissertation, Rutgers University, 1979, 236–237.
60. Brandes, *Immigrants*, 139.
61. Ibid.
62. Herscher, *Jewish Agricultural Utopias*, 113.
63. Brandes, *Immigrants*, 163.
64. *Philadelphia Inquirer*, August 12, 1979.
65. Joseph, *History of the de Hirsch Fund*, 99.
66. Goldhaft, *Golden Egg*, 164.
67. Joseph, *History of the de Hirsch Fund*, 101.
68. Jeffery M. Dorwart, *Cape May County, New Jersey* (New Brunswick, NJ: Rutgers University Press, 1993), 216.

69. Joseph, *History of the de Hirsch Fund*, 110, 112.

70. Report of the Woodbine Community Center, September 1932, 1, Cape May County Library.

71. Goldhaft, *Golden Egg*, 262–263.

72. Marjorie Rosenfeld, interview with the author, May 3, 2006, Woodbine, NJ.

73. Harold Feldman, "Mrs. Meranze Remembers the Old Days in Woodbine," *Jewish Exponent*, August 8, 1958, 2.

74. "Cape May's Poverty-Stricken Community Seeks Industry, Housing," *Philadelphia Bulletin*, October 31, 1977.

Roosevelt: New Deal Town

1. In 1843 a group of weavers banded together in England to form the Rochdale Equitable Pioneer Society. In 1844 they set out the Rochdale Principles, which were influential in the Co-operative movement.

2. Alan Pine, Jean Hershenov, and Aaron Lefkowitz, *Peddler to Suburbanite: The History of the Jews in Monmouth County* (Deal Park, NJ: Monmouth Jewish Community Council, 1981), 107–130.

3. "History of Roosevelt, New Jersey," manuscript, p. 1, Roosevelt Collection, Special Collections and University Archives, Rutgers libraries.

4. Benjamin Brown, as quoted in Russell Lord and Paul Johnstone, *A Place on Earth: A Critical Evaluation of Subsistence Homesteads* (Washington, DC: U.S. Department of Agriculture, 1942), 138.

5. Paul K. Conkin, *Tomorrow a New World* (Ithaca, NY: Cornell University Press, 1959), 120–121.

6. David Dubinsky, as quoted in Lord and Johnstone, *Place on Earth*, 143. Dubinsky's "limitations of contractors" refers to limiting the number of contractors that a jobber could hire so as to avoid unethical competition and the resultant sweatshop conditions.

7. David Dubinsky, as quoted in Ralph F Armstrong, "Four Million Dollar Village," *Saturday Evening Post*, February 5, 1938, 34.

8. Sora H. Friedman, "No Place Like Home: The Foundation and Transformation of the New Deal Town of Jersey Homesteads, New Jersey," Ph.D. dissertation, George Mason University, 2005, 106.

9. George Weller, "Land of Milk and Honey," *Digest*, August 14, 1937, 13.

10. Friedman, "No Place Like Home," 106.

11. Edwin Rosskam, *Roosevelt, New Jersey: Big Dreams in a Small Town and What Time Did to Them* (New York: Grossman Publishers, 1972), 18.

12. Friedman, "No Place Like Home," 109.

13. This film, made in 1983, was produced by Richard Kroehling.

14. Dorothy D. Bartlett, "Tugwell Hands out $1,800,000 for N.J. Commune," *Philadelphia Inquirer*, May 7, 1936, 1.

15. "Housing Project at Hightstown Reported Doomed," *Asbury Park Press*, December 24, 1935, 2.

16. Edmund De Long, *Sun*, July 9, 1936.

17. William Weaver, "Louis Kahn in Roosevelt: Early Lessons of the Historic 1930's Community in New Jersey," *Architectural Digest*, July 1993, 68–74.

18. "At my feet lay a great city. Miles of broad streets, shaded by trees and lined with fine buildings, for the most part not in continuous blocks but set in larger or smaller inclosures, stretched in every direction. Every quarter contained large open squares filled with trees, among which statues glistened and fountains flashed in the late afternoon sun." Bellamy, *Looking Backward*, 18.

19. Walter L. Creese, *The Search for the Environment: The Garden City Before and After* (Baltimore: Johns Hopkins University Press, 1992), 205.

20. Rosskam, *Roosevelt*, 13.

21. Clare Nadler Sacharoff, interview with author, July 15, 2006, Roosevelt, NJ.

22. Rosskam, *Roosevelt*, 41.

23. Helen Kleinman, interview with E. Dalz and F. Hepner, May 7, 1981, Roosevelt Oral History Project, Roosevelt Collection, Special Collections and University Archives, Rutgers Libraries.

24. Helen Barth, interview with author, July 5, 2006, Roosevelt, NJ.

25. Rosskam, *Roosevelt*, 3.

26. Lord and Johnstone, *Place on Earth*, 148, 148–149.

27. Ibid., 149.

28. "Jersey Homesteads Launched as 2,000 Cheer Cooperative Pioneers," *Jewish Record* (Elizabeth, NJ) 8, August 1936, 1.

29. Michael Shally-Jensen, "New Deal, New Life: Culture and History of a Jewish Cooperative Colony in New Jersey," Ph.D. dissertation, Princeton University, 1992, 460–461, 462.

30. George Weller, "The Promised Land," in *New Letters in America*, ed. Horace Gregory (New York: W. W. Norton, 1937), 210. .

31. Conkin, *Tomorrow a New World*, 269.

32. Lord and Johnstone, *Place on Earth*, 150.

33. Armstrong, "Four Million Dollar Village," 38.

34. Lord and Johnstone, *Place on Earth*, 152.

35. Poultry farming was a successful business for Jewish farmers in many parts of the state, and Brown himself had been extremely successful with it.

36. Lord and Johnstone, *Place on Earth*, 154.

37. Leo Libove, interview, 1979 or 1980, Roosevelt Oral History Project.

38. Rosskam, *Roosevelt*, 28.
39. Lord and Johnstone, *Place on Earth*, 155.
40. "Depending on Themselves, Homesteaders Plan Future," *Asbury Park Press*, February 23, 1938, 1.
41. Weller, "Land of Milk and Honey," 12.
42. Armstrong, "Four Million Dollar Village," 7.
43. Shally-Jensen, "New Deal," 476–481.
44. Sol Axelrod, son of homesteaders Joseph Axelrod and Rose Klein Axelrod, interview by Susan Axelrod, Roosevelt Oral History Project.
45. Sol Axelrod, interview. Also, Morris Chasen, interview, June 13, 1975, Roosevelt Oral History Project.
46. Armstrong, "Four Million Dollar Village," 36.
47. Morris Chasen, interview.
48. Nathan Narod, interview, July, 29, 1981, Roosevelt Oral History Project.
49. "Clinging to Paradise Corners," *Everybody's Weekly*, August 18, 1940.
50. Ibid.
51. Helen Barth, interview.
52. Shally-Jensen, "New Deal," 482.
53. Israel Weisman, interview with E. Dalz and F. Hepner, May 21, 1981, Roosevelt Oral History Project.
54. "Clinging to Paradise Corners."
55. "Cooperatives," *Time*, April 22, 1940, 86.
56. Augusta Chasen, interview, June 13, 1979, Roosevelt Oral History Project.
57. Conkin, *Tomorrow a New World*, 273.
58. Clare Nadler Sacharoff, interview.
59. Rosskam, *Roosevelt*, 47–48.
60. Rodham Tullos, interview with the author, October 11, 2006, Roosevelt, NJ.

Rova Farms: Preserving a Culture

1. J. Turner Brakeley (1847–1915) was born in Bordentown, N.J., graduated from Princeton University, and went on to study law. In 1872, after reputedly finding his fiancée in the arms of another man, Brakeley retreated to Lahaway Plantation, his father's 350-acre holding in Jackson Township. There he lived a reclusive life studying nature: wind and weather, plants and animals, and especially insects. His work on wasps and mosquitoes was well known to entomologists. He was consulted by the U.S. government on malaria control during the building of the Panama Canal. Henry Charlton Beck, "Abode of Jersey Hermit Blossoms into New Fairyland," *Newark Sunday Star Ledger*, March 15, 1953.
2. L.D., "The Roova Farm" *Russian American Herald*, May 1934, 3.

3. John Shest, "Down on the Farm," *Russian American Herald*, May 1934, 9.

4. Tatiana Petrovsky, "Russian Americans," in *Ocean County: Four Centuries in the Making*, ed. Pauline S. Miller (Toms River, NJ: Ocean County Cultural and Heritage Commission, 2000), 688.

5. Ibid.

6. Serge Rogosin, "The First Pushkin Monument in the United States," unpublished essay, unpaginated.

7. M. K. Argus, *Moscow on the Hudson* (New York: Harper and Brothers, 1951), 157.

8. Petrovsky, "Russian Americans," 686–687.

9. Ibid., 691.

10. Ibid., 690.

11. *Jackson Times*, June 16, 2000.

12. Helen Zill, as quoted in "Report on Rova Farm," Fellowship in Prayer, Princeton, NJ, 1981, 7.

13. Ibid.

14. Martin Hrynick, interview with the author, October 23, 2006, Rova Farms, NJ.

15. Frank Montarelli, "After 45 Years, Rova Farms Cultural Aura Being Regenerated," *Ocean County Reporter*, September 9, 1978, 1.

16. Jo Ann Moslock, "Russian Center a Troubled Resort," *Asbury Park Press*, February 22, 1987, A1.

17. Ann Vayda, "Hello from Cassville, 'Little Russia in the Garden State,'" *Philadelphia Inquirer*, n.d.

18. Larry Waddell, *Asbury Park Press*, n.d.

19. A. Yarmolinsky, *Russian Herald*, 1954.

20. No one can own more than ten shares in Rova.

21. Moslock, "Russian Center."

22. This case, *Rova Farms v. Investors Insurance*, remains a textbook case in New Jersey law.

23. Carol J. Suplee, "Troubled Times for Little Russia," *New Jersey Monthly*, November 1986, 91.

24. Lydia Wolniansky, interview with author, May 28, 2006, Ocean Grove, NJ.

25. Suplee, "Troubled Times," 92.

26. Martin Hrynick, interview.

Conclusion

1. Richard Hofstadter, ed., *The Progressive Movement, 1900–1915* (Englewood Cliffs, NJ: Prentice Hall, 1963), 1.

BIBLIOGRAPHY

Allen, Frederick Lewis. *Only Yesterday.* New York: Harper and Row Perennial Library, 1964.

Allen, Robert Corey. *Union Today and Yesterday.* Union, NJ: Union Township Schools, 1962.

Argus, M. K. *Moscow on the Hudson.* New York: Harper and Brothers, 1951.

Armstrong, Ralph F. "Four Million Dollar Village." *Saturday Evening Post,* February 5, 1938.

Avrich, Paul. *The Modern School Movement.* Oakland, CA: AK Press, 2006.

Baez, Joan. *Daybreak.* New York: Dial Press, 1968.

Barry, Olive S. "Woodbine, New Jersey: Land Use and Social History." Unpublished college paper. 1975. Cape May County Library, Cape May Courthouse, NJ.

Bayuk Rappoport Purmell, Bluma, and Felice Lewis Rovner. *A Farmer's Daughter: Bluma.* Los Angeles: Havenhurst Publishers, 1981.

Bellamy, Edward. *Looking Backward.* New York: Bantam Books, 1983.

Bercovici, Konrad. "Colonies, Campfires and Theories." *New York Times Magazine,* October 21, 1923.

———. *It's the Gypsy in Me.* New York: Prentice-Hall, 1941.

Bercovici, Rion. "A Radical Childhood." *Scribner's Magazine,* August 1932, 102–106.

Bierbaum, Martin. "Free Acres: Bolton Hall's Single-Tax Experimental Community." *New Jersey History,* Spring/Summer 1984, 39–62.

Bok, Edward. *The Americanization of Edward Bok.* New York: Charles Scribner's Sons, 1931.

Brandes, Joseph. *Immigrants to Freedom.* Philadelphia: Jewish Publication Society, 1971.

Cagney, James. *Cagney by Cagney.* New York: Doubleday, 1976.

Carson, Gerald. *Cornflake Crusade.* New York and Toronto: Clarke, Irwin and Co., 1957.

Champney, Freeman. *Art and Glory: The Story of Elbert Hubbard.* Kent, OH: Kent State University Press, 1983.

Colbron, Isabel Grace. "Adventures in Home-Making: Free Acres Homes." *Touchstone*, August 1918, 438–448.

Conkin, Paul K. *Tomorrow a New World*. Ithaca, NY: Cornell University Press, 1959.

Coyne, Kevin. "Roosevelt's New Deal." *New Jersey Monthly*, May 2003, 48–51, 77.

Creese, Walter L. *The Search for the Environment: The Garden City Before and After*. Baltimore: Johns Hopkins University Press, 1992.

DeFeo, Lawrence. "The Transformation of a Community: A History of the Development and Education of Woodbine." Ph.D. dissertation, Rutgers University, 1979.

Dougherty, Sadie S. *History of Outcalt, 1905–1963*. Pamphlet. Spotswood, NJ, 1963.

Dorwart, Jeffery M. *Cape May County, New Jersey: The Making of an American Resort Community*. New Brunswick, NJ: Rutgers University Press, 1992.

Dunsany, Edward John Moreton Drax. *Five Plays*. New York: M. Kennerley, 1914.

Durant, Will, and Ariel Durant. *Dual Autobiography*. New York.: Simon and Schuster, 1977.

Durant, William J. *The Ferrer Modern School*. New York: Francisco Ferrer Association, 1912.

Eisenberg, Ellen. *Jewish Agricultural Colonies in New Jersey, 1882–1920*. Syracuse, NY: Syracuse University Press, 1995.

Ernst, Robert. *Weakness Is a Crime: The Life of Bernarr Macfadden*. Syracuse, NY: Syracuse University Press, 1991.

Federal Writers' Project. *Monroe Township, Middlesex County, New Jersey, 1838–1938*. [New Brunswick, NJ]: Works Progress Administration, 1938.

———. *Stories of New Jersey: Its Significant Places, People, and Activities*. New York: M. Barrows and Company, 1938.

———. *The WPA Guide to 1930's New Jersey*. New Brunswick, NJ: Rutgers University Press, 1986.

Ferm, Elizabeth. *The Spirit of Freedom in Education*. Stelton, NJ: Modern School, 1919.

Flood, Loren. "Charles K. Landis." *Vineland Historical Magazine*, centennial edition, August 8, 1961.

Floyd, Andress. *The Making of Our Book*. Union, NJ: Self Master Press, 1913.

———. *My Monks of Vagabondia*. Union, NJ: Self Master Press, 1913.

Freedman, Samuel G. "A Requiem for Anarchy." *New Jersey Monthly*, May 2003, 56–57, 104.

Friedman, Sora H. "No Place Like Home: The Foundation and Transformation of the New Deal Town of Jersey Homesteads, New Jersey." Ph.D. dissertation, George Mason University, 2005.

George, Henry. "The Single Tax: What It Is and Why We Need It." *Christian Advocate*, 1890.

BIBLIOGRAPHY

Gilliam, Harold, and Ann Gilliam. *Creating Carmel*. Layton, UT: Gibbs Smith, 1992.

Gilman, Charlotte Perkins. *Concerning Children*. Walnut Creek, CA: Altamira Press, 2002.

———. *Herland*. Mineola, NY: Dover, 1998.

———. *The Living of Charlotte Perkins Gilman: An Autobiography*. Madison: University of Wisconsin Press, 1990.

———. *Women and Economics*. New York: Prometheus Books, 1994.

———. *The Yellow Wallpaper*. Edited and with an introduction by Thomas L. Erskine and Connie L. Richards. New Brunswick, NJ: Rutgers University Press, 1993.

Gold, Michael. "In Foggy California." *New Masses*, November 1928, 162–171.

Goldhaft, Arthur D. *The Golden Egg*. New York: Horizon Press, 1957.

Goldman, Emma. *Living My Life*. New York: Knopf, 1931.

Goldstein, Philip Reuben. "Social Aspects of the Jewish Colonies of South Jersey." Ph.D. dissertation, University of Pennsylvania, 1921.

Hall, Bolton. *Life, Love, and Death*. New York and London: F. Tennyson Neely, 1898.

Harris, Leon. *Upton Sinclair: American Rebel*. New York: Thomas Y. Crowell, 1975.

Harte, Bret. "Tennessee's Partner" and "The Luck of Roaring Camp." In *Bret Harte: Stories of The Early West*. New York: Platt and Munk, 1964.

Hartmann, Sadakichi. *My Theory of Soul Atoms*. New York: Stylus Publishing, 1910.

Herscher, Uri D. *Jewish Agricultural Utopias in America, 1880–1910*. Detroit: Wayne State University Press, 1981.

Hessing, Laurel, ed. *Annotated Anthology of Free Acres Writing*. Free Acres, NJ: self-published, 1992.

———, ed. and trans. With Sylvia Heerens, trans. *The Treasures of the Little Cabin*. Free Acres, NJ: self-published, 1999.

Hicks, Ami Mali. *Color in Action*. New York: Funk and Wagnall's, 1937.

Hinds, W. A. *American Communities and Cooperative Colonies*. Gloucester, MA: Peter Smith, 1971.

Hine, Robert. *California's Utopian Colonies*. San Marino, CA: Huntington Library, 1953.

Hofstadter, Richard, ed. *The Progressive Movement, 1900–1915*. Englewood Cliffs, NJ: Prentice-Hall, 1963.

Houriet, Robert. *Getting Back Together*. New York: Avon, 1971.

Joseph, Samuel. *History of the Baron de Hirsch Fund*. Philadelphia: Jewish Publication Society, 1935.

Kantor, MacKinlay. "My Most Unforgettable Character." *Reader's Digest*, December 1966, 221–228.

Kaplan, Lawrence. "The Helicon Home Colony." *American Studies*, Fall 1984, 59–73.

Kelly, Harry. *The Modern School.* Stelton, NJ: Modern School Association of America, 1920.

Kemp, Harry. *Tramping on Life.* New York: Boni and Liveright, 1922.

Kent, Rockwell. *It's Me, O Lord: The Autobiography of Rockwell Kent.* New York: Dodd Mead, 1955.

Koch Reidel, Gerda. "I Like to Remember Stelton." In *The Modern School Twenty-fifth Anniversary Publication*, ed. Abe Gosner, 28. Stelton, NJ: Modern School, 1940.

Kropotkin, Peter. "Declaration of the Anarchists Arraigned before the Criminal Court in Lyon." In *No Gods, No Masters*, vol. 1, ed. Daniel Guerin, trans. Paul Sharkey. Edinburgh: AK Press, 1998.

———. *Fields, Factories, and Workshops.* London: Nelson, 1913.

Leon, Lillian. "A Free Acres Chronicle." Unpublished essay. 1949. Special Collections and University Archives, Rutgers Libraries, Rutgers University, New Brunswick, NJ.

Lewis, Sinclair. "Two Yale Men in Utopia." In *The Man from Main Street: Selected Essays and Other Writings, 1904–1950*, ed. Harry E. Maule and Melville H. Cane. New York: Random House, 1953.

Liber, Benzion. *A Doctor's Apprenticeship.* New York: Rational Living, 1956.

Lord, Russell, and Paul Johnstone. *A Place on Earth: A Critical Evaluation of Subsistence Homesteads.* Washington, DC: U.S. Department of Agriculture, 1942.

Ludins, David. "Memories of Woodbine: 1891–1894." *Jewish Frontier*, June 1960.

Macfadden, Johnnie Lee. *Barefoot in Eden: The Macfadden Plan for Health, Charm, and Long-Lasting Youth.* Englewood Cliffs, NJ: Prentice-Hall, 1962.

Macfadden, Mary, and Emile Gavreau. *Dumbbells and Carrot Strips.* New York: Henry Holt, 1953.

Macfarlane, Peter Clark. "When Lang Was Six Months from Riley's." *American Magazine*, January 1914.

Manners, Ande. *Poor Cousins.* New York: Coward, McCann and Geohegan, 1972.

Miller, Ray Porter. "My Teachers at Stelton." In *The Modern School Twenty-fifth Anniversary Publication*, ed. Abe Gosner, 27. Stelton, NJ: Modern School, 1940.

Morris, William. *The News from Nowhere and Other Writings.* London: Penguin Books, 1993.

Murray, Ella. "Free Acres Twentieth Anniversary." Brochure. 1930. Free Acres Collection, Special Collections and University Archives, Rutgers Libraries, Rutgers University, New Brunswick, NJ.

Nearing, Helen, and Scott Nearing. *Living the Good Life.* New York: Schocken Books, 1970.

Neill, A. S. *Summerhill.* New York: Hart Publishing Co., 1960.

Oursler, Fulton. "The Most Unforgettable Character I've Met." *Reader's Digest,* July 1951, 78–82.

Perlin, Terry M. "Anarchism in New Jersey: The Ferrer Colony at Stelton." *New Jersey History,* Fall 1971, 133–148.

Pestalozzi, Johann Heinrich. *Leonard and Gertrude.* Trans. Eva Channing. Boston: D. C. Heath, 1895.

Petrovsky, Tatiana. "Russian Americans." In *Ocean County: Four Centuries in the Making,* ed. Pauline S. Miller. Toms River, NJ: Ocean County Cultural and Heritage Commission, 2000.

Pine, Alan, Jean Hershenov, and Aaron Lefkowitz. *Peddler to Suburbanite: The History of the Jews in Monmouth County.* Deal Park, NJ: Monmouth Jewish Community Council, 1981.

Robins, Jacob. "Two Persons and an Ideal." *Modern School,* June–July 1919.

Rogosin, Serge. "The First Pushkin Monument in the United States." Unpublished essay.

Romano, Joseph. "Free Acres Single Tax Colony, 1910–1930: An Experiment in Pleasant Living." Master's thesis, University of Tennessee, 1972.

Rosskam, Edwin. *Roosevelt, New Jersey: Big Dreams in a Small Town and What Time Did to Them.* New York: Grossman Publishers, 1972.

Sabsovich, Catherine. *Adventures in Idealism.* New York: private printing, 1922.

Schnittkind, Henry T. "The Function of a Modern School." In *The Modern School Twenty-fifth Anniversary Publication,* ed. Abe Gosner, 16. Stelton, NJ: Modern School, 1940.

Shally-Jensen, Michael. "New Deal, New Life: Culture and History of a Jewish Cooperative Colony in New Jersey." Ph.D. dissertation, Princeton University, 1992.

Simon, Linda. "Socialism at Home: The Case of Upton Sinclair." *New Jersey History,* Spring/Summer 1989.

Sinclair, Upton. *The Autobiography of Upton Sinclair.* New York: Harcourt, Brace and World, 1962.

———. *The Brass Check: A Study of American Journalism.* Pasadena, CA: author published, 1920.

———. *The Jungle.* Cambridge, MA: Robert Bentley, Inc., 1946.

Smith, Thorne. *The Night Life of the Gods.* New York: Pocket Books, 1947.

———. *Topper.* New York: Ballantine Books, 1953.

Spayth, George W. *It Was Fun the Hard Way.* Dunellen, NJ: Spayth Press, 1964.

The Story of Fellowship Farm. Pamphlet. Twenty-fifth Anniversary of Fellowship Farm and Dedication of Township Park, October 9, 1937, Special Collections and University Archives, Rutgers Libraries, Rutgers University, New Brunswick, NJ.

Suplee, Carol J. "Troubled Times for Little Russia." *New Jersey Monthly,* November 1986.

Taylor, Robert Lewis. "Physical Culture." *New Yorker,* October 28, 1950.

Thurber, James. *The Years with Ross.* Boston: Atlantic Monthly Press, 1957.

Tolstoy, Leo. *Anna Karenina.* Trans. Constance Garnett. New York: Modern Library, 1994.

———. *On Education.* Trans. Leo Weiner. Chicago: University of Chicago Press, 1967.

Veysey, Laurence. *The Communal Experience.* Chicago: University of Chicago Press, 1978.

Waugh, Clifford. "Bernarr Macfadden: The Muscular Prophet." Ph.D. dissertation, State University of New York, Buffalo, 1979.

Weaver, William. "Louis Kahn in Roosevelt: Early Lessons of the Historic 1930's Community in New Jersey." *Architectural Digest,* July 1993.

Weller, George. "Land of Milk and Honey." *Digest,* August 14, 1937.

———. "The Promised Land." In *New Letters in America,* ed. Horace Gregory. New York: W. W. Norton, 1937.

Whorton, James C. *Crusaders for Fitness: The History of American Health Reformers.* Princeton, NJ: Princeton University Press, 1982.

Williams, Michael. *The Book of the High Romance.* New York: Macmillan, 1928.

INDEX

Note: All places named are in New Jersey unless otherwise indicated.

INDEX

ABOUT THE AUTHOR

Perdita Buchan was born in England and came to America as a child. She has published two novels, and her short fiction and articles have appeared in the *New Yorker, Ladies' Home Journal, Harvard Magazine, House Beautiful, New Jersey Monthly*, and the *New York Times*.